The Haunted Queen

By
Leah Toole

The Haunted Queen

Copyright © 2023 Leah Toole. All rights reserved.

All rights reserved. No part of this publication may be reproduced, stored, or transmitted in any form or by any means, whether electronic, mechanical, or photocopying, recording, scanning, or otherwise without written permission from the author.
It is illegal to copy this book, post it to a website, or distribute it by any other means without permission.

**Praise for the Novels of
The Tudor Heirs Series:**

"A brilliant and captivating read! The historical facts remind true with a great element of fiction. Highly recommend. "
- UK

"I like the author's fluid style. She knows how to captivate the reader and describes previously unexplained aspects of the story in a convincing way."
- Germany

"The most amazing book I have ever read regarding Mary I. Leah Toole did an amazing job describing all the good and the bad that came along with Mary's life. I honestly cannot wait to read book #2. Great job Leah."
- United States

"I loved every minute of this book, and I can't wait for the next one! I've read other books that mentioned Mary, but this book made you feel like you were walking in her shoes! This story fills you with the emotions Mary must have felt living her turbulent life. Wonderfully written, I couldn't put it down!!"   - United States

"I love history, the Tudors are one of my favourite eras so I knew I would enjoy this book. Leah has written a wonderful story about Mary Tudor; I couldn't put it down and look forward to the next instalment."
- UK

Also by Leah Toole

The Tudor Heirs Series

I – The Saddest Princess
...

Message from the author:

During the time that I was writing this book, I discovered songs which I believed fit the emotion of certain scenes really well.

Without giving anything away, I would like you to keep an eye out for song titles at the start of some paragraphs. And if you enjoy a playlist while you read, the songs I have suggested are the ones I feel fit the emotion perfectly for that particular scene.

You can enter the titles and artists into YouTube and have it on in the background during that scene, or you can ignore it – whatever you choose to do.

Happy reading!

To, Jessica

If you loved this book please feel free to tell your friends ♡ Don't forget to review on Amazon!

love,
Leah Took

xx

Prologue:

17th November 1558
Tower of London

"Queen Mary is dead," Sir Henry Jerningham says as he kneels before me and presents me with my sister's ring – proof that the Queen of England is dead.

"My sister's ring," I breathe, my voice no more than a whisper, the enormity of this moment weighing heavily upon my conscience.

I take the ring from his outstretched hand and as he rises from his bended knee, mine buckle, and I fall to the ground in a heap.

I sit there, crumpled on the cold, stone floor in my nightshift, the guard's cloak wrapped around me, and I inhale deeply to regain my composure.

As I breathe in and out, I can feel my mind clearing, and after a moment I look up and extend my hand to Sir Jerningham. He reaches for me, his new Queen, and helps me upright before bowing his head at me in respect.

And my chest becomes heavy with dread.

I have never wanted this.

24th March 1603
Richmond Palace, London

"Your majesty," the old physician said as he bowed his head, wringing his hands nervously, "The ring must be removed," he persisted, "It has grown into your majesty's skin!"

Elizabeth snatched her white hand away and shook her head.

"Her majesty must rest," her lady-in-waiting declared as she tried to usher the physicians out of the chambers.

"But… my queen!" the physician called over his shoulder as the lady shooed them towards the door.

"Her majesty shall wear the ring," the lady continued, "every day as she has done over the entirety of her reign. You may remove it when her successor shall need it as proof of his accession. Until then it shall continue where it is!" and she glared at them as though they were naughty children, "Good day!" and she closed the door in their concerned, old faces.

When her lady returned to Elizabeth's side, the old queen smiled faintly and nodded in thanks.

"Do not worry, my queen," the lady said tenderly, "all shall be as you command until the very end."

At that, Elizabeth nodded once more as her eyelids became heavy, and she waved her hand to dismiss her lady. Then she turned her head to the side carefully so as not to smudge her white makeup onto the feather cushions, and closed her eyes to sleep.

Her ladies had noticed that Queen Elizabeth had been in and out of consciousness all day, and though she had feared and avoided rest for many days before finally collapsing of exhaustion, they noticed that she would now fall asleep smiling.

While they could not know what joy she now found in her dreams after many months of being haunted by nightmares, they were glad to finally see her peaceful, and they thought that perhaps she could recover from this latest illness yet.

As soon as Elizabeth closed her eyes, she fell into a deep sleep and found herself reawakened within the same dream she had been dreaming all day. In it she was no longer an old, dying woman, but a beautiful and carefree lady in her youth. She could not say with certainty how old she was in her subconscious, but she boasted a full head of bright red curls, and her face was free of worry as well as wrinkles.

But the biggest difference was not one she could see, but rather one she could feel, for in her fantasy she was liberated from burdens and duty.

In her dream she felt light as a feather as she half ran, half floated across the field towards a figure in the distance. As she ran towards him, he became clearer in her mind's eye just before she crashed into him, and she would see the face of her true love smiling back at her.

And they would kiss.

They would kiss with such passion and completely without fear of discovery, in a world where she had not been queen and he had not been unattainable.

It was a world she would have gladly inhabited if she had had the choice during life.

But instead, her path had led her to the throne of England – a path which had been stained with blood – and she could not have allowed her mother's death to have been in vain.

Even if it had meant the sacrifice of her own happiness and the potential for true love.

The queen awoke then with a start, and as her eyes snapped open and she gasped, her ladies looked towards her apprehensively. But she settled back into the feather cushions and sighed, giving them no further concern to approach her, and they resumed their mundane activities.

Elizabeth lay there in silence, her illness having rendered her completely mute, and she looked up at the ceiling as she felt a strange weightlessness slowly taking over her body.

She allowed it to engulf her as she considered her life as England's longest reigning monarch; and though she had never wanted the throne, Elizabeth hoped she had achieved what she had set out to do when this burden had fallen to her.

She had given her life for the preservation and memory of her mother. She had dedicated herself to achieving greatness in the hope of amending history so that Anne Boleyn's sacrifice would not have been in vain. So that she would not be remembered as Henry VIII's Great Whore, but rather as the woman who had given him the child he had always hoped to have.

Elizabeth had proven that she had been that child, despite having been born a girl.

Yet guilt had haunted her in the final months of her life, her subconscious mocking her that perhaps…it had not been worth it.

And even now, as her soul left her deceasing body, she felt one final moment of regret. And just as queen Elizabeth I closed her eyes for the very last time, she croaked out one incoherent word with her final breath, just as she had promised she would so many years ago.

"Robert…"

Chapter 1

7th September 1533
Greenwich Palace, London

Queen Anne Boleyn had been confined in her birthing chamber just eleven days when her waters broke quite suddenly, and before she even had time to waddle over to the bed and mentally prepare herself for the long hours that it would surely take to birth a baby, her child slipped out from between her legs after just two contractions.

"I've got it," the midwife exclaimed as she expertly bundled up the child and straightened up from her low crouch before the queen.

Anne Boleyn stood frozen, her knees bent, and her feet wet with birthing fluid. Her teeth were chattering from the shock the swift birth had put on her body, and she looked into the midwife's eyes for some reassurance that all was well.

"Is it...?" she mumbled, before groaning suddenly as the pain of it all hit her like a lightning bolt.

The midwife looked down at the pink baby in her arms and smiled when it opened its gummy mouth and squealed.

Anne let out a breathy sigh of relief when she heard the precious sound, and she watched as the midwife peeled back the little blanket she had wrapped the baby in. But Anne's smile faded quickly when she saw the midwife's expression falter, and her stomach lurched in fear.

"What is it?" she croaked as the tears threatened to spill from her beautiful blue eyes.

The midwife looked up at her queen, "She is a healthy and strong baby girl," she confirmed.

At the words, Anne Boleyn's body slumped forward, and she released a terrifying wail, her normally stunning face now twisted and ugly at the news.

The door to the queen's birthing chambers opened then and three more midwives entered the room.

"Oh," one said as she looked from the queen to the young midwife, "Excellent work, your majesty!" she said and then walked over to observe the baby as the other two midwives took their queen by her hands and carefully walked her to the bed.

"Do you wish to hold her?" the young midwife said as she followed her queen closely.

Anne climbed into bed gingerly and sucked air in through her teeth as the pain between her legs throbbed, but she replied with a single nod.

Once she was cleaned and made comfortable, Anne swallowed her tears and raised her arms to receive her baby.

"I want to see my daughter," she said, and though she felt an instant jolt of love for the tiny baby as it was gently placed into her arms, her voice broke at the mention of her unfavourable gender.

"It is but your first child, your highness," a low voice said beside the queen and Anne looked up into the kind face of the midwife who had helped her bring her baby into the world, "There is no need for tears at a time like this," she said, and Anne realised only then that she had begun weeping.

Anne wiped her tears away and looked back down at the babe in her arms as she jerked her little head from side to side in search of a nipple to feed on.

Anne breathed a little laugh and instinctively opened the buttons of her nightshift before placing the baby's eager little mouth over her breast.

"Oh no!" Anne heard suddenly as someone exclaimed from across the room, and her head snapped up self-consciously, "A queen does not feed her child from her own breast!" and the elderly midwife who had praised her not moments earlier, approached swiftly with a disappointed frown etched on her face.

"Especially not a girl!" she hissed before snatching the infant from the queen's embrace.

Immediately the baby wailed, and Anne exclaimed in pain as the abrupt removal of her child tore the skin on her nipple.

"I would feed my own baby!" queen Anne said hotly as she covered up her chest.

"There are wet nurses for that," the older midwife replied without even looking at her queen, then handed the bundle to a plump lady beside her.

Anne watched as her newborn was passed to the red-cheeked peasant who would be the source of nourishment for her daughter, and yet she could do nothing but clench her teeth in anger, for she knew that this was the way of things.

Queens did not keep their own children.

They belonged to their king and country.

"Rest now," the older midwife said as she turned back to the queen, "You must regain your strength if you are to bear the king a son soon."

Anne lay back on her pillows carefully and watched through narrowed eyes as the older midwife escorted the wet nurse and her infant to the other room, her cheeks burning with resentment.

But while she hated the idea that she would not hold, feed, or care for her own baby for most of her life, Anne knew that the midwife had been right – this child had been a girl, which meant that Anne was not yet safe.

Nothing mattered more now than to recover and regain her beauty so that the king would forgive her this failure and attempt once more to put a boy child inside of her.

Only then would she have fulfilled her side of the unspoken bargain – that she remain queen under the promise that she would be the one to give Henry VIII the son he had been denied in his former marriage.

King Henry rubbed his hands over his tired face.

"I can almost hear Katherine and Mary cackling over the news that the queen has borne me a girl!" he said as he pressed his finger and thumb into the corners of his eyes in desperation.

Thomas Cromwell, Chancellor of the Exchequer, sighed beside the king as they walked slowly through the stone corridor towards the great hall.

"Though the queen gave you a daughter this time," he said, his deep voice calm, "The child is alive and healthy. Something your previous wife had often failed to produce."

Henry nodded briefly as he thought, "That, at least," he replied, "is true," but then he exhaled, his aggravation returned once more, "But she *promised* me a male heir! It makes a mockery of everything I have gone through by setting aside Katherine to marry Anne! It matters nothing that she is healthy and strong – she is but another *girl*!"

"Your majesty must remember that whether you have a son this day or next year," Cromwell replied, "To be separated from the darkness of Rome, and to become Supreme Leader of the Church of England, shall be your greatest achievement."

"Parliament has yet to pass the Act of Supremacy…" Henry said, his pale blue eyes staring blindly ahead.

"I can assure you that it will be passed," Cromwell replied smugly.

"But it will mean nothing," Henry suddenly exclaimed as he took a step in front of his advisor and pressed his face just inches from Cromwell's, "if the queen does not grant me a successor to leave it to."

Cromwell cleared his throat, "You are young yet, your majesty," he said tactfully as he felt his heart beating wildly in his chest at the king's outburst, "And your new wife is still in her childbearing years. I have no doubt that many more children will follow."

Cromwell watched as the king's rage evaporated before his eyes and he took a step away from him.

Henry nodded then and scratched at his chin, "Enough talk of this," he said as they entered the great hall, "There are much more important issues to discuss than the disappointment of women."

10th September 1533

"The princess is to be christened in two hours!" Charles Brandon, the king's greatest friend and advisor said, his dark eyebrows furrowed in confusion, "How can you, nor the queen, not know what to name her?"

"She promised me a boy, Charles!" Henry retorted angrily.

"No woman can make such a promise, you know that!" Charles replied, then clenched his jaw shut as his king glared at him.

"She promised me a boy," Henry repeated, "Why then would I consider girl names?"

Just then, there was a knock on the door and a young midwife walked in. She bobbed a quick curtsy as the two great men watched her, dumbfounded by her presence.

"Queen Anne has sent me," she said, and she looked from Charles to the king.

Henry waved his hand for her to go on and she cleared her throat.

"She wishes to name the princess after her mother and yours, your majesty," she said with a smile, suggesting that she very much liked the sentiment.

"Elizabeth?" Henry said aloud, testing the name out. Then he looked the midwife up and down and nodded, "Tell the queen I approve."

The young woman before them curtsied and left the room.

"Elizabeth," Charles echoed, "A great name. A name fit for a queen."

But Henry grunted as he picked up an apple from the bowl by the window, "I'd still rather have had a Henry."

November 1533

Queen Anne and her husband the king sat side by side upon their thrones as they and their courtiers enjoyed the banquet.

The court was merry, their excitement for the birth of the new princess, as well as the upcoming Christmas festivities, growing by the hour with each emptied cup of wine, and before long, everyone was dancing.

Everyone, that is, except for the king and queen.

Though they both displayed smiling faces, the tension between them had grown thick since the birth of their child, and as Anne sat straight-backed beside her once-doting husband, she contemplated all kinds of different ways she could address the obvious, unspoken issue.

But as the hours ticked by her nervousness grew and as the wine flowed without a single word spoken between them, she could no longer contain her emotions, and she strengthened herself for an argument.

"My lord," she said as she turned her head to him, her words slurring slightly, thanks to that fourth cup of wine, "I think it has been rather a long enough time to punish me," she said as she breathed erratically, her chest heaving with each breath.

Henry's gaze fell to his wife's breasts then, and he raised an eyebrow.

"Punish you?" he said casually, as though he did not understand that his silence since their daughter's birth had been torture to Anne.

While she felt frustrated by his sidestepping reply, she was pleased to see that he still felt lustful towards her, and she decided that rather than cause a scene and aggravate his anger for her further, she would use what power she held over him to hopefully regain his love.

She turned in her seat to face him.

"It pains me," she drawled, taking full advantage of his male weakness for her, "That you have not visited my bedchamber of late."

"It pains you, does it?" Henry replied as he moved closer towards his wife and licked his thin lips, and she could see from the glint in his eyes that he was picturing her naked before him.

Anne nodded as she reached her hand towards him and began caressing his upper thigh.

Henry breathed a short laugh as he looked down at his wife's hand reaching nearer his manhood, "You forget yourself," he said quietly, a small smile playing on his lips, "We are in public."

"Are we?" Anne replied innocently as she looked up at him with her bewitching blue eyes.

Henry looked down at her red lips and shifted in his seat so as to move his groin closer to Anne's hand, his eagerness for pleasure overpowering him, just as she knew it would.

But just as she felt his erect manhood underneath his hose, she removed her hand and turned away from him, leaving the king feeling utterly desperate for her.

"Perhaps we should excuse ourselves," the queen said as she looked straight ahead at the courtiers on the dancefloor before them.

Henry looked from his wife to the crowd, as though *he* had forgotten that they were in public.

"Leave them," he said, "They won't miss us," and then he stood from his throne and grabbed his queen's wrist before pulling her to stand, "Come with me, woman," he growled underneath his breath, the anger he felt towards her for the past two months suddenly forgotten, "I won't be done with you until your eyes are rolling back in your head and I can be sure that you are carrying my son in your womb!"

Although Anne still felt tender since the birth of her daughter just two months prior, she allowed the king his way with her.
As he pumped repeatedly inside her with a ferocity she had never known, Anne said a silent prayer that he would believe her cries of pain to be that of pleasure, for her very life depended on the conception of a son, and she would endure whatever she had to to obtain it.
When he finally finished, he collapsed on top of her, their naked body's sticking together with their perspiration – his of exertion and hers of agony – and though his weight crushed her, she did not complain.

"If that did not produce a son," the king mumbled, his face pressed into the pillows, "I don't know what will."
Anne nodded and swallowed, "Yes, your majesty," she croaked.
Eventually he heaved himself off of her and Anne was able to cover herself.
She lay there for a moment and listened to Henry breathing heavily beside her, satisfied and spent.
It was now or never, she thought, as she steeled herself to broach the subject she had long been fearing to raise to her husband. Namely that of the future of their daughter.

"My king," she said as she crawled towards him seductively, "I was hoping for an audience," and she smiled at him as she bit her lip, playing the part of the seductress as she knew he enjoyed the most.

Henry laughed, "I grant you an audience," he said playing along, waving his hand leisurely for her to continue.

"Your majesty is most gracious," she said as she lay down beside him, her naked breasts uncovered for him to see.

He ogled them hungrily and then took one in his hand and squeezed it, to which Anne gasped in feign pleasure to praise his fragile ego.

"What is it you wish to discuss, my queen?" he said.

Anne looked him straight in the eyes as he ran his hands over her naked body and she prayed that his attraction to her would be enough to grant her her wish.

"It concerns our daughter," she said as she pressed her body against his and felt his manhood growing erect once again, "I do not wish her to leave court. Would she not be better kept here with her own mother?"

In an instant, the king pushed her away from him, "For heaven's sake, Anne," he exclaimed as he stood up from the bed, his face twisted in frustration, "Must you bring all this up *now*?"

Anne sat up and grabbed a handful of the sheets, covering herself again, "I only speak of it now because you have denied me your presence until this moment!" she replied.

Henry ran his hand through his thick auburn hair, "Well, whatever your personal wishes may be," the king said, "The girl is to go to Hatfield with her royal household – as any other princess would be expected to –"

"—Yes, but," Anne interrupted, to which Henry's face turned red with rage at the insult, and he stepped towards her, grabbing her by the throat.

"You will listen when I speak, and not interrupt me!" he whispered menacingly as he squeezed her throat, "The girl will go to Hatfield, as is expected of her," then he flung Anne back down onto the bed, "Or do you wish for people to talk? To suggest that she is *not* a legitimate princess, if the king and queen do not send her away as other princesses would be."

Anne ran her hand over her throat and wheezed, tears pricking at her eyes, "Of course not, my lord," she croaked as she looked down at the pillows, her long brown hair like two curtains on either side of her face, hiding herself from him.

They remained in silence for a while as they both tried to compose themselves. But anger overrode Anne's composure and before she could stop herself, she pushed her hair aside, revealing an expression as hard as stone as she confronted him.

"If my child is to be taken away from me," she said hotly, "Then I would insist that the Lady Mary be made one of her nursemaids. If – as you say – there may be doubt as to the purity of our daughter, then we must show the world the order of things. Make Mary a servant to our daughter and establish their rank clearly, so that there may be no doubt as to the legitimacy of *our* children."

Henry stared at his wife in bewilderment as she spoke, his muscular chest heaving in anger at her tone.

All of a sudden, he pinned her down onto the bed, his strong hands grabbing her tightly by the wrists as he pressed his face into hers.

"You dare tell me what to do, woman?!" he screamed, and Anne flinched, trying to squirm out from underneath him.

But he was too strong.

"You're hurting me, Henry!" she pleaded, "Get off me!"

Henry ignored her cries of fear, and instead he pushed her legs apart with his knee.

"Don't, Henry," Anne begged as she knew what was to come.

And then he forced himself inside of her.

Anne screamed out in pain, unable to contain her agony this time, but Henry did not stop.

"You," he said into her ear threateningly as he raped her, "You will learn your place!" he said as he thrust aggressively, "I made you queen! And I can just as easily take it away!"

Then he groaned and shuddered in pleasure, completely uncaring that his wife lay there, motionless and limp, as tears spilled silently from her eyes and blood trickled down her legs.

Chapter 2

December 1533
Greenwich Palace, London

The little three-month-old princess Elizabeth and her household had moved from her place of birth in Greenwich Palace, to the countryside manor of Hatfield House where she would remain under the care of Lady Shelton, queen Anne's aunt.

The Lady Mary, king Henry's daughter by the former queen Katherine of Aragon, had been sent for from her residence in Hunsdon House – just a few miles from Hatfield – to tend to the new princess.

And though it had been Anne's idea to degrade the former princess of England to nothing more than a linen washer to her newborn replacement, Anne could not help but suddenly fear for the safety of her child.

Lady Mary's quick temper had become a matter of common knowledge, and there were nights when Anne would pace up and down her chambers, worrying that Mary would do something terrible to her baby girl.

"Your majesty," the queen's lady-in-waiting, Jane Seymour, said on one of those nights, "you must rest now, it is past midnight."

"I cannot," Anne replied as she chewed on her thumb nail, her pretty face ashen with apprehension, "Is there no word from Hatfield?" she asked for the third time in as many hours.

"No, your highness," Jane replied, "But no doubt they are all asleep at this hour."

"Or perhaps the place is ablaze," Anne replied anxiously, "And my poor Elizabeth among the flames!" then she covered her face with her hands and wept.

Jane Seymour frowned at Anne's irrational ramblings, and she approached the queen, "I am certain," she reassured, "That the princess is fast asleep and dreaming of her mother."

Anne continued sobbing loudly, unable to contain herself, but even while she wept, she knew that she was being absurd, and yet she felt completely inconsolable.

And not even the fact that she had missed her courses that month could bring her joy, for she feared that the child within her belly had been conceived through a terrible act of violence.

March 1534

As the king's Chief Minister Thomas Cromwell had predicted, Parliament passed the king's Act of Supremacy, defining king Henry VIII as Supreme Head of the Church of England, and thereby severing all connections with Rome and the Pope.

This meant that – not only was his marriage to Anne Boleyn finally lawful – but it put his children by her above any others in the line of succession – something Henry knew his former queen Katherine of Aragon and their daughter the Lady Mary would not take lightly.

"It's all working out perfectly," Henry said as he shot an arrow and hit the target dead centre, "With queen Anne pregnant with what will hopefully be a son, and the Act passed by parliament, all will be as it should be very soon!"

"Indeed, your majesty," Charles Brandon agreed casually as he took his turn and pulled the bow string tightly, before releasing it purposefully off-centre to allow the king this minor victory.

"The people must yet sign the oath of loyalty that they recognise your majesty's marriage to queen Anne," Thomas Cromwell interjected, his long black robes flapping in the breeze.

"They will sign," Henry mumbled.

"Not all will be so inclined," Cromwell said under his breath, to which Charles shot him a look.

"Do you mind, Cromwell!" Charles said angrily, "The king is trying to enjoy this moment of peace. Leave your weaselling work to another time!"

Henry laughed and slapped Charles heartily on his broad shoulder, "Now, now, Charles," he said, "Thomas is right. We must make sure everyone signs," then he looked down at the bow in his hand, "How does Katherine take the news?"

"The Dowager Princess of Wales, Katherine of Aragon, has not yet signed," Cromwell replied, "As your majesty may have guessed. She and your bastard daughter Mary have not willingly accepted this news."

"They will," Henry said as he looked up and squinted at the bright sky pensively, "They shall do what their king asks of them, even if I must make them."

June 1534
Greenwich Palace, London

As the queen's belly grew, so did the king's love for her, his anger over her failure to produce a son in her last pregnancy simply forgotten.

But Anne did not forget.

What had happened the night of this child's conception had never happened before or since, but Anne would never forget the hatred in her husband's eyes as he had forced himself on her.

And even now, seven months later, the memory of it still turned her stomach.

Anne knew that people whispered behind their hands about her. She knew what people called her behind her back – the king's Great Whore.

Though it stung to think of herself remembered in such a way, Anne found comfort in her knowledge that she had not willingly pursued the king.

She had seen, first-hand, the shame an affair with the king could bring upon a lady when her own sister, Mary Boleyn, had been bedded by the king until he had become bored of her, sullying her name throughout England.

And Anne had had no intention of becoming the second Boleyn girl whose reputation the king would ruin.

But when king Henry had reared his head towards Anne all those years ago when he had still been married to the former queen, Katherine of Aragon, Anne had known there and then that she would have no say in the matter.

Regardless as to whether she had been interested or not.

And she had not been.

When his lingering gazes from across the room had turned into poems sent to her in secret, suggesting his interest in her to be becoming more intense, Anne had decided that some distance would best be put between them. She had hoped that by leaving court for the sanctuary of her family home, Hever Castle, that he would surely turn his attention onto another lady within the week.

How naïve she had been.

No matter the distance or the amount of time Anne had put between them, it seemed the king would not be deterred, and he had persisted in his pursuit of her by sending her letters and gifts, begging her to return to court.

"He is in love with you," Anne's younger brother, George, had teased her one morning over breakfast when yet another messenger had arrived, this time with a sapphire necklace and a note from the king.

Anne had ignored her brother and peeled open the note.

"Read it aloud," George had said, laughing easily and seeing nothing wrong with the receiving of grand gifts, as the Boleyn family had done during their sister, Mary's, affair with the king.

"No," Anne had replied after scanning the letter's contents, and she had walked away and tossed the letter into the fire.

"Anne!" George had exclaimed, his playful tone gone, "What did it say?"

Anne *tsked,* "It does not matter," she had said.

But it had mattered.

For within that letter, the king had proclaimed his undying love for her and declared that he wished for her to become his royal mistress – something Anne had been fearing for some time when his letters had evolved from whimsical to passionate.

"Send the necklace back," she had told the messenger, who had frowned in confusion, unsure as to whether he had understood correctly.

"Anne," George called from behind her, "What the Devil are you doing?!"

"Send it back," Anne had repeated, ignoring her brother, "Tell the king I must decline his offer. Regretfully," she added at the end, though there had been no regret in her rejection of his request.

But – much to Anne's initial distaste – the king had not given up on his quest for her.

After some time, his letters had grown romantic and, although his poems were by no means exceptional, they spoke of a life together as husband and wife, suggesting that he held true feelings for her, above that of a meaningless affair, as he had had with her sister.

Though she had never wanted him or the promise of the crown, his persistence had begun to wear her down, and slowly but surely she had begun to feel butterflies at the arrival of the king's messengers.

Eventually, after a month away from court, she had given in and returned to court under the pretence that – as a royal courtier and lady-in-waiting to Katherine of Aragon – she had a duty and obligation to serve her queen. And while that was of course true, Anne had also realised that she suddenly wished to see the man who had been wooing her from afar, even if only to ask him to put a stop to his flirtations in person. But her return to court had gone nothing as to plan, and as soon as she had lain eyes on the handsome king, she knew that she was beginning to fall in love with him.

He began promising to divorce his wife for her but a week after Anne's return, and though her stomach churned with apprehension at the prospect, her new love for him blinded her of his true nature. And soon, she prayed fervently that his promise would come to pass before long.

How she wished now that she had listened to her gut and heeded her intuition, warning her of what was to come.

For, of course, the divorce from his wife would not be a simple task.

Katherine of Aragon had put up quite the fight, using all the means at her disposal to argue her marriage to the king to have been lawful in the eyes of God, her nephew the Holy Roman Emperor, as well as all of Europe, supporting her in that claim.

But Henry would not be stopped, and he had turned the country upside down on his quest to rid himself of his former wife.

Many had blamed Anne for this reckless pursuit, and while she could admit that she had played *some* part in the king's

desire for a divorce, she had never initially intended for any of it.
But it would not come to pass for some time, and after seven long years of courting Anne – first in secret and then openly – and stealing kisses and caresses but never allowing the king to claim her fully, it had taken its toll on his obsession with her.
And by the time they were finally wed, it was no longer about his love for her, but about what he had done to attain her, and what she must give him in return.
Anne looked down at her swollen belly then, her mind returned to the present as she walked through the courtyard on her way to bid the king farewell before his hunt.
She had prayed with all her might that this child would be a boy so that her duty to the king would be completed; and even though the child had been conceived of cruelty, Anne would do all in her power to ensure that he would grow up to become a good and compassionate king.
The opposite of his father.

July 1534

It was not meant to be, for but two months before the baby was due, Anne began to suffer intense cramps.
"It is too early," she whimpered, holding her hands over her belly as a gush of warm liquid ran down her legs, and she lifted her skirts to wipe a hand over her thighs.
"Oh God," she whispered as she looked at her blood-stained hand, "Oh God," she repeated and then she began to collapse.
Her ladies caught her and helped her to the bed as a servant ran off to fetch the midwives.
But it was too late.
By the time they had arrived, Anne had expelled the tiny baby from within her, and as the midwives stood frozen in terror at the foot of her bed, their queen lay there shivering, unable to

look at the little baby boy that lay motionless in a puddle of blood between her legs.

September 1534

Anne was scared. And there was nothing she could do to calm her fearful mind.
Since the loss of her baby boy, Henry had become more and more distant, the look in his eyes showing her just how much he despised her for her failure, as though she had somehow been responsible for the death of her own child.
Weeks went by in which Anne rarely spoke to, or even saw, her husband the king. On the rare occasion that she did, it was during a formal setting from which he could not escape attending without her presence, unless he wished for the rumours of their crumbling marriage to rage on.
It was at one such occasion – a jousting tournament to celebrate the passing of the Act of Succession – that the king and queen sat side by side as knights rode towards one another at full speed with great wooden lances for the nobles' entertainment.
But the king paid his wife no attention, and the tension between them was palpable.
Eventually, when the king stood and demanded to be armoured to take part in the next turn, Anne was left to sit underneath the canopy on her own.
She sat straight-backed, with a small smile plastered on her face, and she hoped that she looked the very picture of nobility and calm. But when she scanned the crowd before her and saw her brother's face peering back at her, she could tell that her mask must not have been very convincing.
"You alright?" her brother, George Boleyn, mouthed up at her, to which Anne replied by nodding once.

But he had not been assured, and moments later he stood from his seat beside his wife, Jane Boleyn Viscountess of Rochford, and made his way towards his sister.

"Cheer up, your majesty," he said with a grin as he crouched down beside her underneath the canopy.

"I am cheerful, George," Anne replied tight-lipped, "Don't you see?" and she forced her smile to broaden.

George laughed, his handsome face brightening, "Oh, sister," he said, then leaned forward slightly, "Is it the king?" he whispered.

"Isn't it always?" Anne replied quietly, never tearing her eyes from the king as he expertly swung himself onto his great warhorse.

"Has he visited your chambers since…" George asked.

Anne only shook her head and George muttered something under his breath.

"My only hope," Anne whispered, "Is to betroth Elizabeth to a prince."

George nodded as he considered the idea, "Have you thought of who?"

"I will be asking Henry today if he would consider an alliance with the French," Anne said, "It should strengthen England as well as secure Elizabeth as the rightful princess in the eyes of Europe."

George nodded and then cleared his throat as he ran a hand through his chestnut hair, "Do you think the king will think on it, at least?"

Anne shrugged her slender shoulders, "What other option do I have in this moment?" she replied quietly, "Without a male heir in our immediate future and the king growing more and more restless, I must do what I can to ensure Elizabeth is safe."

"Elizabeth will be safe," George replied as he looked over his shoulder as the king and his opponent crashed their lances into each other savagely, and he raised his eyebrows in appreciation as neither of them faltered from their horses, "she is his daughter."

Then he looked back at his sister as she sat rigidly upon her throne, "It is you who I fear is not safe."

"France will not accept," king Henry mumbled to his queen some weeks later as she stood before him as still as a statue. She watched him continue to read the letter in his hands calmly, and all the while Anne's mind spun out of control at his lack of emotion at the news.

"They won't accept?" she said sourly, unable to comprehend, "But she is the princess of England!"

Henry dropped the letter then and looked up at his wife, the lifelessness in his eyes scaring Anne more than if they had reflected anger.

"In this letter they explain that France, as well as all of Europe, does not see her as such..." the king said.

Anne tried to swallow the lump in her throat, her greatest fear having that instant come true.

"But," she mumbled with a breathy laugh, "That is absurd!"

Henry looked up at her from his seat at the table in his chambers and raised his eyebrows as he waited for her to continue, and when she did not, he inhaled, "Forgive me," he said mockingly, "I thought you would have something else more stirring to add to that pointless remark, but alas..." and he waved his hand to dismiss her.

"My lord," Anne pleaded as she took a step towards him, her voice cracking with fear, "Could we not ask them to reconsider?"

"Damn it, woman!" the king bellowed suddenly as he slammed his fist down upon the table, his eyes wild with anger, "Surely you must understand that to reject her this time was insulting! I will not beg!"

Anne's heart thumped wildly in her chest at his outburst, but it was preferable to his bored emotionlessness, for with his anger at least, she knew what he was thinking.

Anne offered him a curtsy, "I understand," she replied as she remained lowered before him, "Forgive my foolishness," and then she looked up at him, her chest rising and falling as she breathed, and she hoped that a glimpse at her breasts from that angle would calm his rage.

Henry glanced at her breasts and then back into her beautiful, azure-blue eyes, unmoved, "Leave," he said.

Anne's heart broke in two as she realised then that the king no longer desired her as he once had.

And she was suddenly acutely aware that, without an alliance with France, and without the king's love – she was lost.

February 1535

By now, almost all of England had signed the oath to the Act of Supremacy, but there were many who had blatantly refused, proclaiming the act to be ungodly and sinful.

Many were being arrested and tried for their refusal to sign – while others were put to death, including even some of those closest to the king.

Though Anne believed the act to be a vital part of her security as queen, she did not agree with the extremities to which her husband was going to. Beheading one of his dearest friends and advisors, Thomas Moore, having utterly shocked her as well as the nation.

She knew, however, that there was no talking him out of his rage, and that there was nothing she could do that would awaken Henry's forgiving nature.

If, indeed, he even had one.

Since the loss of their baby boy, the king had visited Anne's bedchamber but six times in as many months and had outrightly refused to admit her when she bravely attempted to visit his.

While he still doted on her and gifted her great jewels and magnificent dresses in public, privately, Anne knew just how little he cared for her presence; and their rare couplings had become nothing but transactional in the hopes of conceiving an heir.

But Anne had little hope left that it would come to pass, for Henry's vicious attack on her had left her mind and body traumatized, and when the only sliver of light that had come from it had ended in death, Anne's soul had been crushed.

Which was why, after six months of failing to conceive again, she was certain that it was her heartache that impacted her ability to bear another child.

And she had no idea how to fix a broken heart.

"I wish to visit my daughter," the queen announced to her husband one day, hoping to get permission to visit the only good thing left in her life.

Henry had looked up at her and dropped the meat he had been eating, then sucked the grease off his thumb and forefinger, "Go," he said, "Do as you wish."

Anne had nodded her head in thanks, her stomach dropping at the prospect that he would no doubt entertain his latest mistress in her absence – and she wondered briefly who it may be.

But the very next day Anne and her guards set off to Hatfield, and her heart soared as she approached the princess' residence, just twenty-two miles from London.

Queen Anne had been allowed to visit her daughter only one other time since the little princess' move to Hertfordshire, and otherwise had seen her only briefly during Christmastides at court. But Elizabeth knew who her mother was, and whenever they did see each other, the love and adoration they held for one another was palpable.

"Oh, my darling baby," queen Anne exclaimed as she took her seventeen-month-old little daughter into her arms, "Mummy missed you so much!" and they held each other as Elizabeth squealed with excitement.

"Let me look at you!" Anne said as she pulled away to take in her daughter's changed appearance, "Oh, Elizabeth," she whispered as she kissed the princess' plump little cheek, "You are my whole world."

"The princess is very steady on her feet, your majesty," lady Anne Shelton, the queen's aunt and princess Elizabeth's governess, said.

"Yes, I saw!" Anne replied proudly, a bright smile on her face as she pressed her cheek against Elizabeth's.

"And she is starting to communicate," lady Shelton continued, "Not much, but I see in her eyes that she wants to." Queen Anne put Elizabeth down then and took her hand before walking further into her nursery and sitting down on the floor by the fire.

"Can you say 'Mama', Elizabeth?" Anne said as she watched her daughter play with her wooden horse, "'Mama'?" Anne repeated, but Elizabeth just looked at her.

Anne smiled and stroked her daughter's head, her bright red curls springing at her touch, "What of the Lady Mary?" the queen asked lady Shelton then.

Lady Shelton cleared her throat, "She is often in her room," she said, "And only emerges to tend to the princess' linens, as requested by your majesty, and to attend chapel."

"Has she signed the oath?" the queen asked, to which a short, mousey-looking lady-in-waiting to the princess Elizabeth raised an eyebrow.

"Not that I am aware of," lady Shelton replied.

Anne nodded her head in thought, "She must not touch the princess," she said as she watched Elizabeth play quietly with the wooden horse, "She cannot be trusted around my daughter."

Lady Shelton nodded, "Of course, your majesty," she said, "I will not allow any harm to come to Elizabeth."

Anne nodded and smiled briefly in thanks, then she turned her attention back to her child, and there she remained for several hours as mother and daughter simply enjoyed each other's company.

And all the while Anne's husband the king was back in London, seducing Anne's lady-in-waiting, the lady Jane Seymour.

Chapter 3

December 1535

"My lord," queen Anne mumbled as she bobbed a curtsy to the king, her pregnant belly feeling heavy.

"Come," Henry said as he turned around and began walking out of the queen's chambers and down the dimly lit hallways, "The imperial ambassador brings news."

Anne followed as swiftly as her swollen body allowed, her ladies on either side of her to ensure she did not stumble as the king raced ahead, unaware, and no doubt uncaring, that his wife could not keep up.

By some miracle of God, the king's monthly visits to her bedchamber had granted her another gift of life, and a wave of relief had washed over Anne when, after three missed courses, she could say with certainty that she was with child once more.

She had thanked God fervently for this gift and had asked Him to keep this child safe within her womb for, though she would never admit it aloud, its life was of paramount importance – even more so, perhaps, than its gender. For to continue to fail in the delivery of live children would surely be the end of her, as Katherine of Aragon's same failings had been hers.

"Take my arm, your majesty," Anne's lady, Jane Seymour, said as she offered Anne her support.

Anne snatched her arm away from her, "Do not touch me, lady Seymour," she snapped under her breath, her piercingly blue eyes narrowed with hostility.

By now it had become common knowledge among the court that the king had taken plain Jane Seymour as his mistress, showing her favour above all others, including even the queen herself.

"Do not suppose to be my equal simply because my husband graces you with his… presence," Anne said as she looked the lady up and down, "He may show you favour, but I am his queen. And I carry his son in my belly! Remember that, Jane. You are nothing more than his whore."

Jane flinched at the insult, and Anne was glad to see she at least had the grace to blush and nod in agreement, "Forgive me, your highness," she mumbled and returned to her place among the other ladies.

"Do not count on it," Anne replied snidely over her shoulder as she entered the great hall.

Henry was already sitting impatiently on his throne, tapping his foot petulantly as he watched his wife approach and sit down carefully on her throne beside him.

The imperial ambassador, Eustace Chapuys, entered then; his thick grey hair bouncing as he walked towards them swiftly.

As he approached, Anne noticed that his expression was sombre, and she knew instantly that he would bring news of her husband's former life. She flashed Henry a quick glance to gauge his level of interest in the ambassador's visit, knowing that he too would understand the reason for the man's audience.

"Your majesty," the ambassador said in his heavy Spanish accent, and Anne noticed that he made a point of bowing directly at the king, ignoring the queen's presence entirely.

Anne raised her chin at his disrespect, but she was not surprised, for he had never acknowledged her as the rightful queen, and his loyalty to Katherine of Aragon remained strong even now.

"I bring grave news that Katherine of Aragon is grievously ill," said the ambassador.

Anne noticed from the corner of her eye that her husband sat forward in his seat, unable to hide his immediate concern for his previous wife, whom he had been married to for twenty-four years.

Anne could not help herself. Between the betrayal she felt over the king's affair with Jane Seymour, as well as his obvious discontentment with her over the last year, Anne could not control the anger she felt at her husband's sudden concern for her predecessor, and she narrowed her eyes at him in suspicion.

"Ill?" the king said before shifting slightly in his seat as he felt his wife's disapproving eyes on him.

"Yes, your highness," Eustace Chapuys replied, "I also bring you a letter from the Prin – from the Lady Mary," and the ambassador climbed the three steps to the thrones and handed the letter to the king, "She begs your majesty to allow her to visit her mother on her deathbed."

The king skimmed the letter, and all the while Anne watched him, every second that ticked by giving her greater cause to worry over the security of her position. Her heart beat wildly at the possibility that he had played her for a fool for all these years, and that his feelings for her were nothing more than the fickle promises of a faithless man.

The ambassador and the king exchanged some more words, but Anne could not hear them, for her blood had begun to pump uncontrollably through her body, leaving her ears ringing sharply from it. And as the two men's mouths moved soundlessly, Anne could not help but think that the ringing in her ears sounded unmistakeably like alarm bells.

The king had not allowed his bastard daughter, Mary, to visit her mother, under the suspicion that the former queen's illness was but a ruse to create a plot against the king.

This decision brought Anne some reprieve, suggesting that Henry did not, in fact, harbour any lingering feelings for his former queen.

But the matter of his betrayal with the lady Jane continued to haunt her in her dreams as well as her reality, and her mind was as heavy as her growing belly.

Anne could not help it, but she loved the king.

Even now. After all he had done.

Though she had initially rejected his advances and had had no inclination of becoming his, through his persistence and promises of a lifetime of happiness, she had fallen for him. And yet, even now, after nearly fifteen years of having known him, she could not rightly say what it was that she loved about him.

He was powerful, no doubt. As the king of England, he was the most powerful man in the country, and this of course arose some attraction towards him.

He was also good-looking and well built, his love for jousting and hunting having given him a beautifully sculptured physique.

But Anne believed that despite all that, his greatest gift and most attractive quality was the way he could make someone feel when he turned his attention towards them. As if no one else mattered, or even existed, but them.

She believed now that it had been his attentiveness and persistence which had made her fall for him.

And not his character.

Anne had recently learned that he had very little else to offer other than his all or nothing, his personality having come to light as nothing but that of a petulant, spoilt child, who would discard you at the earliest convenience if he did not get his way.

This realisation brought a knot to Anne's stomach on a daily basis, and though the court was merry for the Christmastide, and she got to spend time with her daughter Elizabeth, she had recently become overwhelmed with fear that she too would be cast aside as his former beloved had been.

Anne dreaded to think of what would happen to her and her daughter if she would fail her king one more time – for she knew that she had already lost his love – and the only thing that was keeping her upon the throne was the child within her belly.

This child was her last hope. The only thing that would keep not only her, but Elizabeth, safe.

And so – for her daughter's sake – Anne spent many hours of every day at prayer, begging God to keep this unborn child from harm, so that her daughter would continue to be safe.

He *had* to be born healthy and strong.

This child would be – *had to be* – their savour.

Her life depended on it.

January 1536

The former queen of England was dead.

When news of Katherine of Aragon's passing broke, Anne noticed that the mood throughout the court was suddenly much less merry, and it dawned on her that the people of England truly had loved their former queen.

To hear that she had in fact been fatally ill when her daughter had begged the king to see her, grieved Anne deeply, for as a mother, she could understand the grief the two women must have felt to be denied one final goodbye.

Only a few days after the news had spread through court, Anne became increasingly aware that people had begun whispering behind their hands to one another, and stopping midway through conversations whenever she entered the room.

But Anne had little energy to waste on the newest court gossip, for she had recently begun to feel the familiar aches that had previously led to the premature arrival of her last baby.

"I should like to lay down," Anne told her ladies one morning when a messenger arrived inviting her to a joust, "Tell the king," Anne said, addressing the messenger, "That I regret to have to decline the invitation."
She carefully climbed into bed as the messenger bowed and hurried away, all the while holding her great belly with one arm, as if to carry the weight off of her own body.
When she finally got comfortable among her feather pillows, Anne breathed in and out deeply in an attempt to calm her mind. Then she closed her heavy eyelids and fell asleep.

She was awoken but an hour later when the same messenger burst through the doors to the queen's chambers, followed closely by her guards who had been standing outside the doors.
"His majesty the king," the messenger wheezed as he tried to catch his breath, "He has fallen from his horse!"
"What?!" Anne exclaimed in panic as she heaved herself upright and stood up from her bed, "Is the king alive?"
The messenger shook his head and coughed as he breathed raggedly, and in that moment, it felt as though the ground fell out from underneath Anne's feet.
"Oh my God," she breathed as her vision blurred, a mixture of intense relief, as well as dread, engulfing her, "No, it cannot be," she muttered, remembering only to show her dread.
It was not until two hours later that she would hear news of the king's miraculous recovery, his physicians being utterly baffled by the strange and sudden reawakening of their king who, just moments before, had been unconscious and practically knocking at death's door.
The ordeal had left Anne spent, the battle of her emotions creating a tidal wave of unease to coarse through her body.
And that night – as the rest of the castle was still – Anne's baby would be born sleeping.

She had miscarried of her saviour.

Anne had sat at the edge of her bed all night, her bloody nightshift sticking to her thighs as she stared blindly at the floor ahead, her last hope of reclaiming the king's love having died along with her infant.
It was only when a servant girl entered her rooms to stoke the fire for the cold day ahead that Anne suddenly realised that hours had passed since her baby had made its untimely arrival. Immediately, she attempted to hide herself and her bloody clothing underneath her bedsheets, but as the servant girl entered the queen's bedchamber to find drops of blood on the floor where her feet had dangled all night, she gasped in terror and ran to the queen's bedside.
"Your majesty," she said, trying to sound calm, "Should I fetch the midwives?" and she tried to peel the cover off of her queen.
Anne grabbed fistfuls of the sheets and pulled them around herself and over her head, "No!" she screamed from underneath the covers, "Get out!"
Just then, the doors to the queen's chambers opened and her ladies made their entrance unannounced, as they would on any other day.
"Your majesty?" her lady, Nan Gainsford, said as she entered the bedchambers to find Anne tucked under her bedcovers, "Are you unwell?" she said as she walked around to the other side of the queen's bed, and then inhaled sharply as she saw a tiny, bloody, bundle wrapped in a blanket on the floor.
Nan looked up at the servant girl across the room and gauged from her expression that she had not yet seen the little bundle, "Leave us," she said urgently, and the girl hurried away.

Nan watched her leave, then peered out to the other rooms before closing the heavy curtain to the queen's bedchamber to gain some privacy.

"Anne!" Nan hissed as she hurried back to the queen's bedside where the bundle lay motionless, "What happened?!"

She picked the lifeless baby up gently, as though it still mattered that it be handled with care, and she looked down at its little button nose and its beautifully pouty, yet purple, lips.

Anne did not reply, and Nan could only imagine the agony her queen must be feeling at the loss of yet another baby, and she allowed the tears to fall for the innocent little life in her arms. Then she slowly peeled back the blanket it had been carefully wrapped in, all the while praying that it would not be another lost boy.

Nan uncovered the tiny baby's little body, and her heart sank, for not only had the child been born male, but it was also deformed from the neck down, its little body twisted and misshapen beyond human recognition.

And Nan knew that as soon as the king would find out about it, Anne Boleyn would be to blame.

2nd May 1536
Greenwich Palace

Queen Anne and her ladies were enjoying the fine Spring air and feeling greatly entertained as her brother George was losing terribly at a tennis match against Sir Francis Weston.

"See how he sulks," Anne laughed over her shoulder at her ladies who giggled merrily at the sight of the great George Boleyn losing his temper over such a trivial matter.

"Now, now, George!" Queen Anne called, "It is but a bit of fun!"

"I seem to recall a similar reaction out of you, your majesty, when we were children," George called back in jest.

"Ah, so you see that I have grown up since," Anne replied as she laughed, to which George bowed grandly and resumed the match.

Just then, as the queen settled herself back into her seat underneath the canopy, a messenger arrived.

"Your majesty," he mumbled as he bowed his head in greeting, "The king requests that you present yourself to his Privy Council."

Anne blinked, "The king has asked for me?" she asked as her stomach dropped.

"No, your grace," the messenger said and then swallowed, "He orders for you to go to the council chamber. To present yourself to the Privy Council."

Anne looked over her shoulder at Nan, her eyes wide with confusion and fear, "Nan?"

Nan shook her head and shrugged, "I do not know," she answered, as if she had read a question in her queen's mind, "But you must go."

Anne looked back at the messenger and cleared her throat before rising shakily from her seat, "Tell the king's council that the queen is underway," and she watched as the messenger sped off ahead.

Anne stood stock still for a moment as she watched him disappear, her feet feeling suddenly as heavy as two boulders.

"Your highness," Nan said quietly behind her, "You must go."

Anne nodded her head and made her way up the path and into the Palace, her throat tightening with each step, for she knew that the king was much displeased with her since her latest loss.

When the queen entered the council chamber and saw three of the king's council members awaiting her, she relaxed slightly at the sight of her own uncle, Thomas Howard the Duke of Norfolk.

"My lords," she said in greeting, but Anne's fear returned in an instant when none of them bowed their heads upon her entrance, suggesting that something terrible was about to happen – and she could do nothing but await her fate.

"Your majesty," one of the men said and Anne recognised him as Sir William Paulet, "You are hereby being accused of committing adultery against your sovereign lord and king Henry VIII, with no less than *three* men, two of which have already confessed to the crime. How do you plead?"

Anne stared at the three men before her, her mouth open in shock. Then she blinked and shook her head slowly before inhaling deeply, steeling herself for the inevitable.

"It is not true," she said simply, her voice as hard as stone, "I would never have committed such crimes against my husband and king, for he is the only man on this good earth to which I have given myself to."

Then she raised her chin defiantly and stared them down as she breathed erratically, and she said a silent prayer that she would be believed.

For surely, she would. Since it was the truth!

The three men looked at one another and Anne rested her gaze upon her uncle, who certainly would not allow this to happen.

He would stand to defend his own flesh and blood.

Wouldn't he?

"Your highness," Sir William Paulet said as he turned to face his queen after a moment of quiet discussion, "You are henceforth under arrest and shall be kept within your royal apartments until the turn of the tide of the Thames, after which you shall be escorted by barge to the Tower of London, where you will remain until your trial."

Anne blinked, unable to understand the words she had just heard. Then she began to laugh, a small laugh at first which she hid behind her delicate hand. But then it quickly grew into a more intense, almost manic laughter as the three men continued to simply watch her through emotionless eyes.

Anne knew that to laugh in the face of danger was her mind's way of coping with the news of certain death, but she also laughed at the irony of where her life had taken her – for had she not been the Boleyn girl who had tried to keep a distance from the king? Had she not been the one who had, all those years ago, not even been interested in him or in becoming his queen?

After all the abuse and heartache he had put her through, when it had been *he* who had wanted *her;* and now to be condemned as an adulteress when it was *he* who blatantly fornicated with her ladies, was too comical for Anne to maintain her composure.

But the laughter soon subsided as the reality of it all became increasingly unavoidable, and she cleared her throat before inhaling deeply.

Then, once the bout of laughter had dwindled and the three men continued to watch her, Anne stared them down, her blue eyes glistening with unshed tears as she breathed raggedly in and out.

Every fibre of her body screamed for her to run, while her soul simply laid down and died as she realised in that moment that she would never see her beloved daughter ever again.

And just like Katherine of Aragon before her, Anne Boleyn, too, would never get to say goodbye to her daughter.

Chapter 4

19th May 1536
Hatfield House, Hertfordshire

The two-and-a-half-year-old princess Elizabeth sat playing with her wooden toys in the garden when the ladies around her suddenly looked from one to another as the sound of galloping horses grew near.
The princess' governess, lady Shelton, hurried inside Hatfield House to greet the messengers, who Elizabeth thought would no doubt have brought her a new dress or toy from her royal mother and father, and so she stood up from the lawn with excitement to see what gift she would be receiving.
But as the little girl toddled inside – two of her ladies walking beside her – Elizabeth was shocked to see a dozen men aggressively ripping tapestries off the walls and shouting commands at one another, while the lady Shelton stood dumbfounded and pale-faced in the middle of the room.
"Did the king...?" one of Elizabeth's ladies asked Anne Shelton.
The older lady turned to face them and nodded before looking down at the little princess' confused and worried face.
Lady Shelton walked towards Elizabeth and took her gently by the hand before turning her around and back to her toys on the lawn.
"Shall we continue playing, princess?" she said cheerfully.
Elizabeth looked up at the plump lady beside her and flashed her a bright smile.
And though lady Shelton feigned happiness as she entertained the little girl as her home was being wrecked, inside she was heartbroken – for queen Anne had been executed, and she knew that Elizabeth's life would never be the same again.

June 1536

Though Elizabeth was but a small child, she could tell straight away that something significant had happened.
Her home suddenly felt different – emptier and bigger, almost daunting – and though the sun had started to feel warmer the last few weeks with the promise of summer, her home now felt strangely cold.
Elizabeth also noticed that many of the faces she had known throughout her short life were suddenly no longer to be found, many ladies and servants having disappeared as if into thin air, and those that did remain no longer called her 'Princess', but 'Lady' instead.
Elizabeth did not know what any of it meant or even why it had come to pass, but her little chest felt heavy with unease as things only got worse each day.

"Elizabeth," her half-sister Mary said as she crouched down before her one afternoon and smiled, "You must be strong now," she said, and Elizabeth frowned briefly.

"Our father the king," Mary continued slowly so that Elizabeth would have a chance of understanding, "has asked me to move back to Hunsdon House."

"Back?" Elizabeth repeated to which Mary nodded.

"Which means I will no longer live here with you," her sister explained.
Elizabeth's eyes grew wide then as the significance of the words sunk in.

"No!" she exclaimed and grabbed Mary by the arm and began to cry.

"That's enough now, lady Mary," Anne Shelton said as she stepped forward and tried to take Elizabeth's hand, "Come now, Elizabeth," the lady said.
But Elizabeth only screeched and held Mary's arm tighter.

Mary pulled her arm free gently and picked her sister up in her arms, "I shall see you soon!" she promised, but Elizabeth's chest tightened at the thought of not seeing her beloved older sister every day.

The strangely cold feeling she had felt of late suddenly engulfed her, and she began to cry louder, burying her face in Mary's neck.

"Now really!" Anne Shelton said impatiently as she pulled Elizabeth from Mary's embrace.

And the little girl could do nothing but let go, her throat becoming raw as she screamed for her sister to stay.

Elizabeth watched from her governess' constricted grasp as her sister mounted her horse and rode out of Hatfield House's gates, and all the while Elizabeth wept, her young mind unable to understand why those that she knew and loved were suddenly abandoning her.

July 1536 *('Goodbye's the Saddest Word' by Celine Dion)*

"A messenger, lady Shelton," Elizabeth's only remaining lady-in-waiting said as she scurried into the nursery, a young man following closely behind.

"I bring news from court," the young man said, addressing the lady Shelton, "The lady Elizabeth has officially been declared as illegitimate by Parliament, following the execution of her mother Anne Boleyn and the king's marriage to the new queen Jane Seymour."

At the mention of her mother, Elizabeth looked up from the toys before her, "Mama?" she said, her eyes searching the room then, in hopes of seeing her.

Lady Shelton looked over at the poor child and pressed her lips together, completely lost as to what she ought to tell the little girl.

"You may leave," lady Shelton said to the messenger, and he turned on his heel and left.

"Mama?" Elizabeth repeated as she looked over at her governess and then stood up from the floor.

Lady Shelton held out her arms, "No, my dear child," she said as Elizabeth toddled towards her, "Your mother is not coming today."

Elizabeth's face dropped but she allowed herself to be heaved onto the plump lady's lap.

"Your mother is with God now," the lady said gently, to which Elizabeth frowned, "She will always be with you. But you shall never see her again."

Elizabeth looked down at her little hands, the meaning of her governess' words too great for her to truly comprehend. But she felt her throat tighten as a sadness washed over her for a reason she could not fully understand.

"Oh, my dear girl," lady Shelton said then as she noticed Elizabeth's tears and she wrapped her protective arms around her, rocking her gently.

They remained there for a long time in silence, little Elizabeth crying silently over the loss of her mother, and lady Shelton crying over the loss of her niece.

And, after a while, when the girl's governess believed that her ward had fallen asleep in her arms, she gently kissed the top of her head and mumbled, "If only you had been born a boy."

But Elizabeth had not been asleep, and she stared blindly ahead, a deep sense of guilt washing over her as she wept.

October 1537
Hatfield House, Hertfordshire

A year later, little lady Elizabeth was running through Hatfield House's garden barefoot and unkempt as the lady Shelton tried desperately to catch her.

"Lady Elizabeth," the lady called, out of breath, "Stop at once!"

But Elizabeth paid her no attention, the thrill of being chased overcoming any desire for etiquette.

Lady Shelton, a woman in her early fifties, gave up the chase easily, her body too aged to be able to keep up with the four-year-old Elizabeth.

When the young girl noticed her governess had given up trying to catch her, she stopped and turned around to face her before sticking her tongue out defiantly.

The vulgarity of the child's actions inspired a new bout of adrenaline to pump through lady Shelton, and she picked up her skirts and began running after the little girl once more, her face creased with irritation.

Elizabeth shrieked with happiness as well as fear, fear of being caught and spanked for her misbehaviour. But she recognised that it would be a while before the old lady would be able to capture her, and unless she tripped and fell, Elizabeth knew they would be playing this deliciously aggravating game for a long time.

Just then, as the lady Shelton missed Elizabeth's arm by but an inch, a messenger rode up to the gates in a cloud of dust, and lady Shelton and Elizabeth both stood stock still as he dismounted and approached them, news from court over the last year having been nothing but blow after blow.

"Lady Shelton, lady Elizabeth," the man said as he bowed his head briefly, "I bring news of the birth of a healthy son and heir to the kingdom. Queen Jane has granted the king a long-awaited heir."

At the news, lady Shelton forced a smile and turned to Elizabeth, "You have a brother, Elizabeth."

"A brother?" Elizabeth repeated as she looked from her governess to the man before her.

"There is more," the messenger continued, "The queen was taken ill since the birth. And though she recovered briefly, she has sadly since passed and is now with God."

Lady Shelton shook her head, "Poor child," she mumbled, then raised her head to address the messenger, "We thank you for the news. Please send the king our deepest condolences for the loss of his wife, the queen."

The messenger nodded, "And congratulations, too?"

Lady Shelton raised an eyebrow, "Yes, of course," she said, "And our greatest congratulations for the birth of a healthy…son."

Elizabeth watched the exchange, unable to gauge the meaning behind the words and the tone in which they were spoken, and she thought briefly how odd grown-ups were.

Then she forgot about the entire conversation and began running around the gardens once again, her little feet feeling no pain as she ran unprotected upon the sharp gravel.

Greenwich Palace, London

England was weak.

Following the death of queen Jane Seymour, the king of England had fallen into a deep sorrow and locked himself in his chambers for weeks, seeing no one but his fool, Will Sommers, who had kept him from the brink of despair with the constant flow of wine and jokes.

When Henry finally emerged, refreshed and clear-headed, he knew that his council and his country would expect him to pursue a new marriage and alliance.

But he could not bring himself to even consider another, for the loss of his dearest wife – the angel who had gifted him his long-awaited son – was still too raw.

Instead, to strengthen the country in any way that he could without subjecting himself to the task, he evaluated what little he could do with the children that he had.

"Councilmen," king Henry said in greeting once all his advisors had entered and taken a seat at the council table, "We must seek to strengthen England – and before you say it," Henry said abruptly as he saw his Chancellor of the Exchequer, Thomas Cromwell, open his mouth to speak, "I shall not be considering new queens for myself."

Henry inhaled deeply then as his chest tightened at the memory of Jane.

"I have considered of late, a betrothal for my daughter, the lady Mary," Henry continued, "It is about time she was wed, and what better time than when England needs it most."

Some of the members of the Privy Council nodded their heads in agreement.

"Any idea who, your majesty?" the Duke of Suffolk Charles Brandon asked, his dark eyebrows raised in question.

Henry wagged his finger in the air, "I have, Charles," he said, "I think we should revive her previous engagement to the second son of the king of France, Henri d'Orleans."

"But their first betrothal was rejected by France itself," Cromwell pointed out, "Why ought they reconsider it?"

Henry narrowed his pale blue eyes in anger, "Because she is the daughter of a king," he said simply, his tone indicating that he would not be challenged on the matter, not even by his favourite.

Cromwell bowed his head in apology, "Yes, your majesty," he mumbled before taking note of the king's orders on the parchment before him.

Charles Brandon smirked as he observed the back and forth between Cromwell and the king.

Charles had no love for Cromwell, never had done. His weasel-like behaviour towards the king had always irked

Charles even before he had received so many unwarranted promotions. So, to watch Henry finally lose his patience with Cromwell was like music to Charles' ears.

But Thomas Cromwell was not a foolish man, Charles would say that much about him at least. Though he was of low birth, he had achieved much in his fifty-two years to be Henry's right-hand man and to have the king's ear – even above Charles himself.

But Cromwell had begun abusing his power of late, going so far as to assume himself above his betters, as though he had not in fact been born of a lowly blacksmith.

Charles had finally had enough of his arrogance, but he knew there was not much he could do, for until Henry had reason to demote him, Cromwell would continue in his glory.

"Might we consider some alternatives? Portugal perhaps?" Charles Brandon added casually, hoping to fuel the flame of doubt Cromwell had ignited in the king, "To ensure at least one response, and if more were to accept then England would have her pick of the best."

"Excellent idea," the king replied and then turned his attention back to Cromwell, "See to it that marriage proposals are sent to France and Portugal, Thomas. In the meantime, I shall consider others. But there is another subject I wish to broach," then he stopped to clear his throat, "While the lady Mary is of age to wed and create an alliance for England, I wish also to strengthen my other daughter's worth for a future alliance."

The members of the Privy council looked around at one another, none of them daring to speak – for the king's love for his children and their mothers wavered from one moment to the next, and to agree with him today about his illegitimate daughter's worth could prove fatal tomorrow.

Eventually, when the silence had dragged on uncomfortably long, Charles Brandon cleared his throat, "A wise decision, your majesty," he said, and he was amused to see the other council members visibly relax in their seats that they had not been the ones to reply.

They were all cowards.

"What do you suggest?" Charles asked.

"Well," Henry said then as he ran his hand through his coppery hair, "She is still a bastard – and a girl – so there is not much necessary in the form of tutoring. However, she must be educated in music, dancing, and languages. It is the very least she ought to know as the daughter of the king if she is ever to be of any use to me. So, I think it's about time that Anne Shelton be discharged from her duties in favour of a more educated governess. For not only is she unable to teach Elizabeth anything of real value, but I also want my daughter released from any and all connections to her mother's family."

Thomas Cromwell stood then, eager to show his support, "An excellent decision, your majesty," he said, and Charles rolled his eyes.

"Sit down, Cromwell," Charles grumbled, "Your arse-kissing will be the death of you yet."

At that Henry roared with laughter and slapped his friend on the shoulder as Thomas Cromwell's face reddened with humiliation. But he resumed his seat slowly as the other advisors sniggered under their breaths.

He shot a threatening glance at Charles, and yet his stomach flipped with unease as he considered the way of all the king's previous favourites: Thomas Wolsey, Thomas Moore, Katherine of Aragon, Anne Boleyn...

And so, he remained silent throughout the remainder of the meeting, all the while fearing that Charles Brandon may very well be right.

March 1538
Hatfield House, Hertfordshire

As the mousey-looking lady-in-waiting got Elizabeth dressed for the day, Lady Shelton watched from across the room and shook her head.

"The girl needs new clothes," she pointed out frustratedly.

"Will the king send some bolts of textile?" the young lady said as she stood and took a step back to assess the ill-fitting dress the little girl was squeezed into.

"I have sent a letter," Shelton replied, "But I received no reply."

The girl raised an eyebrow, "Are you surprised?" she asked the lady Shelton.

Anne Shelton smiled at little Elizabeth then, "Off you go, Elizabeth," she said, "You may play," and then she turned back to the lady beside her as Elizabeth hurried away.

"The king does not even send us pay to care for his child since the execution of her mother. He may be sending enough food to keep us alive, but beyond that I believe he cares little for her comfort."

The young lady nodded, her stomach rumbling as if on cue, and they both fell silent as they thought.

"The lady Mary," the mousey girl exclaimed abruptly, and then crinkled her nose at the memory of Elizabeth's half-sister, who had caused them nothing but bother during her time at Hatfield House, "The king has accepted her back into his favour and she now resides at court."

"What of her, girl?" Shelton asked, irritated.

"Well, she does care for her little sister," she said, "Despite our dislike of her, she would certainly speak on her sister's behalf if we informed her of the situation. The king may not reply to you as Anne Boleyn's aunt, but he may listen to his own daughter."

Lady Shelton raised her eyebrows and nodded, "I had not thought of it," she admitted, then she turned and walked towards the writing desk, "Fetch the messenger," Shelton called over her shoulder, "We must get word to the lady Mary at once, or the lady Elizabeth shall be running around in rags before long!"

Just two weeks later, several bolts of cloth arrived at Hatfield House. Though they were not of the finest quality, and certainly no cloth of gold, they were rich fabrics nonetheless – wool and silk – which gave the lady Shelton some hope for Elizabeth's future and that perhaps the king did care for her after all.
At least a little.
Anne Shelton and the lady-in-waiting got to work immediately, sewing the little girl new dresses. And though it really was the very least a father could do for his child, lady Shelton could tell that Elizabeth was utterly delighted with the gift.
The following day, Shelton was surprised to have received a plate of gold from the lady Mary, with a note attached with a simple 'thank you'.
With it they were able to treat themselves and Elizabeth to a month of hearty meals, which was a long sought-after reprieve from the gruel and stale bread they had been living off for months.
And though lady Shelton and the lady Mary had never once seen eye to eye when she had lived at Hatfield as Elizabeth's nursemaid, Shelton was not too proud to admit that she was grateful for Mary Tudor's forgiving heart.

April 1538

It was a wet and cold morning.

The rain had begun a month before and had been a constant throughout the month of April, leaving the four-year-old Elizabeth feeling bored and increasingly restless.

Elizabeth enjoyed nothing more than to spend the day outside, exploring her surroundings and leaving no stone unturned.

She would spend hours inspecting the different colours of the fallen leaves or sit cross-legged by an ant hill just to count each one as they marched out in single file. Her mind was always searching for more information, and nothing brought her more joy than to learn something new.

And so, when the rain would not cease from falling week after week, Elizabeth began to wonder if she would ever learn something new again, the gloomy insides of Hatfield House bringing her no pleasure to investigate yet again.

One morning, Elizabeth and her governess sat side by side at the small wooden table by the fire, eating their bowl of gruel in silence, when they suddenly heard horses approaching through the constant sound of the rain.

Elizabeth dropped her wooden spoon into the bowl of grey slop and hurried towards a window, her curious mind eager to know who had graced her with their presence, after so many months of solitude.

But all she saw as she looked down towards the gate, were five wet horses, and five cloaked figures upon their backs.

"Who is it, lady Shelton?" Elizabeth asked, her little voice giving away how confused she was at the unannounced and bannerless visitors.

"I do not know," Shelton admitted, "Come," she said as she stepped away from the window and took Elizabeth's hand, "We must be ready to present ourselves."

With Anne Shelton ahead and little Elizabeth trying to keep up, they hurried along the darkened hallways and into the main hall of Hatfield House, where they would welcome their unexpected guests.

The guards opened the doors to the main hall and gave entrance to the five cloaked and soaking wet people, and as they entered, Elizabeth felt a brief moment of fear, the gloomy weather outside evoking an eerie atmosphere upon their shrouded arrival.

But then they removed their hoods and shook the rain off their shoulders, revealing two guards and three women, and Elizabeth visibly relaxed.

"Ah," the lady at the centre of the group said as she exhaled and smiled, "It is good to be out of the rain!" and then she peeled her dripping cloak off her shoulders, "We must apologise for our late arrival," she continued, addressing lady Shelton, "But the weather kept us from making a direct approach."

Lady Shelton's thick brows twitched, "Forgive me, lady –?"

"Ashley," the lady replied, "Katherine Ashley. Please call me Kat."

Lady Shelton smiled tightly, "Lady Katherine Ashley," she said formally, "Forgive me, but I do not understand. We were not given word of your arrival."

At that, lady Ashley frowned and looked at the young ladies beside her, one of which shrugged while the other simply shivered in her wet clothes.

Kat Ashley turned back to the lady Shelton, "The king sent us," she said, as though it would spark the lady Shelton's memory.

"We have been sent to tend to the lady Elizabeth," Kat continued, "To... well, to replace you, my lady."

At the words, Elizabeth's stomach dropped, and her eyes widened as she looked up at her plump governess.

Shelton looked down at her little ward, whom she had cared for since birth, and smiled a sad smile. Then she looked back to the lady Ashley.

"May I see written word?" she asked, though she knew the word of the king did not need proving.

Lady Ashley immediately produced a carefully tucked away leather pouch from which she pulled out a letter, "Of course," she said, and she stepped towards the older lady and handed her the letter with the king's seal, "I apologise for my bluntness, lady Shelton. We did not know that you had not been previously informed."

Lady Shelton raised her eyebrows as she took the letter, "It must have slipped the king's mind," she said, but it was clear by her tone that she did not believe that, and lady Ashley's lips twitched in sympathy for the aunt of the late Anne Boleyn.

As Anne Shelton read the letter, all the ladies remained silent, and Elizabeth looked from one to another, her panic rising as each silent second ticked by.

Lady Ashley offered the little girl what she hoped was a reassuring smile, but the girl only shrunk away behind her governess, and Kat felt her stomach tighten at the loss she knew was about to come to the lady Elizabeth.

Anne Shelton sniffed then as she raised her head from reading the letter and handed it back to lady Ashley.

"It says effective immediately," Anne Shelton said, and Kat was saddened to see tears in the older lady's eyes.

Kat could do nothing but nod, and then she watched as Anne turned back to the confused Elizabeth and bent down to hold her face in her hands.

"Now you listen to me lady Elizabeth," Anne Shelton said, her tone strong yet heavy with emotion, "These ladies have come to take care of you in my stead –"

"No!" Elizabeth exclaimed, interrupting her governess.

"Ah!" Shelton retorted as she held up a finger, "It is unseemly to interrupt, and you mustn't put my teachings to shame before these new ladies."

Elizabeth nodded but she could not control her tears, and they streamed down her face unchecked.

"Listen to me, Elizabeth," Anne continued as she looked her little ward in the eyes, "Your father has sent these ladies to care for you. If it is his will then we must respect it for he is not only your father, but your king. And I have every faith in him that my replacement," and then she looked over her shoulder at the lady Ashley, "will do a much better job of caring for you than I have."

Though she had uttered the words as a statement, Kat Ashley knew them to have been a direct question, and so she nodded in promise that she would do her very best to tend to the little lady.

Anne Shelton looked back at Elizabeth as she silently cried, her little chin trembling with grief.

"It is for your best, Elizabeth," Shelton whispered lovingly, "For reasons unknown to us, the king has given you a new household and a new path ahead," then she wiped the tears from the little girl's cheeks and smiled, "And I believe your days of eating gruel for breakfast is likely in your past."

Elizabeth giggled then, but the sadness overwhelmed her again quickly, "Will you come back?" she asked, her little voice echoing in the great, empty room.

Anne pressed her lips together and shook her head, "But I will always keep you in my prayers. Do you promise to keep me in yours?"

Elizabeth nodded vigorously, "I shall keep you in my prayers along with Mama."

Anne breathed a sad laugh, then she kissed Elizabeth's forehead and straightened up before heading upstairs to pack her things and leave Elizabeth's life, forever.

Elizabeth cried for days.

Violently and loudly at first – so much so that she would make herself sick from it – and then silently and in secret, whenever she thought no one could see.

Elizabeth had known much loss in her short years. First her mother – whose sudden disappearance she still did not fully understand – then her sister and her ladies, and now her dear governess, who had been there to wipe her tears through all the other losses.

But now she too was gone, and with her the only other lady-in-waiting Elizabeth had known.

They had packed up their few belongings three days prior, when the group of strangers had arrived at Hatfield House unannounced and uninvited.

But when Elizabeth's tears had finally run out, her sadness was replaced with red-hot hatred.

"Do not touch me!" little Elizabeth screamed one morning as her two new ladies tried to dress her, "Don't you know who I am?" she shouted, her pale face turned red with anger, "I am the daughter of the king! Do not touch me!" and she stomped her little foot onto one of the lady's toes.

"Ow!" the lady exclaimed, but she let the little girl run off into the corner, her dress hanging off her, half open.

Another lady, the one Elizabeth remembered had introduced herself as Katherine Ashley, approached Elizabeth then and crouched down before her.

"I know you miss your governess," lady Ashley said with a smile, "It is perfectly natural to be confused and frightened."

"I am not frightened!" Elizabeth said and crossed her arms with a *humph*.

"Can you tell me what it is you are feeling, my lady?" lady Ashley asked calmly then.

"I am angry," she challenged.

Lady Ashley nodded her head, "That, too, is perfectly natural," and then she looked over her shoulder and waved the other two ladies out of the room before turning back to Elizabeth, who watched the silent exchange of orders.

"You know," lady Ashley said, "I too lost my mother when I was very young."

Elizabeth frowned, her young mind not understanding, "Where did you lose her?"

The lady laughed, a gentle and warm laugh, "No, my sweet child," she said, "When someone has passed on, we say that 'we lost them'."

Elizabeth cocked her head to one side.

Lady Ashley, sensing the young girl's anger to have dissipated and replaced with curiosity, risked reaching for her slowly and she was glad to see Elizabeth approach her willingly.

"Do you know what it is to die?" lady Ashley said as she pulled Elizabeth's sleeves over her shoulders.

The little girl nodded, "I think so," she admitted, "It is when someone goes to God and you never see them again."

"That's right!" lady Ashley said with a smile, and Elizabeth frowned at her enthusiasm.

"But why do you smile?" Elizabeth asked then, the lady's joy at the prospect of death confusing the young girl.

Lady Ashley shrugged as she tied the front of Elizabeth's bodice, "Death is a part of life," she explained, "One cannot be without the other. And though it is sad for us who remain on Earth, those who go to God are happy in Heaven."

Elizabeth blinked in thought and then said, "So you did not lose your mother. And I did not lose mine."

It was lady Ashley's turn to cock her head, "What do you mean, my lady?"

"Well, if they are in Heaven, and we know where they are," Elizabeth said with a bright smile, "Then they are not lost to us."

Lady Ashley breathed a little laugh at the young girl's insight beyond her years.

"I suppose that is right," Ashley said as she stood, and she felt a flicker of hope come alive inside her as Elizabeth smiled up at her, "You are a very clever little girl, Elizabeth, has anyone ever told you that?"

The girl's smile vanished in an instant, and her light eyebrows furrowed together once more.

"Lady Shelton used to tell me all the time," she said, her icy tone returned, "Before you came and took her away from me," and then she narrowed her blue eyes at lady Ashley and ran off, her disdain for her new governess remembered once more.

Chapter 5

January 1539
Hatfield House, Hertfordshire

It took many months for Elizabeth to fully accept that the lady Ashley and her other ladies were here to stay, but with each month that passed, the little girl thought less and less of those that she had lost and began to slowly but surely warm to her new entourage.
The lady Ashley was by far Elizabeth's favourite, the two having bonded greatly since that first icy encounter, and it was she who Elizabeth ran to if a question needed answering of if she fell and grazed her knee.
But lady Ashley was by no means an easy-going governess.
Not a week went by without her voice cracking assertively over the little girl's whining or whimpering, Elizabeth's years of freedom having allowed her to forget where she had come from and how she ought to behave as the daughter of a king.
And it was lady Ashley's responsibility to rectify that.

"Must we do this again?" five-year-old Elizabeth said then as she slumped her shoulders in defeat, her shoulder-length fiery curls bouncing as she covered her face with her hands, "I just had a French lesson this morning."
Her father, the king, had chosen Katherine Ashley above all other candidates specifically for her skills in languages, as well as her knowledge in mathematics, geography and history. And while the king proclaimed that he cared little for Elizabeth's education, lady Ashley believed that he secretly hoped for great things from his daughter by Anne Boleyn.
And so, she took it upon herself to not only teach the girl how to sew a pretty shirt and to dance to a pretty song, but also to improve the girl's languages so that she may one day be as

educated and confident as though she had never lost her title of Princess.

She began by giving Elizabeth language lessons at least twice a day – much to the disappointment of the stubborn little lady – in an effort to overcome the years of learning that she had missed due to her banishment into bastardom.

"Be grateful it's not Flemish twice today," lady Ashley replied.

Elizabeth exhaled sharply, "Can't we do some Italian instead?" she grumbled, "I much prefer it to French."

Katherine Ashley dropped a book down heavily on the table before Elizabeth, "That is precisely why we are doing *French* today – because you do not like it."

"But, Kat…" Elizabeth whined as she shifted in her seat.

Lady Ashley shot her a look then which silenced the little girl instantly, and she watched as Elizabeth picked up the book before her and opened it.

"What page?" she asked.

Katherine smiled, "Page 18," and then she cleared her throat and began speaking in flawless and effortless French.

Elizabeth sighed heavily as she tried to keep up, her little mind working hard to decipher the gibberish that was being directed at her.

And though she dreaded every minute of her long and repetitive lessons, there would come a day where she would be indebtedly grateful to her governess for her perseverance.

December 1539

Unbeknownst to the little lady Elizabeth, matters of politics were brewing within the king's court.

The offers of betrothal that were sent out by Henry VIII and his council, presenting his eldest daughter's hand in marriage to several princes and nobles of Europe, were all either rejected or ignored entirely – her illegitimacy inciting no noble man to even consider her for a wife – leaving the matter of forming an alliance for England in the hands of the king.

There was talk of many princesses, duchesses and ladies from all around Europe, but none other was mentioned more than the Protestant princess Anne of Cleves. There was much gossip surrounding the German princess, piquing Elizabeth's interest immensely when word finally reached Hatfield that Anne of Cleves would indeed be her father's new queen despite the king's alleged lack of enthusiasm for their union.

The princess of Cleves had arrived in England to a great storm which, according to Elizabeth's servants' gossip, had affected her household's travelling schedule, leaving them stranded at Rochester Castle until the weather had improved.

The king, supposedly overcome with love and impatience, had ridden to meet his new bride to surprise her in disguise.

But what followed the meeting was no romantic tale, leaving Elizabeth even more curious as to its outcome.

"I 'ear she is as ugly as an ol' mop," Elizabeth overheard a servant girl say one evening as they whirled around the rooms stocking the fire and emptying chamber pots.

Elizabeth did not look up from her embroidery, but she watched from the corner of her eyes as they went about their chores, unaware that they were being eavesdropped on.

"How can that be true?" the other replied, "The king saw 'er portrait before agreein' to marry 'er!"

Elizabeth sat forward in her seat and craned her neck as they scurried further away into the adjoining room, but she heard nothing but mumbling as the distance between them grew.

"Eavesdropping, my lady?" her governess, lady Ashley said from the seat across from her.

Elizabeth had been so engrossed in the gossip from court that she had not noticed that while she had been watching the servants, her governess had been watching her.

Elizabeth cleared her throat and shrugged, "I never met queen Jane," she said in her defence, "Is it wrong to be interested in the woman who shall be my new stepmother?"

Lady Ashley watched the young girl turn her attention back to her needlework, but she did not answer, for the matter did not need to be said aloud.

After all, it was only natural that the young girl would be curious.

After having lost her mother at the tender age of two-years-old, and then the only other mother figure she had ever known – her former governess, lady Shelton – Elizabeth was desperate to find a meaningful motherly bond with someone that would not abandon her.

Lady Ashley had tried to be that for the little Elizabeth over the years. She had opened her heart to the former princess, believing her to be in desperate need of healing. But while Elizabeth liked and trusted her new governess immensely, she knew that her position within her household was fragile, and that at the whim of her father she, too, could be removed from her life from one day to the next.

Lady Ashley understood that the iciness she sometimes felt from Elizabeth to be nothing more than her way of coping with all her loss.

She had observed very early on in her position as Elizabeth's governess, that while the girl longed to have a mother figure in her life, she did not forget easily. And the brutal lessons she had learned in her short time on this earth were shaping her right before the lady Ashley's eyes.

As the years had gone by and Elizabeth's understanding of the world had grown, the topic of her mother's death was never far from the young lady's mind.

Since the very first time that lady Ashley had broached the subject during her first week as part of Elizabeth's household, it had been raised again and again by the little girl; and with each year that had passed, her understanding of its circumstances grew.

It had begun with simple questions, thrown about out of the blue during mealtimes or during lessons.

Lady Ashley had never met the former queen whom the country referred to as the Great Whore, and while she had been old enough to understand the incidents in which she had become queen, she had never given it much thought at the time of the scandal.

At the queen's downfall however, lady Ashley had mourned. She had personally found it very hard to believe that a woman so intensely in love with the king and so deeply destroyed by her babies' deaths, could willingly and brazenly have coerced several men to bed, when she must have known that the punishment for it would have been... well, exactly what had happened.

Lady Ashley had not believed her, or anyone, so careless – especially not when they had a child's future to consider.

But despite Katherine Ashley's beliefs on the matter, she never once allowed her personal views to cloud her answers to Elizabeth's questions. Instead, she had taken care to reply with nothing other than what was considered fact upon the matter, shrouded – of course – with a blanket of discretion according to the girl's age.

But many years had passed since her mother's beheading, many years in which she had insisted on details and facts and points of view to shape her own knowledge of the tragic occurrence.

And by now, Elizabeth knew what no child ought to know – that her father had ordered the death of her mother, and that Anne Boleyn's downfall had begun when she had birthed a useless and inconsequential girl.

Her.

July 1540

Elizabeth never did get a chance to formally meet her German stepmother, for only six months after their elaborate wedding, news came from court that the king had been granted an annulment.

"What is to become of her?" Elizabeth asked her ladies one morning as they dressed her, "Is she to go back to Cleves?"

One of her ladies, Blanche Parry, pulled the sleeves over Elizabeth's arms and tied them to the shoulders of the dress, "I believe she is to remain in England," she said, "Under the agreement that she be known as the king's Beloved Sister."

"His sister?" Elizabeth echoed, "Why?"

Her lady shrugged. Blanche was a girl of fifteen years old and had been one of the shivering ladies who had arrived along with Kat on that rainy evening, two years ago.

"It is said," she whispered, her brown eyes focused on tying the dress' sleeves, "That because the princess of Cleves was so amicable about the annulment, that the king has granted her a large annual allowance... as well as a castle."

Elizabeth gasped, her almost invisible eyebrows raised, "What castle did she get?"

The lady cleared her throat uncomfortably then, and Elizabeth frowned.

"Hever Castle, my lady."

Elizabeth blinked at the information.

"My mother's childhood home," she mumbled, her young heart tightening at the memory of her beloved mother.

"He marries again?" Elizabeth asked Katherine Ashley as they strolled through the garden of Hatfield House two weeks later.

"In Italian, my lady," lady Ashley replied, "The agreement was that we enjoy the summer air but not to pass up on the lesson."

Elizabeth huffed but did as she was bid and repeated the question in perfect Italian.

Lady Ashley smiled and replied fluently, "*Si*," she said in the foreign language, "He is indeed. To a young lady of the former queen's, it would seem."

"Does he have no shame?" Elizabeth asked under her breath, "To wed another so soon... and on the same day as his favourite's...execution?"

Thomas Cromwell – the king's right-hand man for as many years as Elizabeth had been alive and longer – was said to have been executed by beheading for treason against his king and country.

The political details for the gruesome occurrence had not made its way to Elizabeth's residence in Hertfordshire, but that had not stopped the accounts of the man's demise to be shared through gossip and whispers. And it was not long before all of England spoke of the gruesome butchery that was Cromwell's execution, the axeman having missed the poor man's neck the first swing and hacking away at his back several times before he was finally dead.

Elizabeth and lady Ashley were silent for a while as they walked along the hedgerows.

"Is that how my mother was beheaded, Kat?" Elizabeth asked then, breaking the silence.

Kat Ashley did not even flinch, as though she had been preparing for that question all her life.

"No, Elizabeth," she replied simply, continuing to look ahead.

Elizabeth nodded slowly, "It was quick then?" she asked, her voice no more than a whisper, "She did not suffer as Sir Cromwell did? I heard the axeman missed his neck four times, gashing the poor man's back open again and again before he died."

Kat Ashley sighed and raised an eyebrow as she looked down at the ground, "Your mother was granted a much more...painless death," she said, "Your father requested a French executioner for the beheading. Your mother died by the sword, and not by the axe. And there was no pain other than the heartache I imagine she will have felt at not seeing you grow up."

Elizabeth breathed in and out deeply, her chest beginning to ache as it did whenever the subject of her mother was broached.

"I wish I had known her," she said then in English, the burden of the conversation outweighing the necessity for scholarship.

Kat Ashley stopped in her tracks and turned to face her ward, "You shall," she said as she took Elizabeth's hand in hers, "You know enough now about how she died. I think it would do you good to no longer question me or others about it. Instead, you should try to learn more about how she lived. Her death was a tragedy – no one can dispute that, not even those who hated her – but it is time to let it go. Remember it. But focus on her memory while she lived – that is where you will find the answers to the questions in your heart."

Elizabeth smiled faintly as tears welled in her eyes, "I am grateful to you, Kat," she said then, "Though I wish my mother still lived, I am glad to have you in my life."

Kat Ashley smiled, her heart soaring at the words she had long hoped to hear from the young girl she had grown to love.

"I am glad to hear it," she said sincerely, and she squeezed the little girl's hand in hers before continuing their walk, "*Vieni*," she said in Italian once again, "Let's not forget our duties. For one day you shall be the wife of a nobleman or a prince... and to do that you must be as educated as any daughter of a king."

December 1540

The lady Elizabeth was sitting before the fire in her chambers, her feet dangling off the edge of the chair as she carefully stitched gold thread into the shirt she had been working on all month as a Christmastide gift for her little brother, prince Edward.
Though it was but 5 o'clock in the afternoon, the sun had already set for the day, causing the manor to be enveloped in darkness, when there was a sudden knock at the door.
Elizabeth and her governess jumped at the sound, and looked up in confusion when a young man entered and bowed his head.

"A letter, my lady," he said, and lady Ashley rose from her seat and took the note from his extended hand.

"It is from court," Kat said after a moment, and when she looked up, her face was as pale as the paper in her hands, "The king invites us to court for the Christmastide, Elizabeth."
In one fluid motion, Elizabeth was on her feet, "To court?" she said, her heart beating wildly in her chest.
Kat nodded in response, "He requests our immediate presence to meet the new queen."
Elizabeth's stomach flipped with apprehension, and she covered her mouth with her little hands.

"My father wishes to see me?" she asked giddily, unable to contain her happiness at the news, "He wants me to come to court? After all these years?"
Lady Ashley nodded, "It is what the note says."
Elizabeth squealed then and jumped up and down, "We must pack!" she said as she grabbed her governess by the hand and pulled her to the bedchamber.

"Ladies!" Elizabeth called, and her two ladies-in-waiting, Blanche and Lettice, appeared as if out of nowhere, "Pack all my best dresses, shoes and jewellery."

The ladies curtsied and dispersed into different corners of the rooms to begin sifting through the young lady's few possessions.

"My lady," Kat said to Elizabeth as the young girl watched her ladies excitedly, her hands clasped tightly before her, "We must remain calm and collected."

"How can I?" Elizabeth replied happily, "This is wonderful news!"

Kat took a step closer and smiled, "Elizabeth," she said, her voice low so that only she would hear, "This is the chance to prove yourself to your father."

Elizabeth frowned but her governess went on.

"You will remain composed at all times, and not behave as a silly girl," she said, "Do you understand? This is your moment to make an impact on the king and the court – to prove that you are as worthy as any of his children. And that though he removed you from the line of succession, you are as royal and scholarly as a princess of England."

Elizabeth inhaled and raised her chin as she listened. Then she nodded once as her governess' words sunk in, and she hardened herself, squashing her childish excitement inside her like a bug between her fingers.

"I understand."

Greenwich Palace, London

Early the following day, lady Elizabeth and her small household travelled from her home at Hatfield House in Hertfordshire to Greenwich Palace in London, and all the while Elizabeth's heart thundered in her chest and her feet trembled uncontrollably with the excitement that she had promised not to show.

But when the carriages and horses finally arrived within London, Elizabeth could not contain her curiosity and she peered out of the carriage window, eager to set eyes on the great city.

But the streets of London were nothing like what she had imagined, and after a moment of staring at nothing but dismal, narrow streets packed with tall buildings, she shrunk back into the carriage, disappointed.

Finally, they emerged out from the timber-framed houses of the city and through a gatehouse which guarded the royal entrance to the Palace. The carriages continued shortly through a wide path lined on both side with trees, and at the end of the straight path, Greenwich Palace stood in grandeur.

"It is so grand!" she said, her voice no more than a breathy whisper as she looked up at Greenwich Palace.

Kat Ashley only nodded and allowed the young lady this moment of astonishment.

When they entered through the gate and the riding party stopped, Kat took Elizabeth's hand and squeezed it gently.

"Remember what I told you, Elizabeth," she said, "For this moment may shape the rest of your life."

Little Elizabeth walked through the large wooden doors and into the great hall with her head held high and her hands clasped before her gracefully; her two ladies and Kat following closely behind. While her dress was far less exquisite than those of the noble ladies among the court, the little red-headed girl's poise was, to the surprise of the crowd, that of a princess of England.

She made her way through the throng of courtiers – all of which turned to watch her arrival, curious to lay eyes on the formerly forgotten daughter of the king – and headed directly towards the two great thrones at the end of the large room.

Behind the gold thrones was a big stainless glass window which reached as high as the tall ceiling, and though Elizabeth continued ahead with her back straight and her chin raised, at the sight of that grand window, she felt suddenly quite insignificant and small.

Upon the two thrones sat the king her father, and the queen which would be Elizabeth's new stepmother; and as Elizabeth approached, she could see by their faces that, so far, she had impressed them.

"Elizabeth!" her father boomed as she neared, his face beaming with happiness, as though he had never shunned her from his life.

Elizabeth, having dreamed of this very moment for as long as she could remember, smiled sweetly at her father, and then dipped an elegant curtsy.

"Your majesty," she said when she straightened up, and behind her the court mumbled in approval.

For a moment Elizabeth and her father simply looked at one another, both of them assessing the other through stranger's eyes.

Elizabeth could not remember the last time she had laid eyes on her royal father, but somehow, she had always had an image of him in her mind as a great, glorious, and handsome king.

That image was suddenly stricken from her memory as she looked up at the man's face and saw a fat, bearded old man gazing back at her.

His eyes were a pale blue she had only ever seen staring back at herself in the looking glass, and his hair – though it contained patches of the same red as her own – was mostly grey and wiry underneath his feathered cap.

But despite the visual disappointment, Elizabeth had to admit that to be in his presence felt anything but, and as he sat on his gold throne, he exuded a greatness that felt eerily like how she imagined it would feel to be in the presence of God.

"May I present to you," the king said then, pulling Elizabeth out of her trance, "My new bride and queen of England, Kathryn Howard."

Elizabeth looked from her majestic father to the little lady beside him on her great throne and felt instantly at ease. The queen – if one could even call her that – was a dainty young woman whose feet dangled before the throne as she sat upon it, her legs too short to even reach the floor.

"Your majesty," Elizabeth said once more in greeting and bobbed a curtsy at the young queen, "It is an honour and a pleasure to meet you."

Before Elizabeth had even straightened up from her curtsy, her father's laugh boomed through the great hall and for a brief moment Elizabeth's stomach dropped in fear that she had committed a comical error.

But as she looked up at her father's round face, she saw a glint in his eye as he laughed not in mockery but in pride, and Elizabeth relaxed once again.

"Come," he said then as he waved his hand for her to approach.

Elizabeth looked over her shoulder at Kat and saw her nod briefly, giving the little girl the courage to approach the great and God-like father she did not know.

King Henry heaved her onto his knee with a *humph* and Elizabeth could not help but giggle, the sudden intimate moment with her father flooding her with joy.

"I hear you are a very clever little girl," her father said, to which Elizabeth blushed.

"I do not doubt it," he continued, "For you are my daughter after all."

Elizabeth smiled broadly, her cheeks red with happiness at his public acknowledgment.

Then he turned his attention to her governess, "You have done your duty well I see, lady Ashley."

Katherine Ashley curtsied, "Your daughter is a joy to be around, your majesty," she said, and she flashed a small smile at Elizabeth, "She has certainly inherited your majesty's intellect and hunger for knowledge."

"Indeed," he said as he looked down at his young daughter's face, "Well," he said, "I am glad to hear it."

He then gently lifted Elizabeth off his knee, and she descended the three small steps, resuming her place by her governess before the two great monarchs. But when she looked up at her father's face once again, she was suddenly alarmed to see that his smile had vanished, and his proud expression was replaced with a dark look of contempt.

"I am pleased to learn of your good character, lady Elizabeth," he said, his tone so ominous that it caused a shiver to run down her spine, and she stared back wide-eyed, "Had you shown me even an inkling of your mother's disposition, I may have reconsidered my invitation today."

Elizabeth could do nothing but blink, the mention of her mother and the look of hatred in her father's eyes rendering the poor child completely mute. After a moment's silence where Elizabeth racked her brain for the correct answer, her palms beginning to sweat with anxiety, the king finally broke the deafening stillness with a loud sigh, and he sat back heavily in his throne.

"There is no place at this court for a great whore such as your mother was," he said, the words slapping Elizabeth in the face, "And should I ever see any similarities between you and that she-devil...well, let's just say...you shall not be welcomed back in my presence."

January 1541
Greenwich Palace, London

The Christmastide came and went and though Elizabeth's initial invitation to the royal court had been solely for the Christmas festivities, she and her household were not told to leave after the celebrations were over.

Elizabeth had been given magnificent apartments during her stay, with high and beautifully carved wood ceilings. There was a great hearth in one room, which was furnished with fine seats and a large wooden table. Her bedroom was smaller but just as grand, with a large four-poster bed in its centre.

Though the rooms themselves did not differ greatly from her chambers in Hatfield, the furnishings and decorations were clearly of much greater value – most of her valuable belongings at Hatfield having been confiscated after the death of her mother.

But it was not the insides of her chambers which brought Elizabeth the greatest joy, but rather the many wonderful dresses and jewels that she had been gifted by her father and new stepmother for the Christmas and New Year celebrations.

"Is this what it feels like to be a princess?" seven-year-old Elizabeth asked as she danced around her apartments as she wore one new gown and held another against herself, twirling.

"You tell me," Kat Ashley replied with a smile, "You are one…"

Elizabeth stopped in her tracks and turned a confused face to Kat.

"You may not be *proclaimed* legitimate," Kat said quietly, looking over Elizabeth's shoulder to gauge the ladies' distance far enough that she would not be overheard, "But you are the daughter of the king and formerly crowned queen of England. Born within their legally binding wedded union. If that is not the definition of princess, then what is?"

"But Parliament denies me the title," Elizabeth countered, "And what king and council say is law."

Not for the first time, Kat looked down at the young girl's face and thought how incredibly advanced her little mind was for one of such a young age.

"You are right of course," Kat concluded, judging it best not to push her own beliefs onto Elizabeth when she was clearly not ready to accept them, "But remember where you came from. For one day, perhaps even sooner than you think... you may be gifted more valuable things than just beautiful dresses."

Though Elizabeth had had her doubts regarding her governess' sudden remark, it remained in the back of her mind like a low flickering flame. And when, just a week later, Elizabeth received word from the king that she was to remain at Greenwich Palace to continue her formal education, she could not help but feel a burst of love for her father.

"Isn't he just the most benevolent and generous king there ever was?" Elizabeth said as she hopped up and down with excitement after having passed the letter to Kat, who was still busy reading it.

Kat looked up from the note with a tight smile, "This is indeed a most generous gift," she said, though her tone was not entirely convincing.

Elizabeth did not notice however, for she was too blinded by the shine of a doting and loving father – one whom she ought to have had throughout the entirety of her life, Kat thought.

But Kat did not wish to tarnish the wonderful feeling of acceptance that her young ward was finally feeling, with her own fears of dread.

Though she too believed it to be in Elizabeth's best interest to further her education in areas she herself may be lacking to teach, Kat was not unaware of the consequences remaining at court might have.

To be in the midst of the lion's den was never a good or safe thing, and though the lion may be temporarily distracted by its latest prey – Kathryn Howard – there would come a day when its greedy head would turn to others. And if Elizabeth was anywhere near it when that happened, she may very well be forfeit as its next meal.

Kat would have to keep a close eye on the little lady if she wished to keep her safe, for she knew all too well that in the world surrounding King Henry VIII, it only took one small mistake to be cast aside.

Or worse…

March 1541

Kat need not have worried about Elizabeth.

Just as she had known she would, Elizabeth exceeded all her new tutors' expectations, and before long it was the word about court that the king's bastard daughter was as sharp and astute as a prince.

"She is a daughter to be proud of," king Henry gushed as he stuffed a handful of sugared grapes into his mouth, "Certainly she gets these attributes from me!" and then he roared with laughter, the chewed grapes in his mouth bobbing up and down on his tongue for everyone to see.

The many advisors before him nodded and joined in with his guffaw, some clearly forcing the emotion while others were simply glad to see their king so happy – something that was becoming increasingly rare over the years since his fall during the infamous joust where the king of England had lain unconscious for over two hours.

But among the members of the Privy Council there was only one who knew him well enough and long enough to really see a difference in the old king.

Charles Brandon had been the king's close friend and confidant ever since they had been young men, and he had seen the king evolve from the second-born, immature young prince to the great and majestic king he now was.

He had seen Henry through all his ups and downs and Charles was more than slightly aware that the king of England did not linger long in one emotion or the other – the pressures of leaving a nursery full of successors becoming a heavier burden with each year that passed.

But Charles was pleased to see that since marrying his fifth wife, the young Kathryn Howard, Henry had become – once again – a most patient and generous monarch, gifting his favourites with new lands and titles, and embracing the children he had formerly abandoned to fend for themselves.

"With queen Kathryn finally with child," Henry said proudly, "I can now relax in my old age. Prince Edward is thriving and with this future spare, all things will be well."

"Hear, hear," Charles Brandon called in agreement as he nodded his head, his wavy dark hair flopping over his brow.

"But there is the issue of the lady Mary and lady Elizabeth," one of the Privy Council members interjected.

All heads suddenly turned to the man who had spoken, and had he been a lesser man, he may have flinched, but Sir Edward Seymour felt no such unease at being the centre of attention.

"What of them, Seymour?" the king asked then, stuffing another handful of grapes into his mouth and chewing loudly.

"If your majesty is content with the heir apparent, your son by my late sister, Jane Seymour, and the child in the queen's belly," Edward Seymour explained, "Then would it not be in the best interest of the kingdom that the ladies be betrothed to form new alliances?"

King Henry waved his fat hand in the air dismissively, "No one will have my bastard daughter Mary," he said, "We already sent out enough proposals – all of which were dismissed or ignored, as you well know…"

Edward Seymour, the Earl of Hertford, bowed his head in agreement, "While that may be true, there is the lady Elizabeth who has not yet been betrothed or indeed offered to anyone…"

Henry's face turned suddenly red, and in an instant two things happened – the king's groom, Thomas Culpepper, jerked forward, his hand raised high while his eyes searched the king's expression, thinking him to be choking on a sugared grape; and but a split second later the king's great bulky frame was standing tall at the head of the table, his red face having been one of anger and not of choking.

"You do not speak to *me* of matters concerning my daughters, Seymour!" he boomed, his rage darkening the formerly calm atmosphere, "The lady Elizabeth shall not be betrothed to anyone – for surely if no one will marry my daughter by a royal princess of Spain, then no one ought to want the bastard daughter of a common whore!"

Edward Seymour looked utterly aghast; his normally smug expression completely wiped from his face.

"Of – of course not," he stammered as he stood and bowed his blond head again and again in apology, showing his king that he knew his inferiority.

The king sat back down heavily in his great chair, his groom holding it steady with the weight of his own body before resuming his place in the shadows.

"Now," the king sighed, "enough talk of betrothals. Let us organise a celebratory hunt for the conception of my son!"

And Henry watched as the members of the council nodded and murmured in agreement, and as they went about their business, discussing details and signing papers, the king sat back and considered his position of power in this his 50th year of life.

In truth, Henry had other reasons why he did not wish for Elizabeth to become betrothed, but they were reasons he would never freely voice to anyone – not even to Charles.

Elizabeth – though her mother had broken his heart with her betrayal – held a special place in his heart.

He had not wanted to admit it for many years, but when he saw her that day, walking up to him in the great hall, all his doubt as to whether she was his had blown out like the flicker of a candle.

Her extraordinary accomplishments – for a *girl* – only enriched his adoration for her further when her tutors recited to him how advanced her thinking was for a child of her age and gender.

It pained him to even think it, but her attributes were all he had ever hoped for in a successor – and though it irked him still that she had not been born a boy, Henry had made up his mind that to marry her off to some foreign land where she was of no use to England, would not do for this extraordinary daughter.

Instead, he would keep her here – where he could make sure she would not stray from her bright path – and he would continue to nourish her clever little mind in case she could ever be of use to him.

For though he hoped for a boy child to be born from queen Kathryn's womb, he knew all too well that the women in his life had a reputation for disappointing him. And if the year were to pass and he would still only have his son Edward to succeed him, Henry would have to consider all his other options for a strong line of succession.

Yes, Elizabeth would remain in England where he could keep an eye on her.

She may not have been born a boy, but if she could be taught to continue to think like one, she would – if need be – one day become an excellent contender for his spare heir.

May 1541

When news broke that the young Kathryn Howard was not in fact with child, Elizabeth finally got to experience what she had often heard about her father's ever-changing temper – and the ominous atmosphere that vibrated throughout the court frightened her more than she had been prepared for.

"Just keep your head down," Kat Ashley said one morning as Elizabeth confided her unease to her, "And focus on your studies. If you are perfect, then the king will have no qualm with you."

Elizabeth nodded, "Be perfect," she said, "I understand."

They were both silent for a moment while Elizabeth stood still, her ladies dressing her in one of the fine silk gowns she had received from her father during the Christmastide.

When she was dressed and her ladies scurried away on another errand, Elizabeth cleared her throat to get her governess' attention, who had been straightening the young lady's bed covers.

Kat looked up and met Elizabeth's gaze.

"I have been thinking of late," Elizabeth said, her voice so low that Kat could hardly hear the words, "That if this is but a trifling of how my mother's final days felt, then I should not like to imagine the fear and heartache she must have experienced."

Kat's mouth twitched as her mind raced with how best to answer the child's remark.

Sometimes Kat believed that Elizabeth was too in tune for her own good, and that if only she were a less wise child, she would not have to suffer half as much.

"Your mother – God rest her soul –" Kat said slowly as she thought, "I have no doubt that what she went through in her final days was nothing short of terrifying. But this is why I made sure you understood the importance of impressing your father, for to fail to do so... it is not a mistake one makes twice. And whether he shun you or behead you... the outcome of his distaste is never an outcome one should seek out."

Elizabeth blinked and sniffed then as she turned her head away, staring blindly out of the window.

"Sometimes," she said, her melodic voice breaking with unshed tears she was trying hard to keep from falling, "Sometimes I wish I had never been born."

Kat tenderly took the girl's face in her hands in one swift motion and made Elizabeth look at her, "Do not ever say that, Elizabeth!" she said, "Do not presume to know that had you not been born, your mother would still be alive, because believe me, my sweet child, nothing could have saved her!"

"But had I been born a boy," Elizabeth whimpered then, her mouth twisted downwards as the grief engulfed her, "Then she would have been spared."

Kat folded the little lady into her warm embrace and shushed her gently, "Now, now," she cooed, "Sweet girl, do not think of what could have been, for it does not matter."

Elizabeth was now sobbing into her governess' shoulder and Kat could do nothing but rock her and pat her back.

It was an extraordinary thing, Kat thought, to observe a young girl as her eyes became opened to the tyranny of one's father, and the knowledge that would suddenly be made clear in her young mind after years of having known the facts but failing to understand the emotional significances of them.

The details of her mother's death had been drip fed to Elizabeth throughout her secluded years in Hatfield, and she had been kept protected from its whys and wherefores to the best of Kat's ability.

But, just as Kat had known, life at court would not be entirely of glitz and glamour. It would prove to be a challenge.

Especially for a young child who had not yet had the chance to face her demons.

The royal court had made preparations to leave the city of London during the hot and plague-riddled months of summer.

The king and queen and over four thousand of their household rode off on a long journey to the north, for a politically motivated meeting with the Scottish king, king Henry's nephew, James V.

Although Elizabeth had been under the same roof as her beloved half-sister, Mary, since her arrival in December, they had not spent much time together, conversing only briefly if ever they crossed paths in the hallways or at banquets. But Elizabeth did not begrudge her sister, for there had been talk among her ladies since their arrival that the lady Mary and the new queen had more than once butted heads, and the gossip surrounding it was scandalous.

"She is left with just the one lady-in-waiting now," Blanche Parry said as she folded dresses neatly into the travel trunks in preparation for their departure from the Palace, "The queen removed one from Mary's service as punishment for disrespecting her."

"Which one?" her other lady, Lettice Knollys, remarked with a giggle, her long straight nose crinkling with delight at some inside information Elizabeth was unfamiliar with.

"The one she would least want to keep, I would imagine," Blanche replied, and then she closed the lid of the trunk and turned to open another.

"Poor Francis," Lettice said, "But I am sure she would contribute more to entertaining the lady Mary than Cecily would at least."

Blanche laughed, "Yes, at least."

Elizabeth, having little insight to what her ladies were talking about, lost interest quickly, and while they continued to gossip quietly among themselves, Elizabeth shrugged her shoulders and walked out of the bedroom and into the adjoining room where her governess stood looking out of the window.

"What news?" Elizabeth asked as she approached and looked to where Kat was staring.

"We leave in an hour," she said as she continued to stare straight ahead, "Your father has arranged for new additions to be made to your household."

Elizabeth frowned, "Who?" and she finally understood why Kat was staring at the group of people surrounding her carriages.

"I am not certain who," Kat admitted, "That is what I am trying to see now. But I am told it will include children of your own age, to study with and befriend."

Elizabeth gasped, her pale blue eyes wide with excitement, "Children my age?"

Kat nodded.

"Oh," Elizabeth sighed, her face bright, "I must admit, Kat," she said then as she looked excitedly out of the window to catch a glimpse of who would be her new friend, "Though to displease him is fearful, to be in favour with the king of England is truly a magical feeling."

And Kat shook her head, frustrated to see her young ward blinded once again by her father's gifts.

Just as so many others had been.

Chapter 6

June 1541
Hatfield House, Hertfordshire

  Elizabeth met the boy who would be the love of her life shortly after she and her household arrived back at Hatfield House.
As it turned out, what she and her governess had presumed would be several children joining her household was in fact only one. His father was John Dudley, who served king Henry VIII as Master of Horse to the queen, and it was through his current favour with the king that he was able to arrange this prestigious position for his son.
When Elizabeth entered the tutor's chambers to commence her formal education a week after their return to Hatfield House, she found her new peer already sitting at his assigned desk.
Though it was Elizabeth's childhood home and Elizabeth's tutor, upon entering last and finding all eyes on her, she felt suddenly as though she might burst into flames, his gaze causing her cheeks to burn red with self-consciousness.
  "My lady," her tutor, Roger Ascham, said in greeting and he waved his hand for her to take her seat.
She did as she was bid and, as she sat down, she braved a look at the boy beside her, "Hi," she said with a small smile, expecting him to – at the very least – look up from his writing book and greet her. But he did not, and instead, he kept his attention fixed at the open book before him, giving off a distinctly disinterested aura.
Elizabeth frowned at the blatant snub at her greeting, and she wondered just who this boy thought he was to think he could act as such towards a lady.

But despite his rudeness, Elizabeth could not help but think that he was the most handsome boy she had ever seen.

His wavy hair was a chestnut brown. It bounced when he moved his head. He had a straight nose and a thin-lipped mouth, and though Elizabeth had not yet had the chance to observe the colour of his eyes, they were bordered by eyelashes so dark it made Elizabeth think of the pirates she had read about in books who operated in the European waters and sported heavily darkened under-eyes, no doubt from refusing to wash for several days, which – judging by the agreeable aroma that surrounded him – was not the case for this boy.

But despite his obvious good looks, Elizabeth thought he was severally lacking in decorum, and she wondered just how this rude boy had managed to attain the right to receive an education such as hers.

She turned around and faced the front, having already given him more of her attention than he deserved.

November 1541
Hatfield House, Hertfordshire

Though the boy – whose name Elizabeth had found out through the tutor the day they met, was Robert – and Elizabeth had spent each day together in close confinements during their lessons over the last few months, they had yet to utter a single word to one another.

Each evening Elizabeth would confide her frustrations to her governess, who would tell her to focus on her learning and not on the boy who clearly had little of interest to say.

But the young lady did not take well to being overlooked, her newfound favour with her father, the king, having shown her that all the years she had spent alone and unwanted at Hatfield House must have been some terrible mistake, and to once again be disregarded – no matter by who – opened old wounds Elizabeth wished to never have to bandage again.

But on the other hand, Elizabeth was too stubborn to be the first to initiate conversation after his clear snub of her greeting some months ago, and she would rather suffer in waiting than be the one to break their mutual silence.

It was on a day like any other – as the two children had their heads bent over their Greek textbooks – that news of the young queen Kathryn's arrest arrived at Hatfield, which would ultimately spur the two to neglect their stubbornness.

"Leave," a voice called suddenly as Kat Ashley stormed into the chambers.

Roger Ascham looked up from the paperwork he had been perusing at his desk, his old eyes wide with confusion as he looked from side to side, wondering who Elizabeth's governess was addressing so brusquely, for surely, she was not dismissing *him* from his own chambers…

When he met her gaze and felt, rather than saw, her eyes boring into him like daggers, the tutor scrambled up from his seat and hurried out of the room, muttering incoherently under his breath.

"The queen has been arrested," Kat said, addressing Elizabeth, who briefly glanced in Robert's direction.

Kat waved her hand, dismissing Elizabeth's thoughts as though she had heard them clearly in her mind, "He likely already knows."

"I did not," the boy said beside Elizabeth, his voice cracking slightly, as though he had not spoken all day.

Kat shook her head, "It does not matter," she said, "Soon it will be all over England."

"What has she been accused of?" Elizabeth asked, her eyes brimming with sadness for the young queen she had grown to know as 'stepmother', though she had been but seven years her senior.

Kat pressed her lips together and frowned, her kind eyes looking at Elizabeth in a way which suggested that the accusation against the queen was one the young lady would not want to hear.

"Adultery," Kat said quietly, giving voice to what Elizabeth had already concluded from the sadness in Kat's eyes, the pain of having to convey the message of another young woman meeting her end so similarly to Elizabeth's mother, "Treason."

"There is no hope for a reconciliation, then?" Elizabeth asked. There was no need for an answer.

For a moment all three were silent before Kat inhaled sharply and cleared her throat, "You are dismissed, both of you. No doubt your minds have had enough stimulation for one day."

She watched as the two children stood from their seats and began tidying away their books, quills and parchment, and as they walked side by side to the bookshelf, Kat noticed the boy's eyes darting to and from Elizabeth, no doubt thinking desperately of what to say.

"Marriage," he scoffed then, a small smile darting on his lips.

Elizabeth turned to look at him, uncertain that what he had said was directed at her, but finding his dark eyes on her, she could not help but frown.

"I beg your pardon?" the young lady said, baffled by his sudden need to address her at such a time. Did he wish to antagonise her? Or perhaps – had he sensed her distress at the news?

"Marriage," Robert repeated, his smile wiped from his face as he watched Elizabeth's cheeks redden with ire, "It is supposed to be for life."

Elizabeth's eyes suddenly blazed at the insinuation that her father was to blame for the failure of his unions, and she opened her mouth to reply viciously when the image of her mother burst into her mind, causing her words to become stuck in her throat like a fishbone.

She swallowed her rage, "Queen Kathryn committed adultery against her king," she said matter-of-factly, the words leaving a bitter taste in her mouth.

Robert blinked his dark eyes at her, and Elizabeth noticed that it was barely possible to distinguish the line between the iris and pupil, "Do you truly believe that?" he said quietly as he pushed one of his books back into the space between two others on the bookshelf before them.

Elizabeth inhaled and raised her chin, "It is not for us to decide."

Robert nodded his head and extended his empty hands, offering to take her books from her. Elizabeth handed him the pile of thick, leather-bound books and papers.

"Thank you," she mumbled, and as he put them away Elizabeth glanced over his shoulder at her governess who was watching them with a sad smile.

"What do you think of it?" the boy said then.

"What?" Elizabeth replied, quickly returning her gaze to him.

"Marriage," he said casually.

Elizabeth, sensing her heart beating harder all of a sudden at the wildly inappropriate topic, scoffed a little laugh and began to sidestep him.

"I do not believe in marriage," she said as she walked around him, her eyes never straying from his, "And if the choice were mine, I would never marry."

February 1542

The king of England put forth a bill of attainder – which was swiftly passed by Parliament – that declared it treason for a queen consort to fail to disclose her sexual history to the king within twenty days of their marriage.

It was with this bill that the seventeen-year-old former queen Kathryn Howard was sentenced to death on all grounds, regardless as to whether she had, in fact, committed adultery or not, since she had failed to divulge her past sexual relationships within the allotted timeframe.

"I do not understand," Elizabeth admitted to her governess one evening as they sat together by the fire, playing cards, "It is as though he is insistent that she committed treason in one way or another – though there is no proof."

Kat raised an eyebrow, "I know it is hard for you to hear," she said, her heart heavy ever since the news of the queen's arrest had reached them, "But it brings back memories of your own mother's imprisonment. There was never any proof of her adultery either. Your father simply grew tired of her, just as he has no doubt grown tired of little Kathryn."

Elizabeth sat back in her chair with a *humph* and Kat fanned out her cards, watching the young girl battling within herself as she tried to come to terms with her father's undeniable shortcomings.

"So he marries," Elizabeth said while looking down at the cards in her hands, unable to meet her governess' gaze, "with the intent of... what? Getting rid of them shortly thereafter."

"He marries because he is desperate for heirs," Kat said.

"But he had a male heir by Jane Seymour," Elizabeth pointed out, "And yet she ended up dead too."

"Queen Jane had a long and traumatic birth," Kat replied.

Elizabeth raised her eyebrows, "I am no longer sure I even believe that," she mumbled.

Kat folded her cards together then and lay them face-down on the table, concluding their game finished.

"It does not matter what you believe, my lady," she said, her tone stern, like a warning, "I tried to caution you about your father, but he blinded you with gifts and adoration, just as I knew he would, for you are an exceptional child. But let this be a lesson to you... your father will do what he pleases, whether it mean the death of someone he loves or not, it will not stop him from achieving whatever goal he seeks. Remain in his good graces or remain out of sight – your sister Mary learned that many years ago on her own path and with her own heartache. If you do not believe my counsel, she will tell you that the only way one survives your father is by being perfect, and if you cannot be perfect then remain unnoticed. Hatfield House is your sanctuary, just like Hunsdon House is the lady Mary's. Remain here whenever you can unless he calls on you. And then, when he does – because he will – that is when you apply your mask, and you dance to his tune."

Elizabeth's tears ran down her face uncontrollably, her governess' words having opened a floodgate of emotions the young girl had been holding in for as long as she could remember. She had wanted nothing more than to believe that her father was not the monster he appeared to be, and for a time, while he openly cherished her, it had been easier to believe.

But this new development was one Elizabeth could not easily disregard, and the spontaneous execution of yet another of his innocent wives was too severe to ignore.

It was as though the bill passed by Parliament condemning Kathryn Howard as a whore had nicked a vital artery in Elizabeth's body; and she could not figure out how to stop the bleeding.

February 1543
Hatfield House, Hertfordshire

It had been a year since the former queen's untimely death at the order of her husband, and in that year, Elizabeth did little else than dedicate herself to her studies, her governess' words of warning and perfection having etched themselves into her core.

She had developed a keen interest in languages above all else, her ability to learn them quickly and efficiently giving her great joy, and she happily showcased her knowledge to anyone who would listen.

Her tutors praised her daily on her achievements and reported back to her father that her intelligence surpassed even their highest expectations.

She and Robert, though they had spoken little since that first time upon Kathryn Howards' arrest, studied together amicably, and he even went so far as suggesting she widen her passion to more than simply languages, showing her what beauty she could find in mathematics.

"Some might say it is the language of the world," he said, his eyes lighting up at the subject.

Elizabeth laughed, "It is not the same as a language."

"Why not?" he said with a shrug, "If I do this," and he held up three fingers, "and speak not a single word, the whole world will know I mean 'three'."

"It is still not the same," Elizabeth insisted stubbornly, although she could see his point.

Robert shrugged again, "My father doesn't understand me either," he said, and Elizabeth frowned, noting a hint of sadness in his tone.

"No matter," he said more cheerily then, "it is still a fascinating subject."

Later that same day, as her ladies undressed her for the night, Kat entered her chambers holding a note in her hands, her face as hard as stone.

"The king invites you back to court," she said, her green eyes communicating to her ward that it was time to apply her perfect mask and dance, "He is to wed again – a lady Catherine Parr."

Elizabeth only nodded in response, and Kat could see the young lady hardening herself against the fear that overwhelmed her at the prospect of returning to court, and to face her father.

July 1543
Greenwich Palace, London

On the 12th of July, the fifty-two-year-old king of England married his sixth wife most intimately. There was no celebration, no decorations, and virtually no guests.

The lady, a wealthy widower, was proclaimed queen that same day, though there were no plans made for a great entry into London to introduce the new queen to her people, and certainly no talk of a coronation.

"Is it not odd," Elizabeth asked Kat quietly, as the courtiers made their way into the great hall, the king and his new queen walking several steps ahead, "That he has not had any of his wives inaugurated since my mother?"

Kat flashed her a look, suggesting it was unwise to make such comments in the presence of certain people, and Elizabeth ducked her head, wordlessly apologising for her foolishness.

As they made their way to the long tables set up for the banquet, Kat was pleased to see that Elizabeth had reapplied her mask gracefully, a mask that suggested she had no thoughts in her head other than those of contentment for her father.

January 1544
Greenwich Palace, London

"The lady Mary," Elizabeth's guard announced, and Elizabeth turned to find her half-sister entering her chambers.
Elizabeth and her siblings had been called back to court for the Christmastide at the request of the new queen and they had spent most of December feasting at banquets, dancing and attending masquerades.
But now that Christmas and the New Year celebrations were over, life had returned much to normal, with daily tutorage for the lady Elizabeth.
That morning, however, it seemed there was something in the air the moment her sister entered the room, for her normally sullen expression was brighter, in a way that Elizabeth had never seen before.
"Elizabeth," she said as she approached, her thin lips pulled into a subtle smile, her cheeks rosy with what Elizabeth believed was excitement – and she wondered for a brief moment if Mary was about to announce that she was *finally* engaged to be married... for real this time.
"I bring great news," she breathed, taking Elizabeth by the hand and pulling her to sit by the window for some privacy, away from her ladies.
"Sister," Elizabeth said once they had sat down, beaming, "You are cheery," she pointed out, "Are you getting married?"
For the briefest of instances, a darkness flickered over Mary's face and Elizabeth's stomach dropped as she knew she had spoken out of turn.
"No," Mary admitted sadly, but her smile returned quickly, "It is greater than that."
Elizabeth raised her brows and nodded eagerly as Mary gripped her hands in hers.
"The king has restored us to the line of succession."

Suddenly, Elizabeth's stomach dropped with dread, "He – he has?" she stammered, unable to believe her ears.

Mary grinned in response, unaware of Elizabeth's lack of enthusiasm, when Kat entered the rooms.

"Why are you not at lesson –" Kat began, but at the sight of the lady Mary she bobbed a curtsy, "Forgive me, my lady, I did not know you were present."

"Kat!" Elizabeth croaked before swallowing down the lump of fear which had begun to form in her throat, "Mary and I, we are restored to the line of succession!" and she dropped her sister's hands and rose from her seat, willing herself to feel happiness for such great news, and she forced a smile to her lips.

"Is it true?" Kat asked the lady Mary, her eyes wide with shock.

Mary nodded, "He told me at the Christmas banquet."

Elizabeth, suddenly remembering Mary's great curtsy to the queen on the dancefloor, gasped in realisation, "Is the queen responsible for this?"

"She is indeed," Mary beamed, but Elizabeth could not bring herself to match her sister's gratitude, for when it came to the prospect of attaining the crown, ten-year-old Elizabeth did not share her sister's desire for it. In fact, the very thought of the throne caused bile to rise in her throat.

"The king told me so himself," Mary continued eagerly, "that the queen had 'opened his eyes to the greatness of his children – whether they be female or male'."

Elizabeth blinked, her cheeks hurting from holding a smile of forced happiness.

"Are we to be princesses again?" she breathed, her hands clasped together tightly before her as the only detail she cared for from this news – her legitimacy and her mother's rightful title as *wife* to king Henry, and not mistress – hung so near her reach.

At the question, Mary's smile disappeared, "No," she admitted, "The king specified that though we are restored as heirs, our legitimacy is to remain denied."

Elizabeth's brows jolted together, and she wiped the false smile from her face, unable to hide her disappointment any longer.

"It does not matter," Mary said then, suddenly rising from her seat in one fluid motion, no doubt fuelled by the anger she too felt at the king's denial of their legitimacy, "Edward is still to succeed our father as king, and his children after him. The king claims our restoration is but a precaution," and Mary's mouth twitched at the word as it stabbed at her heart, "But it is great news nonetheless."

Elizabeth only nodded solemnly in response.

"Thank you, sister," she said coolly, "It is great news indeed."

Kat *tsked* beside them then, noticing her lack of enthusiasm.

"My lady," she said, and she grabbed Elizabeth's chin gently between her thumb and forefinger, raising her head to meet her gaze, "Surely this merits a smile."

Elizabeth sighed deeply, unable to shake the feeling of dread at the potential prospect of one day becoming queen of England. Nevertheless, she forced a great smile for her governess' sake.

But, just like a corset that does not quite fit, it pinched.

Chapter 7

August 1545
Hatfield House, Hertfordshire

Court had become a dangerous place to be when the king of England had declared war not only on France but also on Scotland the year before, leading to a long-winded war on both countries, and to a disastrous defeat at Acrumn, Scotland. The invasion of France had begun well however, English troops having managed to siege the city of Boulogne almost immediately, the city becoming another addition to England's growing territory in France, along with Calais, which had been captured by Edward III in 1347.
But the victory did not extend any further when England's ally in the war against France – Spain – turned on England and made their own peace treaty with the French, leaving England with no other choice but to retreat; the war concluded as practically futile.

"The king is sick with fury," queen Catherine told Elizabeth and Mary, when they came to visit Elizabeth at her home at Hatfield House, eager to escape the king's line of sight, "And without an heir in my belly," she continued with a sigh, "There is nothing that will appease him."

"You may bear him a child yet," Elizabeth said, her melodic young voice sounding hopeful.
The two older women shared a knowing look, as though they knew something Elizabeth did not, but she did not pry.

"It has not been a good year for our king," Catherine continued as she raised her cup of wine to her lips and took a small sip, "The death of his good friend, Charles Brandon, has given him more distress that even the failed war on France."
Elizabeth looked at Mary who nodded sadly at the comment.

The three ladies grew silent then, each of them in their own thoughts as they imagined the king's grief.

Though Elizabeth knew that he had been personally responsible for the death of her mother – as well as countless other innocent people – she found herself feeling sorry for the fat, old king as he grieved the death of Charles Brandon – who had been, without a doubt, his most loyal and unwavering life-long friend.

Such a grief was painful.

Such a grief was soul-crushing.

And though her father had been the cause of her own grief in her short life, she would not wish that sorrow on anyone.

January 1547

Thirteen-year-old Elizabeth and her friend Robert Dudley were practicing their falconry, her ladies observing behind them, when the thunder of horse hooves approached at a deafening speed.

Kat emerged suddenly out of the side entrance to Hatfield House and ran towards the two teenagers, one hand holding her skirts while the other waved frantically above her head to catch their attention.

"Kat," Elizabeth called in fear as she approached, her eyes wide with horror, "What is it?"

She pulled her leather falconry glove off and tossed it to the ground.

"There is news from court," Kat said as she breathed raggedly, "Come," she said, taking Elizabeth by the hand, "Do not make me utter the words, in case they are not true."

Elizabeth was pulled away from the falconry lesson, and as she hurried after her governess, she glanced over her shoulder at Robert who had, over the years, gained the peculiar ability to soothe Elizabeth's nerves.

Seeing her pale face frozen in fear, Robert raised his hand in farewell and shook his head at her slightly, a mischievous smile playing upon his lips as though this had been a strategic move on her part to get out of the lesson.

Elizabeth tried to smile back but instead she clenched her jaw and inhaled as she and Kat hurried inside the mansion to receive her messengers.

"My lady," the four men said in unison as they bowed before her on bended knee, their heads hanging low, "We bring grave news from London."

"Is it the king?" Elizabeth says, unable to keep her words from bubbling over.

"The king is dead," one of the messengers said, and the announcement felt like a punch to the stomach.

She looked bewildered at her governess beside her, the news having driven the breath right out of her, and her vocabulary dispersed from her mind like leaves blowing wildly in a storm. Kat, coming to her rescue, took a step forward, "You may rise," she said eloquently, as though she had been raised for this day, and not Elizabeth.

"Send a message to the Dowager Queen that the lady Elizabeth sends her deepest sympathies, and that we shall make our way to London on the morrow, to attend the funeral of the late king, and the prin—King Edward's coronation."

The men stood and dipped their heads before turning on their heels and leaving.

It was then that Elizabeth's knees buckled, and she fell on the floor in a heap, shivering so hard that Kat had to fetch Robert from the yard, for he would be the only thing that might lessen this gut-wrenching blow.

February 1547
St. George's Chapel, Windsor Castle, London

Elizabeth walked slowly behind her late father's many-wheeled hearse, her half-sister Mary beside her as Henry VIII's lead encased body – which lay beneath a wood-carved and expensively-robed effigy – was pulled through the city of London by eight strong horses.
She and her sister wore black mourning gowns, their faces covered with a black veil to hide their grieving faces from the hundreds and thousands of people who had come to witness the funeral of the sovereign who had reigned over them for thirty-eight years.
The city of London was in complete stillness, the only sound being that of bells tolling in the distance, signifying the death of a royal, and the muffled blubbering of the lady Elizabeth.
While Mary and Catherine Parr continued in solemn silence as they all made their way to St. George's Chapel, Elizabeth could not contain the intense sadness she felt.
It was a strange feeling, Elizabeth thought, to mourn someone though they had been responsible for the gaping hole in her heart.
But he had been her father, and she would always think of him as the greatest lord who had ever lived, despite his shortcomings as a husband and parent, and despite the fact that he had ruined her life.

The world was suddenly a different place.
Though there had always been conflict between those who practiced Catholicism and those who practiced Protestantism since her late father had broken from Rome to marry her mother Anne Boleyn, it had never been quite as evident to Elizabeth until now.

Since her brother's accession to the throne as the first Protestant king, England began to readjust to the new order of things, and those that had previously practiced their Protestant beliefs in secret, were now openly and proudly announcing their opinions to the world.

Catherine Parr, being one of them.

Elizabeth had always known that her stepmother had shared hers and her brother's religious beliefs, and had even translated the Dowager Queen's protestant book 'Prayers of Meditations' into Latin, French and Italian as a New Year's gift for her father the year before.

But even then, though Henry VIII had condemned the Pope a heretic and removed England from Rome's protection, there had still been confusion as to whether practicing one or the other religion would send someone to the block, the late king's decisions as to which religion was the right one changing from one instant to the next.

But now – as his nine-year-old son, king Edward VI, sat upon the throne, his Protestant uncle, Edward Seymour, serving as Lord Protector until the young king came of age – the people of England finally knew that Catholicism was a thing of the past, and that to be a Protestant was not only accepted, but encouraged.

Elizabeth, though she too had been raised a Protestant, could not understand the importance people put onto which religion someone practiced, for she believed that as long as they all spoke to God, did it really matter *how* they chose to let Him into their hearts?

But she knew better than to voice her opinion aloud, and she maintained a neutral approach with both of her siblings, unwilling to cause discontent with either of them.

Especially now that they were the only family she had left in the world.

May 1547
Chelsea Manor, London

It had been but a few months since her father's death when Elizabeth received an invitation to her stepmother's newly inherited estate, Chelsea Manor.

When Elizabeth arrived, her governess, ladies and guards in tow, she was pleased to see her half-sister, Mary, had also been invited.

Upon being announced by the usher, Elizabeth hurried into the beautifully decorated hall and headed directly towards the two women as they stood by the window with cups of wine in their hands.

"Stepmother," Elizabeth said with a curtsy, "Sister."

And then she embraced them both.

"I am pleased to have received an invitation!" Elizabeth beamed, happy for the first time since her father's death.

But as she looked from one to another, she noticed that, while Catherine's pretty face was warm and welcoming – as always – Mary's expression was sour, as though she held a slice of lemon in her mouth.

"What is it?" Elizabeth asked then, worried there was more grave news.

Mary waved her hand then and scoffed, "It is our brother!"

Elizabeth glanced at Catherine as Mary walked away from them, and Catherine shrugged in response, shaking her head lightly.

"The king's council have instructed all bishops that services must no longer be performed in Latin but in English," the lady Mary explained, her face and neck blotchy and red with anger, "They have ordered for all 'superstitious' images and Latin bibles to be removed from churches! It is blasphemy!"

Elizabeth watched her older sister rage at the new developments within the country, but she was not surprised.

She knew that Mary would feel strongly about the new laws claiming Protestantism to be the 'true faith'. But being brought up a Protestant herself, Elizabeth knew it best to simply remain quiet on the matter when in Mary's presence, for nothing would alter her sister's staunch Catholic beliefs.

"It is an atrocity," Mary continued, "what the king's council are allowing in his name."

Elizabeth and Catherine were spared from voicing a reply when a handful of servants entered the chamber carrying trays of food and pitchers of wine, and Elizabeth breathed a small sigh of relief.

"Shall we eat?" Catherine said, turning away from Mary and taking a seat at the head of the exquisitely set table.

Elizabeth took a seat beside her stepmother, her eyes darting from one delicious plate of food to another, "I am pleased to be here, Catherine," she said again, "Thank you for the invitation."

"You are always welcome, Elizabeth," Catherine replied with a warm smile, "Please eat," she said, waving her hand over the table before her, and Elizabeth and Mary both filled their plates.

A silence ensued in which Elizabeth noticed that her widowed stepmother donned a beautiful maroon garb embroidered with expertly stitched gold thread.

As she admired the gown's handywork, it dawned on her that the lady's year of mourning had not yet ceased, and that the time for Catherine to wear anything but her widow's weeds would not be for another eight months.

"I hope you do not find me impolite," Elizabeth said, breaking the tense silence, "But I have noticed that you are no longer in your black mourning dress," and she looked up from her plate, her doe eyes questioning, "Ought it not be a year before a widow proceeds to wearing her normal attire?"

Catherine slowly placed her fork down and wiped her mouth with a handkerchief as Mary, too, looked up from her food and frowned in confusion, having failed to see past her own rage to notice the lady's garments.

"Catherine?" Mary asked then, "What is going on?"
Catherine took a deep breath, "Well," she said slowly, "This is the reason why I invited you both here today. I am no longer wearing my mourning dress because I am no longer in mourning."

"But you are in your widowhood," Mary pointed out and she looked at Elizabeth to back her up, but the young girl only dared to meet her older sister's gaze with a sideways glance, Mary's temper needing no encouragement.

"You are to mourn for a year," Mary concluded.
Catherine nodded, "While that is true," she said, "I came out of mourning early once before if you remember? To marry the king."

It was true. The king had set his sights on the lady Parr – known then as Lord Latimer's widow – and he had insisted on marrying her despite being in her year of mourning for her former husband.

Elizabeth watched the two women batting replies back and forth like a ball in a tennis match.

But when another silence befell them and Catherine looked to her young stepdaughter, Elizabeth knew better than to take a side, and she averted her gaze back to the food on her plate and continued eating slowly.

"I have news I wish to share with you," Catherine said after a sigh, "And I hope with all my heart that you can be happy for me, for I have re-married, and I have never been as happy as this in all my life."

Elizabeth's head snapped up at the announcement and then she jolted at a loud clanging sound when Mary dropped her fork in shock. Mary's face was completely drained of colour and her mouth hung open in disbelief.

But despite her sister's obvious horror at the news, Elizabeth did not share her disappointment, and she flung her arms around her stepmother's neck.

But Mary was quick to interject her disapproval, "How could you?" she said, and Elizabeth felt Catherine's shoulders tense. She resumed her seat beside Catherine.

"Mary," Catherine replied, "I know this won't be easy to hear, but I am in love, and I have been for years. I did my duty by marrying the king and I was a good wife to him and a good queen to the country. But I am getting older, and I could not wait another year before I began living the life I wanted. I believe I deserve this time now, to be happy."

Elizabeth stared wide-eyed in admiration for the brave lady as she spoke so passionately of loyalty and devotion to the king and country above the very love she had borne another.

But Mary did not see it that way.

"You were queen of England," Mary pointed out sharply, "What more could you have wanted?"

"Being queen was not my choice," Catherine explained, "It was never what I would have wanted for myself. But I accepted your father's proposal, as was expected of me, and I devoted my life to him while he was with us, God rest his soul. But he is gone. And it is my time to be selfish."

Elizabeth licked her dry lips and watched the two stubborn women as their locked eyes blazed with passion for what they believed to be right.

And then Mary scoffed, "You are right," she said, standing abruptly, her chair scratching at the wooden floorboards, "It is selfish. But above all else, it is disrespectful. I cannot believe that Edward would have given his permission for this union!"

Catherine looked away, "We did not ask…" she admitted, and Mary shook her head and then continued to bombard the former queen with insults and disdain, but Elizabeth's ears grew numb to it, Mary's rage buzzing loudly in her ears.

Elizabeth could not understand Mary's reaction. Though it was true that to marry without the king's permission was indeed an undermining of the crown's authority, surely Mary could excuse their stepmother's impulsive actions of love, after having spent a lifetime of being married for duty.

"Who is it?" Elizabeth said then, after a moment of silence had arisen. For though she partly did not agree with how the marriage had taken place, she was curious to know what great man had incited such desperate need for a lady to go against her king, "Who is it that you love more than any other?"

Catherine smiled and breathed in deeply, "It is Thomas Seymour," she said, her face beaming with joy, and her cheeks reddened with passion.

The young king's own uncle.

"It is so romantic," Elizabeth sighed sincerely, though she felt that familiar pinch of aversion at the topic of marital bliss – something she did not fully believe truly existed.

"You are a fool, Catherine," Mary suddenly announced.

Elizabeth turned to her sister in shock, "Mary!" she exclaimed, but Mary's expression was unapologetic.

"She is, Elizabeth!" Mary replied hotly, "Married for love? The king and his council will not take this news well no matter what reason she married for!" then she turned to Catherine, "I will be the first to admit that my father was not a kind father and as we can all attest, he was not a good husband."

Elizabeth's chest tightened as the image of her mother flashed in her mind's eye, and she dropped her gaze.

But Mary continued, "But this betrayal to his memory – it is a distinct lack of respect for our late king and the monarchy itself, and I will not stand for it."

And then her sister turned on her heel and stormed out of the hall, calling to the servants to ready her horse.
Elizabeth turned to Catherine slowly, "I am happy for you," she said simply, to which Catherine breathed a small laugh.
"Thank you," she said, "Though I am not surprised at Mary's reaction. I just hope she will forgive me one day."
Elizabeth nodded her head slowly, "I am sure she will," but even as she spoke the words, she knew her sister better than that, and she knew that, once Mary had formulated an opinion on something, there was no changing her mind.

A week later, it was widely known that the former queen of England had besmirched her name by marrying a man below her station, and without the permission of the king. And though her chosen husband was the young king's own uncle, the couple was banished from attending court, though Catherine had previously been named as Regent in Henry VIII's will until Edward came of age.
"Your brother could not have planned it better himself," Catherine said as she paced up and down the length of her chambers, her new husband, Thomas Seymour, watching her through beady eyes.
"Your brother, *Lord Protector*," Catherine said mockingly, anger overcoming her need to act lady-like, "has now attained sole control of the young king! By banishing me, I have no way of giving my advice if he were to need it!"
"By banishing *us*..." her husband, Thomas Seymour added, "He has banished us both, my love."
Catherine rounded on him, "Does it matter how I word it, Thomas?" she said angrily, "The fact remains the same! My stepson, whom my late husband entrusted me to keep safe, has deemed me unfit to be near him…"
Thomas knew what she wanted to say, "Because you married me," he stated matter-of-factly.

Catherine sighed angrily, "It does not matter," she said again, and Thomas wondered if she was trying to convince him or herself.

They were silent for a while during which Thomas began chewing at the cuticles of his nails, deep in thought.

Catherine took a seat by the window and picked up the bible she had previously discarded, hoping to regain her calm through the words of God.

But then Thomas took a seat before her and placed a hand on her knee, "The king and my brother have disallowed us to attend court," he stated, "But there are other ways in which you may continue to be in your stepchildren's lives."

Catherine looked hopefully into her new husband's eyes, and she raised her eyebrows in question.

"The lady Elizabeth," Thomas said with a small laugh, "Send for her to come live with us!"

Chapter 8

December 1547
Chelsea Manor, London

"I am pleased to be here!" Elizabeth said as she walked the gardens with Catherine the day after she had arrived at her new residence in her stepmother's care.

"It was the right thing to do," Catherine replied as she looked up, a flock of birds having abruptly flown out of a tree nearby, "You are but a young girl, and you need someone to look after you. And while I know you did not have any direct care before your father's death, other than from the lady Ashley, his passing made your lack of a parental figure all the more clear to me. And while I know I am technically no longer your stepmother; I do hope that you still see me as such."

Elizabeth smiled at Catherine, "You have always been very kind to me, and I am grateful for your hospitality," she said, "I promise to be a good and loyal guest in your home."

Catherine waved her hand, "Oh, Elizabeth," she said playfully, "You are not a guest. This is your home now, too."

"Nevertheless," Elizabeth said, her face suddenly serious, "I want you to know that you will not regret having me here."

Catherine smiled, "Of course I won't!"

January 1548

Life at Chelsea Manor was nothing short of entertaining. Almost every week, lady Catherine and the Lord Admiral Sir Thomas Seymour, organised banquets, and masquerades – some of which Thomas dedicated to his wife, while others he dedicated to Elizabeth, and the young lady could not help but blush at the generosity.

But Elizabeth was not the only young lady to become ward to Catherine Parr and Thomas Seymour.

Lady Jane Grey, who was the niece of the late king Henry VIII, and cousin to Elizabeth, arrived to reside at Chelsea Manor but two days after Elizabeth herself, and though they had never met before, their closeness in age and relation helped to create an immediate connection.

They would often sit together at banquets, and enjoyed each other's company greatly, their giggles filling the hall as the musicians played cheerful songs during dances.

Though they were both red-headed, Jane was much plainer than Elizabeth, and while neither of them were obvious beauties, Elizabeth had an air about her that encouraged the eye to linger – something Jane lacked completely.

But though she was not much to look at, she was a sweet-natured and well-behaved young lady, with a pretty singing voice and a talent for cards which Elizabeth enjoyed greatly.

But despite their friendship, Elizabeth could not help but wonder why Catherine and Thomas Seymour had wanted to take guardianship of young Jane, when, unlike herself, both Jane's parents were still very much alive.

"Perhaps it is for your sake," Robert Dudley had said to her one afternoon when Elizabeth had voiced her question aloud.

"My sake?" she echoed, frowning.

He had shrugged, "For you to be around more people your age?"

"I have you for that!" Elizabeth pointed out and flashed a grin.

Robert winked at her mischievously, "But seriously. What other reasons could there be?"

Elizabeth had not replied but her stomach had lurched at the question, and she had sat in thought for a while, chewing her lip as she considered why the former queen of England, and the uncle of the young king would want to have not only the second but also the third in line to the throne under their roof.

But as the days had passed and no foul play had come to light, Elizabeth pushed her curiosities aside, and chose to believe that perhaps it truly was merely for her benefit, for though she did not know Seymour well, he had been nothing but kind to her since her arrival at Chelsea.

During the days, Elizabeth continued with her learning, and she and Robert would often resume the lesson's discussion into the late hours of the afternoon even after their tutor had left, both engrossed in the knowledge of the world.

"Knowledge is power," Robert stated causally one afternoon in conclusion to their conversation as the two teenagers sat before a roaring fire.

"Knowledge is power," Elizabeth echoed, "what makes you say that?"

Robert shrugged, pursing his lips, "Is it not?" he said as he picked the dirt from under his nails with the tip of his dagger.

Elizabeth watched the flames for a moment, "I suppose it is in a way," she admitted, "But I simply find it interesting… to know as much as I possibly can."

"With a brain like yours," Robert said as he shifted in his seat, his dark eyes focusing on Elizabeth beside him, "I have no doubt you will ever know enough to quench that thirst for knowledge."

Elizabeth laughed, "It is not a bad characteristic to have," she said playfully, with a hint of defensiveness.

They sat in a comfortable silence for a while then as Elizabeth watched the dancing flames, and Robert watched her.

"Do you think," Elizabeth said suddenly, breaking the silence, "That the lady Catherine is unwell?" and she looked at her friend, her pale eyebrows creased together in worry for her stepmother, who had been laying in bed for a couple of days.

Robert cleared his throat, thrown by the sudden change in topic, "Uhh," he said as he thought, "I do not know her well enough to comment. Is she not normally so indisposed?"
Elizabeth shook her head slightly, her coppery locks bouncing, "If she is, I have never noticed before."

"Well, you have not always lived with her," Robert pointed out, resting his chin on his clenched fist to observe the king's daughter again as the firelight flickered on her pale skin.

From the first time Robert had set eyes on her all those years ago at Hatfield House, the first thing he had noticed were the white, almost invisible eyelashes surrounding Elizabeth's pale blue eyes.

Like ghosts dancing around a frozen lake, he had thought.

And though he had instantly noticed her strange beauty, Robert had felt no desire to get to know the young lady who he had believed, at the time, would be nothing but a pampered little brat.

But in time he had been proven utterly wrong, and the girl he had been assigned to live with had turned out to be anything but.

In fact, he had begun to sincerely enjoy listening to her discuss matters of language and astrology with the tutors, her voice rising an octave when she spoke of a subject that excited her. And he would listen intently to every word, as though she were speaking directly to him.

When he had finally had the courage to speak to her that dreadful day when news of Kathryn Howard's arrest had spread across the country, he could have kicked himself for the stupidity of his chosen first words to her.

Marriage. It is supposed to be for life.

He shook his head at his younger self then, his stomach clenching with embarrassment.

He may as well have gotten down on one knee and proposed to her there and then, so suggestive had been his words.

But in hindsight, he had learned a valuable lesson in that moment.

Though it pained him to recall it, he had learned that the lady Elizabeth was not keen on the prospect of marriage. What had she said?

If the choice were mine, I would never marry.

At the time he had not fully understood. But as the years had passed and they had grown to know each other, Robert had learned much about what the youngest daughter of King Henry had quietly endured. And it made him feel guilty to have believed *his* relationship with his father to have been strained…

In Elizabeth's case, to have been the outcome of a second marriage attained through such a passion that it had ripped England from the clutches of Rome, only to see her mother cast aside – which was putting it lightly – for the sake of another who ended up dying in childbed, followed by another who was quickly divorced in pursuit of another, only for her too to be made a head shorter, just as her own mother had been.

It was fair to say that Elizabeth had not had many positive examples of the prospect of marriage.

And while *it is supposed to be for life* as he had so stupidly pointed out, her father's actions in life had suggested – rather aggressively and without remorse – that perhaps it was not, and that it was instead, a place where women could be misused and mistreated at the pleasure of their husbands.

Robert shook his head at his own train of thought, his chest aching as he thought of Elizabeth's distress throughout the years.

But she seemed happier of late, ever since her household had moved in with her beloved stepmother and her new husband – their marriage finally showing Elizabeth up close and personal that surely not all unions ended in heartbreak.

And though her brow was creased in that moment as she thought of Catherine Parr's wellbeing, Robert could see a slight change in her, and he allowed himself to hope that there would come a day where Elizabeth might reconsider her view on marriage.

"Do you think she might be with child?" Elizabeth asked then as she snapped her head around to face him, her eyes so wide he could see the outline of her irises.

"With child?" he echoed, needing a moment to compose himself at her sudden intense eye contact.

Elizabeth nodded, "She has been unwell for days, she looks pale and cannot stomach her breakfasts."

She was suddenly standing, "Yes!" she exclaimed, answering her own question, "She must be," and she hurried out of the room, leaving Robert dazed in her wake.

On her way through the hallways, Elizabeth could hardly believe her stepmother's luck.

To have been married thrice before her wedded bliss to the love of her life, and to conceive only now – it must be a blessing from God – and Elizabeth prayed she would be right, for though she herself never wished to marry, she knew Catherine had always longed to be a mother.

"Stepmother?" she called, entering Catherine's darkened chambers, "Are you still abed?"

"Come in, Elizabeth," Catherine's voice croaked from within the shadows.

"I had the most wonderful thought and I just had to enquire, I hope you do not find me bold..." the young girl said, her cheeks flushed with happiness. She sat on a chair beside Catherine who sat slumped by the fire, which was the only source of light in the rooms.

"How do you feel?" Elizabeth asked.

"I am no better," Catherine replied, but she smiled, another point to prove Elizabeth's theory that it was not an illness of death, but of life.

"I must ask," she said, "Are you with child?"

Catherine breathed a laugh, "You are very astute," she replied, "Not even my lord husband has come to that conclusion."

"So you are?" Elizabeth gasped.

"The physician will examine me later today, but I do believe I am."

"I am so happy for you!" Elizabeth exclaimed as she stood and embraced her stepmother, "It is all so romantic too! To have never conceived until your union with your most beloved."

Catherine smiled back at her elated young stepdaughter.

"You mustn't tell anyone until I have had confirmation from the physician and have told Thomas," Catherine said.

"I can keep a secret," Elizabeth replied, her smile wide with excitement for the wonderful news.

February 1548

A month had passed since their conversation, and by now all of London knew of the former queen's condition. And no one was more overjoyed than her husband.

In his joy he had made it his routine to wake early most mornings – before even the servants had had a chance to light the fires and empty the chamber pots – and he would brazenly barge into his wards bedchambers as they slept, banging pans, and singing at the top of his lungs.

"My lord!" Kat Ashley had called in fright the first time it had happened, her eyes wide with shock at the gentleman's boldness, "The lady is not yet dressed!"

His gaze had fallen onto Elizabeth, who, in her confusion, had breathed a nervous laugh, and she was suddenly painfully aware of the dishevelled mane upon her head, and the fact that her nipples were visible through her nightshift.

In Kat's opinion, Thomas Seymour's gaze had lingered one beat too long, but he had nevertheless apologised profusely and exited as quickly as he had entered.

However, the same behaviour occurred again but two days later, and this time, Elizabeth had had no reason to laugh.

Upon barging into her bedchambers, he made a direct beeline towards the young woman as she still lay asleep in bed, the bang of the door waking her with a jolt. But before she could even sit up, her stepfather was on the bed beside her, tickling her sides and slapping her rear over the covers.

"Kat!" Elizabeth had screeched in fear as Thomas continued to laugh out of breath.

"Sir!" Kat had shouted, "This is most inappropriate!" and she bundled Elizabeth's gown around her as soon as she had escaped his grasp.

"Oh, lady Ashley," he had said, waving his hand about as though they were discussing the weather, "It is but a bit of fun."

Kat raised her chin and moved Elizabeth to stand behind her, "Though we live under your roof, sir," she said steadily, "You are not to enter the princess' chambers until she is decent or indeed invites you in."

Elizabeth stared at her governess, love swelling within her chest for Kat's protectiveness over her.

"*Princess?*" Thomas spat back.

"She is the daughter of a king!" Kat replied fiercely, "Despite the circumstances, *that* fact does not change. And she shall not be demeaned while she is in *my* care."

For a moment they stared at each other, a silent battle ensuing right before Elizabeth's eyes between the man who had offered her a place to live among her peers and with her beloved stepmother, and the woman who had raised Elizabeth as her own.

But after a moment the Lord Admiral stood up from Elizabeth's bed, his hands raised as though in defeat, and he walked out of the door, leaving Elizabeth and Kat tense, like two little birds ready to take flight.

"What were you thinking?" Catherine asked her husband later that day, "She is the daughter of the late king!"

Thomas dismissed her comment with an aggressive wave of his hand, "Argh! Don't speak to me of him."

"Him?"

"Your beloved king," he said, his voice dripping with jealousy.

Catherine scoffed, a smile of disbelief forming on her lips, "You cannot be serious…" she said as she heard her husband's tone, "Jealousy does not suit you, Thomas."

"And pregnancy does not suit you!" he spat back, and the comment hit Catherine like a slap in the face.

"I don't know what has come over you," Catherine replied steadily, her vision blurring with unshed tears at her husband's remark, "But I stand by my point: She is the daughter of the king. And you shall not humiliate or disgrace her as such again."

Thomas did not reply, but simply stared at the roaring fire in the hearth as he chewed on his thumb nail.

"Did you hear me, husband?" Catherine called in anger.

Thomas turned to her, "I heard you," he said coldly, "*Wife*."

Catherine inhaled deeply to steady her nerves and nodded, glad to have had some agreement at least.

But a small voice in the back of her mind whispered frantically, reminding her of what she already knew: that men – as she had learned from her three previous marriages – were creatures that acted on impulse, and she was suddenly no longer sure that Thomas could contain his sexual desires until after their child was born.

Catherine could say with certainty that Thomas Seymour was the love of her life.

Not only was he handsome, with thick dark hair and a full beard, but he was also the most charming man she had ever met. He had an aura about him that settled over her like a blanket, one that promised security and calmness, like the warming effects of that third glass of wine.

It had been that aura that had made her fall for him, all those years ago, before she had even married Henry.

It had been that aura that had seen her through the darker times of her marriage to the late king.

And it was that aura that she needed above anything else in that moment.

But, for the first time, Catherine was seeing him in a different light, one she had been warned about by those who had been against their union, but who she had not listened to.

It sent a shiver down her spine to think that perhaps he would seek another to warm his bed while she was with child, and though it was not uncommon for a husband to do so, she had never believed him to be so inclined.

Nevetheless, Katherine thought suddenly as she sat down by the fire and watched her husband in her peripheral vision, *He is my lord husband, and he may do as he pleases. So long as it does not involve Elizabeth.*

March 1548

A month later, fourteen-year-old Elizabeth and Robert were walking side by side through the field behind Chelsea Manor, strolling slowly over the freshly cut grass and without a specific destination, as they discussed the recent change in atmosphere.

"Has he intruded again since?" Robert asked, turning his head to look at Elizabeth so that he could see her expression clearly, her eyes often saying things her mouth was too afraid to voice.

"No," she said simply, but she looked down at the ground before them, "But at dinners and such, his stare lingers sometimes."

Robert dropped his own gaze then, his cheeks burning to think he was making her uncomfortable with his own lingering look.

"He cannot mean anything by it," Elizabeth concluded matter-of-factly and shrugged, "In a way, I guess it's flattering."

"He is married," Robert pointed out, his upper lip curled up in disgust, "to your stepmother."

Elizabeth shrugged one pale shoulder, "He is only looking," she mumbled, hoping to diffuse the anger she could hear rising in her friend's voice.

"As long as that's all he does," Robert replied, and Elizabeth looked up and offered him a little smile.

They turned the corner of the manor then, hoping to continue down to the archery stand, when they noticed Seymour approaching, his eyes fixed on them as though he had been awaiting their arrival.

"Ah," he announced, "Children!" and he waved his hand to call them over, "Isn't it a wonderful day for archery?"

Elizabeth nodded once and Robert grunted.

"Join me for a game?" Seymour said, flashing his perfectly straight teeth.

Robert looked from Thomas Seymour to Elizabeth, and sensing evasion from her, he said, "The lady just mentioned she was cold," he announced, his chest puffed out slightly as he addressed the grown man before him, "We are underway to fetch her furs."

Thomas' smile twitched slightly at the rebuttal, but he moved aside to allow them past.

They hurried past him.

"Next time, then," he called after them as they walked back inside the safety of the manor, and though Elizabeth relaxed visibly as they entered the gates, Robert could not help but hear the hint of danger in those three little words.

April 1548

The weather was turning and Spring was in the air, leading to many more leisurely strolls in the gardens, and the beginning of the hunting season.

Elizabeth would often seek to spend any free moment she had in Robert's or Jane Grey's company – depending on her mood – to avoid being alone in case Sir Thomas requested an audience.

Lately, it had become a custom for Elizabeth and Robert to meet by the lonely wych elm tree in the field behind the manor in the afternoons after lessons – weather permitting – to discuss the day's teachings, or to simply breathe the crisp air.

But on this particular afternoon, Elizabeth had not expected to meet him, for that morning, she and her tutor had received word from Robert's servant that he would not join them, due to being struck down with nausea.

Elizabeth sat by the open window of her chambers, embroidering peacefully, as Kat and her ladies hovered nearby, folding linens, or brushing down her dresses.

They were all silent, the only sound to be heard coming through the window in the form of birdsong, and Elizabeth felt serene for the first time since Thomas Seymour's unwanted advances two months prior.

Her peace was disturbed, however, by a gentle knock at the door and the entrance of a messenger.

"My lady," he said, as he handed Elizabeth a note, then turned and exited the rooms.

She peeled it open to find a hurriedly scribbled message bidding her to meet behind the manor. Signed *R*.

Elizabeth smiled and shook her head as she balled up the paper and tossed it into the unlit fireplace.

Had Robert faked being unwell to miss the lesson?

That hardly seemed like him.

Perhaps he was better and needed some fresh air?

Elizabeth could not guess what his story would be, but she headed towards the door, nevertheless.

"I am going for a wander," she announced, "I'm meeting Robert."

"Is he not unwell?" Kat asked, glancing at the balled-up note sitting atop last night's ashes.

Elizabeth shrugged and left.

Though the days had started to grow longer, there was a distinct chill in the air once the sun began to set behind the tall trees, and as Elizabeth emerged from the manor's side entrance into the gardens, she grumbled at herself for forgetting her furs.

She looked up into the sky as she continued through the empty gardens, the pinks and oranges of the sunset casting a magical glow onto the wispy clouds above, and she inhaled the crisp air deeply as she made her way past the rose bushes.

Upon turning the corner to the back of the manor, Elizabeth cast her eye over the field, searching for her friend; but failing to immediately spot him she headed towards the great wych elm tree in the centre of the open field, hoping to find him hiding behind it.

Elizabeth remembered then, as she made her way towards it slowly, how Catherine had told her when she first arrived at Chelsea Manor that the trunk of the tree was so broad because it had been there for more than two hundred years, its trunk having grown wider each year into a thick wall of wood.

Normally, she found the lonely tree in the centre of the field rather beautiful; but approaching it now in the pastel evening light caused an unnerving feeling to come over her.

Upon noticing the growing distance between herself and the manor with each step, her chest tightened slightly as she considered whether to continue ahead or double back.

"Robert?" she called as she approached, craning her neck, trying to see around the tree without having to get too close, "I don't find this funny," she said, hoping to coax him out of hiding with her authority.

But no one emerged or replied, and as the anxiety left her body, she felt a little foolish, and she hoped that no one had seen her talking to no one but a tree.

Elizabeth took a step closer to the great wych elm, its long branches casting a shadow over her then as she entered its shelter, and she perched herself on the unnaturally shaped trunk to await Robert's arrival.

Suddenly, a hand flew over her face from behind while another grabbed her by the waist, pulling her backwards and further behind the thick tree.

She let out a small screech, her heart jolting so abruptly it felt as though it had jumped into her throat, but the hand over her mouth muffled the sound of her protest, and she was held tightly as she tried to wriggle free.

"Shhh!" a voice hissed into her ear. A voice she knew, and her eyed widened with recognition.

Elizabeth bit down as hard as she could into the soft, fleshy palm covering her mouth, and – as she knew he would – the voice let out an angry yell, confirming who she knew it to be.

"You little bitch!" Thomas Seymour said through gritted teeth then as he swirled her around to face him and pushed her hard against the trunk of the tree, hiding them from sight.

"Let go of me, sir!" Elizabeth demanded; her eyes wide with what she hoped was conviction.

He held her tightly by the shoulder with one hand as he sucked on the pad of the hand she had just bitten, "You've drawn blood," he said with a small laugh, "Feisty, aren't you?"

Elizabeth inhaled deeply and raised her chin, "Let me go," she said again, this time lower, her voice breaking slightly as she knew that he would not, and she looked over his shoulder, hoping someone – anyone – would be passing by to save her.

"You know," Seymour said slowly as he moved his free hand over the front of his hose and began pulling at the buttons, "When I am done with you, no one will have you."

Elizabeth watched, frozen to the spot as he removed his erect manhood from his trousers.

She winced visibly at the sight of it.

Thomas, noticing her reaction, narrowed his eyes in humiliation, "Look at me!" he ordered angrily, just an inch from her face, "Once I am done with you, you will be mine to do with as I please. If Catherine does not die in childbed, then I shall simply divorce her – "

Elizabeth squealed in fear, her face turned as far away from him as her craned neck would allow. As he spoke, she tried her hardest to push him off of her, but to no avail, for she was but a fourteen-year-old girl, and he a great, big, brute.

He breathed a laugh into the side of her face as she tried to push him, and Elizabeth grimaced with disgust as the hot, moist feeling of his breath wafted against her ear.

"I will divorce her," he repeated, "And we shall be wed instead. And *you*," he hissed angrily as she tried once again to wriggle free, "Shall have no say in it! For I will have claimed you! And no one else would ever want to marry a little *whore*! The daughter of the Great Whore!"

"Please," she whimpered then, her final attempt to stop what she knew was to come, "Don't."

He took her by the throat then, not hard, but it held her still nonetheless, and he caressed it with his thumb as the palm of his hand pressed lightly against her frail windpipe.

Then he swiftly pulled up her skirts and pushed her legs open with his knee, to which Elizabeth responded by trying to call for help, her fear overwhelming her to fight back one more time.

But he pressed his fingers around her throat, muffling her cries into nothing but a whisper in the breeze, and a tear trickled down Elizabeth's cheek as Thomas forced himself into her urgently.

The pain that followed was like nothing she had ever felt before.

It both burned and ripped all at once, her body completely unwilling to cooperate to the act she was being forced into.

And yet he did not stop, and his grunts fell like drops of poison into Elizabeth's ear as he pumped inside her again and again.

Though her mind was screaming, her body began to slump as each second ticked by, her knees giving way beneath her despite his insistent thrusting to keep her upright.

It only lasted for a minute, but Elizabeth would have wagered it had persisted all evening, time having stopped as her soul had been ripped in half by the man who had claimed to love her like a daughter.

When he finally stepped away from her, his brown hair hanging over his eyes like curtains, Elizabeth, having nothing to hold her steady, fell to the ground, a wrinkled mess on the dirty ground.

"There," he said breathlessly, a smile spreading across his face like a wolf who had just killed his prey, "Now tell me you did not enjoy that."

Elizabeth stared unseeingly into the distance, but she did not respond.

Thomas brushed his hair out of his eyes, straightened his back and sniffed deeply.

"Make your way back," Thomas said casually then, as he stuffed his exhausted manhood back into his hose, "Your ladies will be wondering where you are."

And just like that, he stepped out from beneath the confinement of the tree and headed towards the manor, leaving Elizabeth crumpled on the ground like a child's forgotten doll: used, broken, and left to do nothing but gather dust.

"I saw you!" Catherine hissed at her husband the moment he walked through the doors of their chambers.

"I beg your pardon?" he said, raising an eyebrow disdainfully as he poured himself a cup of wine.

"You," Catherine fired back angrily, "Hiding behind that tree –"

"Leave us!" Thomas called then, and like cockroaches, three servants emerged from the shadows and hurried out the door.

"Go on," he said then, upon hearing the faint click of the door closing behind them, "You saw me?"

Before she could stop herself, Catherine slapped him, her hand cracking loudly against his cheek.

His head whipped to the side, and he remained that way for a moment before turning back to face his wife with a smile on his face.

It was the smile Catherine had fallen in love with.

And yet somehow it was different, his eyes no longer radiating that same adoration he had previously shown her.

"I probably deserved that," he chuckled as he rubbed his cheek and turned away from his wife.

"What did you do?" Catherine whispered hoarsely.

Thomas shrugged casually and licked his lips before collapsing into a chair, "You said you saw me," he said arrogantly, "So what did you see?"

Catherine looked down at him, "I saw you lurking behind the tree. I saw Elizabeth approaching and then – I saw neither of you emerge until several minutes later."

Thomas nodded his head thoughtfully as he listened, "So you saw nothing," he concluded, and he grabbed his cup of wine and knocked it back with one gulp.

Catherine felt sick, and it was not from morning sickness.

She could not remember leaving her chambers or even walking down the hallways, but suddenly she was headed through the archway to the manor's hall when she collided with someone.

"Forgive me," she mumbled and then, as her eyes adjusted to the figure before her, she saw her young stepdaughter, "Elizabeth," she whispered, and a lump formed in her throat.

The young lady bobbed a quick curtsy at her stepmother before hurrying around her and up the staircase to her chambers.

Catherine followed her with her gaze, and though the girl left in haste, Catherine saw, as she sped up the staircase, two little leaves nestled in the mane of the young Elizabeth's hair.

And her worst fear had been confirmed.

Chapter 9

May 1548
Chelsea Manor, London

"It pains me to say this, Elizabeth," Catherine said one morning as she entered the young lady's chambers unannounced, a month after the incident, "But I think it's best for you to leave."

The room fell silent, Kat, Elizabeth, and her ladies all staring back at their host.

Kat was the one to break the confused silence, "Leave?" she said, looking from Catherine to Elizabeth as though she would gauge what had happened through the look in their eyes.

"Yes," Catherine said, her voice breaking with anger as well as sadness, "I am finding pregnancy does not agree with me, and I need rest."

Elizabeth blinked the tears from her eyes before they could fall, "If it is your wish that I leave," she said, "Then I will obey."

Catherine raised her chin, "Good," she said, her throat closing as the guilt overcame her, "I have made arrangements for you to reside at Cheshunt under the care of my good friends Sir Anthony and Lady Denny. They expect you there by the end of the week," and with that she left, her swollen belly leading the way.

Catherine knew her stepdaughter was not to blame for what had happened.

She was as innocent in this game of cat and mouse as Catherine herself had been, Thomas' true colours having finally come out now that he had wedded and bedded the former queen of England, only to set his sights on the sister of the king. Catherine felt a wide range of emotions surrounding this secret scandal – rage, betrayal, sorrow – but above all else she felt an intense guilt for having failed to protect her young stepdaughter.

She should have seen Thomas for what he truly was – for God knows she had known him long enough, and had been warned often of his womanising.

But love had blinded her – as it was known to do to lovesick fools – and she had been unwilling to accept what had been right before her eyes for so long.

With this act, Catherine had learned that, at his core, Thomas was a weak man, threatened by his brother's success as the Lord Protector of the realm; and that Thomas was desperate to attain his brother's power.

But, by nature, her husband was not a deep thinker, and in his hurry to surpass his peers, he took control in the only way he knew how – through the glory of others.

She had been played for a fool.

He had used her adoration of him to attain a higher rank, which alone he would never have achieved, and by marrying the Dowager Queen of England he had inherited all that she had been worth.

He had used her love for her stepchildren to take wardship of not only Elizabeth, but of little Jane Grey too – and in hindsight, that should have been Catherine's first clue that his intensions had not been pure. Especially when she later learned of his plans to marry Jane to the king…

She shook her head at her foolishness.

But despite the clues of his desperate need for power, she had had no idea of the depths of his depravity, and the guilt for the part she had played in it by allowing him anywhere near her stepdaughter weighed heavily on her conscience.

But Thomas Seymour was her husband. And she was pregnant with his child.

She could no sooner eject him from this house as she could command the rain to fall.

And so, she did the only thing she still had a say over, and that was to eject the lady Elizabeth instead.

Elizabeth would no doubt know the reason for Catherine's decision, and while it broke her heart to let her believe that she was angered with her, Catherine would give her stepdaughter this one last departing gift by keeping her husband's indiscretion to herself. And as long as Elizabeth knew to never speak of it, she may be spared the disgrace of having to admit it to the world.

For Catherine knew that a man would never be to blame for his carnal actions, and that if people were to find out what he had done, it would be Elizabeth's name that would be dragged through the mud.

September 1548
Cheshunt, Hertfordshire

Catherine Parr was dead.

When the news came that her dear stepmother had given birth to a little daughter just five days prior, Elizabeth was so happy for her that she had cried tears of joy.

But word soon followed that Catherine had not had an easy birth, and that after the babe's arrival, she had developed a fever which did not break; and Elizabeth could not help but hear her stepfather's words echoing over and over in her head.

If Catherine does not die in childbed, then I shall simply divorce her.

Her stepmother's tragic death shook Elizabeth to the core, and she immediately began to fear that perhaps her death had been orchestrated.

Was Seymour making plans this very moment to wed Elizabeth instead?

A shiver ran over Elizabeth's spine as she considered who he may have already told about his transgressions towards her.
Perhaps he had even spun it into a love story; that *she* had pursued and invited him…
Elizabeth felt suddenly sick, and she hurried to her chambers at Sir Anthony and Lady Denny's manor, hoping to avoid vomiting all over their beautiful wood flooring.
But once she reached the sanctuary of her own room, away from prying eyes, the nausea faded away, and she was left to collect her thoughts.
There was no reason to allow something that had not yet happened to overcome her entirely. For all she knew, her absence had allowed Catherine and Thomas' love for one another to rekindle, and so the death of his beloved wife may have left him utterly heartbroken. His betrayal against her may even be causing him devastating pain.
From what Elizabeth had seen of the man, it was unlikely.
But she had to hold on to hope, and she could do nothing but wait before taking her next step.
For whatever way the tables turned, she was not in charge of its spinning.

January 1549
Greenwich Palace, London

Elizabeth need not have worried, for it seemed out of sight truly meant out of mind for the shallow and dim-witted Thomas Seymour, for soon after his wife's death, news broke that Catherine Parr's widower had finally lost his mind.
"He wants to marry the lady Elizabeth?" Lord Protector Edward Seymour, Thomas Seymour's older brother, asked, his brow furrowed in confusion.
There was silence around the council chamber as all eyes turned to the young king.

King Edward was but eleven-years-old, hardly old enough to marry, never mind run a country. But his word mattered when it came to his sisters, for until he married and produced an heir of his own, they were his successors.

The blonde-haired, blue-eyed young king looked from his uncle Edward Seymour to the other bearded men before him, one by one staring at him, awaiting his ruling.

"Well," he said, his voice breaking, and he quietly damned puberty. He cleared his throat and tried again, "He is, of course, *not* to marry my sister."

Edward Seymour banged his hand onto the wooden table, "Precisely. The king has ruled it so."

"What makes him think it would even be considered?" one member of the council said.

Edward Seymour raised one eyebrow and looked down at the paperwork before him, "He claims the lady is in love with him," and he sat down in his chair, his interest in the conversation about his brother now gone, "Let us discuss other matters, your majesty–"

"Does he not wish to marry the king to his ward, the lady Jane Grey, too?" John Dudley duke of Northumberland said, interrupting the Lord Protector, "Now, *that* I believe to be a good match, your majesty," and he shot Edward Seymour a sly sideways glance.

Edward Seymour narrowed his eyes at him but then turned his attention back to the boy king, "Your majesty should consider a bride from a foreign land, to strengthen England against invasion."

"Your majesty should do what is best for Protestant England," Dudley interjected once more, "Jane Grey is a Protestant, and as cousin to the king she has ties to the crown."

"I don't think –"

"Let's not forget –"

"Perhaps –"

The members of the Privy Council began their usual bickering, and the little king sighed, resting his hairless chin onto his closed fist, and watched through bored eyes as the grown men before him argued like small children.

"Gentlemen," he said, but no one paid any attention.

"Gentlemen!" a voice called from across the table, and all the men turned to look at Edward Seymour, "the king wishes to speak."

King Edward stood from his throne, which looked too large for his little body, "The matter of a bride may wait! I wish to discuss the country's reception of the Book of Common Prayer."

And with that the councilmen settled into their seats once again, eager to tell their king that England's path to a fully reformed country was well and truly underway.

While, in reality, those who secretly practiced Catholicism patiently awaited the rise of their Catholic princess, the king's eldest sister, Mary Tudor.

March 1549
Cheshunt, Hertfordshire

The thunder of horses approaching was heard before it was seen, and in one fluid motion Elizabeth flew from her seat by the fireplace and looked out the window, hoping to see who was approaching.

"They fly the king's banner," she said, frowning as she craned her neck.

Within moments there was a loud commotion in the hall downstairs and then the sound of heavy footsteps running up the stairs.

Elizabeth and her governess stood perfectly still as they awaited the men's entrance, and though they knew nothing as to the reason for their arrival, the two ladies were rigid, uncertain how to receive the uninvited guests.

But when the doors to Elizabeth's chambers banged open and a handful of guards rushed in, followed by Edward Seymour and member of the Privy Council Sir Robert Tyrwhit, Elizabeth and Kat knew something terrible must have happened.

"My lords?" Elizabeth said as she tried to maintain her dignity by not breaking eye contact, "What is the meaning of this?"

"Lady Elizabeth," Sir Robert Tyrwhit said, "Thomas Seymour has been arrested for orchestrating a plot to kidnap the king."

"Kidnap?" the young lady echoed but Kat placed one hand on her arm, silently warning her not to speak.

"He broke into the king's chambers, armed and with malicious intent, and we have reason to believe that you may be involved in the plot."

Elizabeth turned to look at her governess with bewildered eyes, seeking permission to speak, and when Kat nodded that now was the time for answers, Elizabeth turned her attention back to the men before her.

"I, Elizabeth Tudor, daughter of our late sovereign lord King Henry VIII, and sister to our most beloved and good King Edward VI, did *not* and would not *ever* seek to bring harm or malicious intent onto my dearest brother," she said, her head held high, "Whatever my late stepmother's widower," and then she purposefully looked directly at Edward Seymour, "and brother to my Lord Protector, has planned or attempted to do, I can assure you that my hand played no part in it! So help me God!"

The two men stared back at her, Edward Seymour visibly chomping at the bit to chastise her for connecting him to his brother at such a time. But neither of them spoke.

Instead, Robert Tyrwhit began slowly walking around the room, picking up small trinkets and rolling them in the palm of his hand before dropping them back onto their former place again.

Edward watched him, his eyes two narrowed slits, as he wondered what they ought to do when the evidence against the lady was minimal and the passion of her conviction so great.

Finally, Tyrwhit returned to his place beside the angry Lord Protector and nodded his head at one of the guards, "Take the lady Ashley for questioning."

Without hesitation, the guard beside them grabbed Kat by the arm and began forcing her out the door.

"You cannot do this!" Elizabeth wailed as she watched, helpless, as her governess was manhandled downstairs.

"We can," Edward Seymour replied, turning his back on Elizabeth and walking out the door, leaving Robert Tyrwhit behind.

Elizabeth followed them, "Kat!" she called over the banister of the hallway in hopes of stopping her governess from leaving through the terror in her voice.

"Elizabeth!" Kat called back, "I will be alright. We are innocent—" and then she was shoved outside and bundled onto a horse to be taken to the Tower of London for questioning.

When Elizabeth turned back around, Sir Tyrwhit was standing menacingly by the entrance of her chambers, a wry smile on his lips as he stepped aside and swept his hand through the air, gesturing for her to re-enter her chambers.

"Take a seat, my lady," he said, and Elizabeth did as she was told.

"Confess all…" the man ordered as soon as Elizabeth had sat down.

But the lady did not reply.

Tyrwhit inhaled and walked towards her slowly until he was standing tall before her, his dark eyes looking down at her threateningly, and Elizabeth noticed there was a jagged scar near his right eye. But she would not be intimidated.

"Thomas Seymour claims that you and he planned to wed," he said, to which Elizabeth's upper lips twitched slightly in distaste, "Which would put you in the midst of his plot to kidnap the king…"

Elizabeth raised her chin and met the man's gaze, "I had no involvement," she replied steadily, and yet all the while her heart thundered wildly in her chest.

Tyrwhit nodded and took a step back, occupying the seat opposite her.

"If you confess," he said with a smile Elizabeth believed was supposed to come across as friendly, no doubt trying to get her to lower her guard, "you would be forgiven, for you are only young and… foolish. The blame lies with your servants, who should have protected you."

Elizabeth's throat tightened at the insult to her governess. But at the same time, his words echoed in her mind, since it was, in part, true that Kat had failed to protect her from Thomas.

Just not in the way Tyrwhit assumed.

But Elizabeth would never admit to any failings or lapse in protection, for to do so would mean to admit that something had occurred of which she had needed protecting from.

Instead, Elizabeth would take this opportunity to demonstrate the wit and wisdom of which she had often been praised for to her father, using her 'boy's mind' to her advantage against men who would seek to bully her into a confession of their choosing.

"I shall admit that the Lord Admiral Seymour had mentioned – vaguely – of the possibility of marriage," she said, meeting the bearded man's intent gaze, "But I referred him to broach the subject with the King's council, for I would have no say in the matter…as a mere woman," she paused then to observe Tyrwhit's reaction, and judging him to be listening intently for any detail he may use against her, she inhaled deeply, readying herself to skilfully deny the accusations of treason by voicing her very real hatred of Sir Thomas Seymour.

"In truth," she summarised eloquently, "I care nothing for the Lord Admiral. And if the council would see fit to have him executed for his crimes against the king, I shall be the first to admit that he surely deserves such punishment for all his wrongdoings against the crown."

May 1549

While a confession from Elizabeth would have aided the proceedings along, the council did not need her affirmation of involvement to execute Thomas Seymour for his crimes against the king – for breaking into the king's apartments with a loaded gun was reason enough alone to insinuate murderous intent.
His own brother, the Lord Protector Edward Seymour, followed him to the executioner's block shortly thereafter when members of the Privy Council successfully orchestrated a coup to replace him with John Dudley, to which Edward Seymour retaliated by trying – and failing – to assassinate Dudley.
And so, Edward Seymour – like his brother before him – was arrested and executed for his crimes against the crown, causing the young king Edward to lose both his uncles in a matter of weeks.

1550
Hatfield House, Hertfordshire

With the Seymour scandal behind her, young king Edward VI permitted Elizabeth and her household to return to her former residence of Hatfield, where she spent the following three years keeping her head down and focusing on her studies.

She would spend her days at lessons, sometimes alongside her friend Robert, while other times in private. If she had learned anything from her time at Chelsea Manor it was that self-preservation was an important thing, and that to rely on oneself was a necessary skill to master in this world of men.

At night, she would spend an hour at prayer where she would often thank God for her escape from the clutches of a self-obsessed man who had tried to ruin her.

But above all else, Elizabeth would pray for her mother, of whom she had been thinking of more and more since her vicious encounter with the Devil.

Through *him*, as well as her father, Elizabeth had learned that the world was a dangerous place for a woman, and lately there was no doubt in the young lady's mind that her poor mother had likely suffered similarly at the hands of those who had wished to use her. Just as she had been used.

That day behind the great wych elm tree would stay with Elizabeth for the remainder of her life – of that, she was sure.

She could feel how it had distorted her soul in ways she could not explain.

But she vowed to her dead mother's memory that it would remain an experience she would never speak of for as long as she lived. For she would do anything to keep her reputation untarnished from the vile acts of men.

She – the daughter of the proclaimed Great Whore – would not be painted with the same brush that had been used to sully her mother's name!
And so, to the world, Elizabeth Tudor was a virgin.
And she would remain as such to the better knowledge of all.
While only she herself knew the damning truth.

Chapter 10

July 1553
Hatfield House, Hertfordshire

"The king is dead," Kat Ashley whispered as she looked up from the letter before her to meet Elizabeth's gaze, her face suddenly drained of all colour, "Edward," she said as if in explanation, "He is dead."
Elizabeth, now a young woman of twenty-years-old, snatched the letter from her governess' trembling hands and creased her brows together as she scanned the hastily scrawled note from court.
Then she looked up, her face as ashen as Kat's at the realisation that she was next in line to the throne after her sister – her Catholic sister – and that her life was suddenly in danger.
"Then Mary shall be queen," Elizabeth whispered, "England will be a Catholic country once more…"
Kat swallowed and shook her head, knowing what Elizabeth was fearing, "Do not fret, Elizabeth," her governess soothed, though her heart beat rapidly in her chest, "She is your sister," she said.
As if a monarch had never before sentenced their own sibling to death.
Since her father, Henry VIII's passing, England had been an openly reformed country under the reign of his only son, the young king Edward VI, and his Protestant council.
Much religious doctrine had been abolished and superstitious Catholic teachings had been deemed illegal.
It had been a glorious beginning to what many had hoped would be a new age for England and its people. For it meant that not only would England continue to be free of the Pope's

authority and taxations, but it also allowed the common folk to read the Bible for themselves, since the reform called for the Bible to be translated into English: Edward VI's book of Common Prayer.

And though there were those who had opposed the changes – like her half-sister Mary who held onto the old, Catholic faith – Elizabeth believed that many, if not most, in England, wished for a fully reformed country.

Though Edward had been a young king at his accession, there had been much hope for the future as he had grown into adulthood, and had recently been considering ladies and princesses for his bride.

A new alliance had been on the horizon, and with it the hope for a new Protestant generation...

But God had seen fit to take the boy-king from this earth before he had had the chance to further the Tudor line as their father had entrusted him to.

And now the country was to take a step back. Back into the past and under the darkness of a Catholic ruler.

Elizabeth cleared her throat then, her eyes remaining wide, alarmed at the news and at what she knew was to come.

"What do we do?" she asked her governess, searching for comfort in her kind eyes.

Kat inhaled, calming her racing heart, "As I said: Mary is your sister. She would not force anything onto you or her subjects, I cannot believe that. For now, we must wait and learn what her next step will be. And then... you must be yourself."

Elizabeth blinked, unsure what part of herself Kat wished for her to put forward after so many years of wearing different masks.

Henry VIII's perfect daughter?

Edward VI's favourite sister?

The virgin?

"What would you do," Kat continued, sensing doubt in the young lady before her, whom she had cared for and loved for most of her life, "If I was not here to guide you."

"I would offer my support to my sister," Elizabeth stated without hesitation, "Regardless as to our differences in religion, I would support her claim to the throne."

Kat nodded approvingly, though she was unaware that it was Elizabeth's aversion to the idea of the crown which strengthened her support for Mary, rather than what morals she had instilled in her.

"Then we wait," Kat concluded, "And watch from afar if the need for your presence arises."

August 1553

Elizabeth did not have to wait long before word reached her at Hatfield House that her sister Mary was facing immense opposition from the late king's council upon her attempted entrance into London to claim the throne of England.

Rumour had it that their cousin, the young Jane Grey – who Elizabeth had grown to know during their time together at Chelsea Manor – had taken the crown for herself, claiming to be the true and rightful heir to Edward VI.

"Jane Grey?" Elizabeth said, her eyes wide with disbelief, "Little Jane Grey has usurped Henry VIII's own daughter?" then she shook her head, "No, I cannot believe it."

"Believe it, Elizabeth," Kat said as she poured Elizabeth a glass of small ale, "Believe the worst of these rumours so that you may be glad when they are untrue."

But they had been true, and word followed shortly thereafter that their seventeen-year-old cousin Jane Grey, as well as her few supporters – including John Dudley, Robert's own father – had been executed for their crimes.

Elizabeth exhaled sharply as they received the news, troubled by her sister's actions towards the young girl. But she hardened her heart, for though she felt sorrow over the girl's death, Jane Grey had committed a mortal sin against the true queen, and she had to demonstrate – even to her governess – that she felt nothing for her poor, dead cousin.

"If her crimes were confirmed then she did not act alone," Elizabeth stated matter-of-factly, resolving to focus on facts instead of feelings.

Kat raised her eyebrows in silent agreement, knowing full well that the world turned at the behest of men, and not of young women.

"Should I be concerned for my safety?" Elizabeth asked her governess quietly then, "As a protestant heir to the throne as Jane had been, would Mary think me involved in Jane's plot to supplant her?"

Kat sat down by the roaring fire and bit her lip, "It is a strong possibility," she said as she thought, her forehead creased, "Mary will need a strong Catholic following behind her now to regain her rightful throne. And she will be looking to all those who are Protestant to see who openly did not show her their support. Jane Grey may have surpassed both Mary *and* you in Henry VIII's line of succession by trying to claim the throne for herself, but we cannot presume that Mary believes you had nothing to do with this based solely on that fact."

Elizabeth picked up her cup of small ale and sipped it pensively, "Then it is time I showed my undying support to my sister," she said as she stood from her seat by the fire.

"Guard!" she called, and a tall man entered the room, "Send word to the stables to ready our horses for the morrow," Elizabeth said, "On the break of dawn we shall ride out to join the support for my sister, the rightful Queen of England."

3rd August 1553
London

Elizabeth rode into London beside her half-sister Mary with her head held high, her wild red curls flowing freely down her back.
She observed with quiet admiration how the people and lords of London and the surrounding areas had flocked together in support of their rightful queen, as declared by king Henry VIII.
It was an eye-opening experience for Elizabeth – to see with her own eyes how the people clearly welcomed and supported the daughter of the Catholic Katherine of Aragon, though they had – most of them – claimed to be a Protestant people under the rule of their brother just a few weeks prior.
She watched their excited faces as she and Mary trotted in on their horses through the gates of London, their households following closely behind while guards surrounded them on all sides.
The people were falling over each other to catch a glimpse of their new queen. Women and children were weeping with joy and holding up their hands to wave at Mary as she glided by, looking more majestic than Elizabeth had ever seen her.
People were calling her by her name, they were calling her 'Princess Mary', they were calling her 'Queen'.
Elizabeth upheld a sweet smile throughout, for though the people's acceptance of Mary had stunned her, she was undoubtedly happy for her sister to have finally achieved what she had so long been waiting for, though she dreaded the very thought of it for herself.
But their acceptance of a new Catholic queen came as a surprise to Elizabeth, for in all her twenty years she had believed that the people of England had wanted to *escape*

from the dark clutches of the Catholic faith. She had been told on more than one occasion, and by many people – tutors, ladies-in-waiting, even by Kat – that England united in their hatred for Catholicism.

But she could see now that what she had been told had been a folly, words said in whispers by fools who wished for it to be true rather than knowing it to be fact.

It seemed that, in truth, the people of England were divided.

Some practiced religion in the old ways, while some embraced the reformation.

Did every household maintain a differing belief?

For years so many had claimed to be Protestants, and now they cheer for their Catholic queen.

And there was no doubt in Elizabeth's mind that many Protestants would now claim to be Catholic to keep themselves safe under Mary's rule.

The to-and-fro was a shambles, Elizabeth thought as the crowds continued to grow in support for their new monarch.

Surely it mattered not how ones' subjects chose to speak to their God, as long as they continued to do so?

Elizabeth inhaled deeply, filling her lungs with the slightly foul London air, and she said a silent prayer that Mary was having a similar epiphany in that very moment, so that the people of England would not have to suffer too much at the changes which would no doubt come to pass under her rule.

Perhaps Mary would be a lenient queen. Perhaps once she was married and with child, she would learn to obsess over something other than her mother's religion.

Elizabeth looked over her shoulder at the mass of ecstatic people scrambling to get a visual of them when a breeze whipped her locks in front of her face.

She pushed her hair aside and offered the people of London another smile, to which many cheered and called her name.

She felt suddenly curious as to who within the crowd would now be a secret Protestant.

The people all looked the same – there was no telling them apart.

Their differences were all within them – and Elizabeth thought then, *how can what is in one's heart stand to offend another?*

January 1554
Hatfield House, Hertfordshire

The people's love for their queen did not last long.

Five months after her coronation, Mary, despite her subject's opposition to it, insisted on marrying prince Filipe of Spain, the son of Mary's former betrothed and cousin, the Holy Roman Emperor.

England was in an outrage. They did not trust that the Spanish king, Holy Roman Emperor Charles V, would abstain from involving England in its foreign war against France. Rumours had spread that Charles V intended to use English troops in his war as arrow fodder, and it was not long before the people's discontent was made clear when a rebellion ensued.

Elizabeth kept herself informed of the going-on at court as best as she could while remaining out of sight at Hatfield, for though Mary bore a sisterly love towards her, she knew that as her Protestant heir – until she produced her own heir through her marriage – she would always be considered as a threat to Mary's rule.

And to be named as potentially being involved in any Protestant rebellion could very well mean the end of her.

But thankfully, the Wyatt Rebellion – as it had become known as – did not last long, and her name was never linked to the Protestant uprising.

Within weeks, the rebels were arrested, their leaders Thomas Wyatt and Henry Grey beheaded for their crimes against the crown.

September 1554
Hatfield House, Hertfordshire

Queen Mary was with child, and the country was overjoyed.

"With the queen married and an heir underway," Robert Dudley said as he and Elizabeth wandered the gardens of Hatfield House, "Perhaps now you too may consider marriage for yourself?"

Elizabeth looked up at Robert with narrowed eyes before playfully smacking his arm.

"I told you already," she replied, "I am not ever going to marry."

Robert nodded sadly, though his smile remained, "Yes," he said, "You told me."

Robert, a now twenty-one-year-old, handsome young man, had given up on waiting for Elizabeth to change her mind about marriage, and had taken a wife some four years prior, as had been expected of him.

As the fifth son of John Dudley – Duke of Northumberland, and former Lord Protector of England during Edward VI's reign – Robert Dudley had been considered lucky to have married anyone at all – the youngest son being very rarely bestowed any of his father's lands or titles, and therefore considered a worthless candidate for marriage.

And according to his late father, 'worthless in general.'

So, when he and his betrothed, Amy Robsart, married, it was deemed advantageous for *him*, even though she was no more than the daughter of a noble Norfolk farmer.

Robert had hoped to finally gain some respect from his father, John Dudley, through this marriage. But to no avail, John

Dudley caring for little other than himself. And certainly not for the mediocre achievements of a fifth son.

Though it had initially been perceived to be a love match, Robert had been unable to form a deeply emotional connection to his wife, for his heart had always and would always belong to the fiery daughter of King Henry, who he had met when they were just two stubborn eight-year-olds.

And from what he could tell, she continued to maintain her stubbornness even more than ten years later.

He had hoped, now that her sister the queen had been successful in conceiving her own Catholic heir, that Elizabeth would no longer feel obligated to maintain her virtue, since she would be pushed back down the line of succession behind any child the queen and her king consort would produce.

"Surely you must wish for a child of your own?" Robert said as they continued walking lazily past the hedgerows, the sun warming their backs as they went.

Elizabeth looked at her friend and frowned, wondering – not for the first time – if she ought to share her secret fear of the future.

Underneath the dark beard that now grew on his chin and cheeks, Robert Dudley was still that same young boy she had grown up with.

His eyes may have become wiser over the years, but they remained as dark and mysterious as they had always been, shadowed by their chestnut eyelashes, as though to keep his own secrets vaulted away under their protection.

"I do not wish for children," Elizabeth replied, though speaking the words aloud for the very first time, and in Roberts' presence, tightened her chest for a moment, and she wondered if perhaps she was fooling herself.

But she shook her head and inhaled, drowning the doubt with a long intake of air.

"What do you wish for then, Elizabeth?" Robert asked, her name on his lips sounding like honey to Elizabeth's ears.

"What do I wish for?" she parroted.

Robert shrugged, "Is it the crown?"

Elizabeth's eyebrows shot up, panic rising within her at the mere thought of it, "The crown?"

"Is that what you are waiting for to bring you happiness?" he asked, "If you do not seek marriage and you do not wish for children…?"

Elizabeth shook her head and stared down at the ground before replying, "I cannot say that I have ever considered it," she lied.

"With your sister now with child," Robert continued, "It is unlikely you will ever attain that goal – if it is what you seek."

If only he knew that the very idea of sitting upon the throne of England caused bile to rise in her throat, and raised the hairs on the back of her neck.

"To even speak of this is treason," Elizabeth pointed out quietly, hoping to deflect.

But Robert's question gave her pause.

What was she hoping to achieve out of life?

Would she be content to wander the gardens or play cards for the remainder of her days, without a clear goal in sight?

If marriage and children were out of the question, then what would her future hold for her?

The uncertainty etched a frown between Elizabeth's brows.

She took a moment, then, to consider what she would do if the crown *did* ever fall to her.

But in an instant her throat closed up and her stomach lurched, her fear for it too great to bring herself to even imagine the possibility.

She had witnessed the demise of too many others who had willingly reached for it.

"What of you?" Elizabeth said carefully, breathing in deeply to settle her troubled mind, "Have you and Amy discussed having children…?"

Uttering the words gripped her heart, but she ignored the jealousy she felt towards her friend's wife – for Robert was just that to Elizabeth: a friend.

He waved his hand and *tsked*, dismissing her question, "It is not like that," was all he said.

"Oh," Elizabeth replied, and they fell silent, both wondering what the future would hold for them, and neither of them brave enough to admit that they wished for nothing more than for their walk together to never end.

October 1554

"You have a letter," Kat said as she handed Elizabeth the letter stamped with the royal seal, "From your sister, the queen."

Elizabeth took it sheepishly and looked at her governess.

"Is it – ?" she said, but was unable to finish her question.

Queen Mary had recently put forth a bill that called for the revival of the Heresy Act, which proclaimed that: to be a Protestant was a crime punisheable by death, and that all Protestants who refused to convert to Catholicism were to be executed by burning. The Heresy Act had previously been repealed by king Henry VIII on his quest to reform the country, and it had been considered a thing of the past during Edward VI's reign.

But it seemed England's new Catholic queen would not be stopped on her journey to destroying the very thing which had made their father's divorce from Mary's mother possible.

And in a way, Elizabeth understood her conviction very well. For it was the very reason why she could not give up on her own beliefs, since to do so would truly condemn her as a bastard – the only thing keeping her legitimacy safe being the very thing that threatened Mary's: their religious beliefs that *their* mother was legally married to the king of England.

"Open it," Kat said quietly, and Elizabeth suddenly noticed how old her dear governess had become, her forehead featuring deep lines of worry and exhaustion.

Elizabeth did as she was told and read the letter carefully, moving slowly towards the window, as though the contents on the parchment were closing in on her and consuming the very light of day.

"It says," she said then as she looked up from the letter in her shaking hand, "That all Protestants have until the new bill is passed by Parliament to convert to Catholicism, and all that refuse shall be burned alive. Mary writes that her council are putting pressure on her to convince me to convert, and if I do not, that not even she will be able to save me."

January 1555

No one was safe.

The revived Heresy Act had been passed by Parliament, and it became the official law of the land once again, as it had been for centuries before Henry VIII had repealed it.

And the people of England were plunged into terror.

It began with the arrests of the Protestant bishops that represented the extreme reforming party of England. John Hooper, John Rogers and John Cardmaster were all taken to the Tower and condemned as heretics by Queen Mary's Lord Chancellor, bishop Stephen Gardner, after they refused to give up their Protestant beliefs.

They were all burned alive at the stake.

Next to follow was their father's long-time advisor Archbishop Thomas Cranmer – who Elizabeth knew Mary had always hated for the part he had played in the dissolution of her parent's marriage; as well as the union he had sanctioned between Elizabeth's.

It was not long before Elizabeth learned that many within London now referred to their formerly adored queen as 'Bloody Mary'.

"It's highly distasteful," Elizabeth commented one evening as she and her ladies sat by the fireplace, the low flickering flames in the hearth casting dark shadows on the walls as they embroidered and gossiped.

Elizabeth was not normally one for trivial chit chat and whispered 'facts', but considering the current circumstances, she could not afford to be caught off guard by anything.

"How is she *bloody*?" she continued, "When those put to death are being burned?"

A chuckle ensued from the small group of women.

"I heard," Blanche said while leaning into the circle, "That it was a member of her own council that suggested the nickname to the people."

Elizabeth frowned while Lettice sniggered, "Why would a member of her own council do that?" Elizabeth asked, the remark causing her stomach to tighten at the idea that not even a monarch's council could be trusted, "They are all Catholic. They are all in accordance that Protestants ought to be burned alive. It is *they* who pushed her to such measures!" she continued in her sister's defence, her cheeks flushed, "What member of the Privy Council is said to have begun this?"

Blanche shrank back into her chair, hesitating for a moment, "Her Imperial Ambassador, Simon Renard, my lady," she whispered, sensing Elizabeth's irritation at the news.

Elizabeth stared wide-eyed at Blanche, "Renard?" she repeated, the Catholic snake's name leaving a bitter taste on her tongue.

The lady only nodded, but Elizabeth needed no more explanation to believe it to be true, for that man had been nothing but a thorn in her sister's side that she could not seem to pull out, or even see.

Had it not been he who, as imperial ambassador, had pushed for a union between England and Spain?

Had it not been he who – according to Elizabeth's ally at court – kept insisting that Mary act against her 'heretic sister'?

Elizabeth sat back in her seat and sighed, she could absolutely believe that Renard would be to blame for causing a rift between Mary and her people, for he and his true master – the king of Spain – gained a great deal more out of a broken England that a united one.

A weakened England would lean heavily onto its allies – namely Spain – while a strong England would not. A weakened queen might leave the running of the country to her king consort if presented with too much opposition, a strong queen would not.

The advantages to Spain at a faltering Queen of England were vast.

And Elizabeth realised then that to marry for an alliance, even with a country as powerful as Spain, did not guarantee a stronger England, and that perhaps Mary would have been wiser to focus on strengthening her own country from within, rather than relying on others who would ultimately care little for England's advancements.

The following day, Elizabeth received a letter from the queen herself, summoning her to attend court to discuss her conversion to Catholicism.

As soon as she read the letter, her throat tightened, and she looked up at Kat with eyes so wide Kat could see the outline of her pale blue irises.

"It has come then," Kat stated, knowing immediately that the sister of the queen would not be overlooked in this show of power.

"What do I do?" Elizabeth asked, her blood turning to ice in her veins.

"You go," Kat said. There was no other choice but to obey.

With a nod of her head, Elizabeth swallowed her fear and headed out the door of her chambers, giving word to her guard to fetch the stable hand, and her household's horses.

Elizabeth arrived at Greenwich Palace that same day, and though she walked into the great hall with her head held high, inside, she was shaking like a leaf in the autumn breeze.

Her older sister sat awkwardly on her great oak throne at the back of the great hall, her dark-haired king consort sitting beside her on an identical throne that measured a fraction shorter than the queen's, suggesting to the world that while he was a man, he held no power over England's Queen Regnant.

Upon Elizabeth's entrance, the crowd of courtiers that had been casually gossiping or playing chess and backgammon within the hall, turned to watch as the younger, prettier daughter of the late king Henry glided towards their monarch, their activities forgotten in the presence of a potentially much more entertaining show which was about to unfold.

By now, the entire court – in fact, the entire country – knew that the queen of England had one clear goal in mind: to destroy Protestantism during her rule. And due to the very public burning of near two-hundred heretics, the people of England believed that she was not willing to show mercy to anyone.

Not even, it would seem, to her own flesh and blood.

"Your majesties," Elizabeth said sweetly as she curtsied elegantly, dipping so low that her fingertips brushed the floor before her.

"Lady Elizabeth," Queen Mary said, her own speech sounding deep and unattractive compared to her young sister's own, made clearer still by her husband's abrupt flinch at the sound of her voice.

But the queen seemed not to notice and instead flashed Elizabeth a black-toothed smile, "How were your travels?"

"Swift, your majesty," Elizabeth replied, carefully returning a tight-lipped smile to avoid showing off her own perfectly white teeth, "I am honoured to have received your invitation to court."

The queen's smile vanished, and her husband shifted in his seat, raising his eyebrows in anticipation.

"You won't be feeling honoured when you hear what I have to say," queen Mary said, unconsciously placing a hand over her swollen belly.

Elizabeth steeled herself and raised her chin, meeting Mary's tired gaze with what she hoped was confidence as her queen inhaled deeply.

"You are to attend Mass," Queen Mary announced then.

Elizabeth blinked.

"Mass?" she echoed, unsure if she had heard correctly.

Was she not to be condemned to die as so many others had done before her for denying the Catholic faith?

"Yes!" Mary boomed, "I order you to attend Mass. You must convert to the true faith, Elizabeth. The future of England and the salvation of your soul depends on it."

Elizabeth inhaled shallowly, forcing herself to appear calm.

She had been certain that to attend court today would have meant the beginning of her end. She had envisioned the worst – death by fire – but hoped for the best – arrest.

And so, to be greeted with a simple command to attempt to change Elizabeth's ways, she breathed a sigh of relief, for her chance to live another day had just presented itself.

Elizabeth gave an exaggerated, slow curtsy, and in doing so she applied her most innocent mask, one she had perfected over the years.

"My dear sister," she began, "My most gracious queen. I am but a fool and therefore ignorant of the Catholic faith," she looked up at her older sister's sharp gaze and continued, "I beg your majesty for instruction, for my ignorance is due to a lack of teaching on the doctrines of the ancient religion," even as she spoke the word 'ancient', she could have kicked herself, and she heard a snicker emerge from among the crowd. Mary frowned slightly but said nothing, so Elizabeth continued, "If your majesty would be so good as to give me books so that I may educate myself, I promise to attend Mass."

The queen's mouth twitched approvingly at Elizabeth's public promise, and her Spanish husband beside her inhaled deeply, puffing out his chest as though he had achieved a great deed.

"Very well," Mary announced with a nod of her head, "You are to remain at court then so that I may see this new dedication for myself," and she sat back heavily in her throne, folding both hands over her bump, "You may also attend me during my confinement, when my time is near."

Though this placed Elizabeth directly in the line of fire, she offered another deep curtsy to suggest her gratitude.

But inside, she was screaming.

January 1555
Greenwich Palace, London

Three weeks later, the queen's council and her entire court believed the young Elizabeth to be toying with her sister's generosity to keep her alive, when so many others had been put to death for a much lesser offence than simply refusing to attend Mass.

The queen's councilmen were baffled then, when their queen continuously allowed Elizabeth to avoid the fiery fate they all believed she deserved.

But they would never understand the inner turmoil Mary battled with daily, between the love for her sister and the devotion to her religion.

The matter was never far from discussion, and with queen Mary's confinement creeping near, her advisors were restless to understand what her plans for the future of England were.

For if she or the child were to die in childbed – which was likely due to her old age – then the country would fall back under the reign of a Protestant ruler.

All their hard work to return to the glory of Rome would have been for naught!

And though their queen verbalised that she was in agreement, Mary's willingness to overlook her sister's ignorance and to keep her alive suggested otherwise…

"The king consort has begun making plans for the succession," the queen's Lord Chancellor, bishop Gardner said as he looked down at his documents before him on the council table, "In case of your majesty's –"

Queen Mary waved her hand, cutting him off, "Yes, yes," she said, unimpressed by the subject of discussion, "in case I die in childbed," she sighed angrily, "As Queen Regnant, it is rather tasteless, is it not? Being as it imagines my death."

The advisors gathered around the council table looked at each other, the situation being new to all of them; for no one in England had ever served a Queen Regnant before, and the protocol was completely foreign to even them.

"Indeed," the imperial ambassador, Simon Renard braved, raising his dark eyebrows in exaggerated horror, "However, it is imperative that the line of succession is clear if it were to happen."

"Once my son is born," Mary said as she placed her hand upon her heavily swollen belly, "there will be no doubt as to who will follow my reign."

"There is the question of your half-sister," Renard mentioned boldly, the lady Elizabeth's absence at Mass being the most talked about thing at court.

"What of her?" Mary demanded, daring the imperial ambassador to voice what she knew they were all thinking.

"Well, she has not converted to Catholicism –" he said brazenly.

"Argh!" Mary exclaimed angrily, "The stubborn girl will say one thing and do another. She expressly promised me, to my face, that she would attend Mass, then has a stomach sickness every time. What am I to do?"

The question was rhetorical, yet every one of her councilmen looked down or raised an eyebrow, each of them silently suggesting that the only action left to take was the one so many others had already suffered.

But they all knew – just as they believed Elizabeth knew – that the queen would not sentence her little sister to such a fate, no matter how many threats she spewed in anger.

Chapter 11

May 1555
Hampton Court Palace, London

  The queen and her household travelled to Hampton Court Palace in preparation for her confinement.
Elizabeth had been invited to attend the queen, to which she felt both honoured and terrified, knowing that to be in close proximity to her Catholic sister for six weeks meant she would easily see through Elizabeth if she wished to know for certain whether she was studying the Catholic doctrines or not.
And she was not.
Elizabeth refused to.
It was a matter of pride for the young lady, one which was etched into her very core with the understanding that the religion she had been brought up with – Protestantism – was the very foundation of the validity of her parents' marriage and therefore her legitimacy.
It was the only thing she cared to hold onto from her parent's marriage. Unlike Mary, Elizabeth cared little about attaining the throne, but she did care to be acknowledged as Henry VIII's legitimate child, but only for the sake of her mother's memory as his true and lawful wife. And not his whore.
Elizabeth knew that Mary would at least understand that, since her strong stand on Catholicism stemmed from the exact same reason. But whether there would be enough understanding to keep her from signing Elizabeth's arrest warrant – that she did not know.
But the threat of arrest alone was not enough to change Elizabeth's mind, and she would not so easily give up her mother's faith.

In the meantime, she would continue to smile and curtsy and say all the right things. She would fight to keep herself alive, but she would not sully her soul…or her mother's memory.
Her own life was not worth that much.
She needn't have worried though, for as soon as Mary and her household settled into Hampton Court and she, her ladies and servants enclosed themselves into the warm, dark birthing chamber, Mary spiralled into a melancholy no one could explain.
She sobbed day and night, rocking herself back and forth as she hugged her knees to her chest – an action Elizabeth found odd considering a child ought to be in her great belly, and therefore to hug herself so tightly… *How was that even possible?*
Entire days went by where Mary would do nothing but cry or sleep. And even in her slumber she would often whimper and wail, leaving her ladies-in-waiting, Cecily and Frances, to take turns in the night to soothe her back to sleep – as though they were the parents and she their child.
Elizabeth maintained her distance as much as she could during the confinement, preferring to observe from the dark corners than to offer aid, since she knew nothing of the birthing of children.
And likely never would.
The thought popped in her head like a burst bubble, and immediately she thought of Robert.
She had not heard from him or seen him since their last encounter at Hatfield where their conversation about children and the future had weighed more than would have been considered appropriate.
They had left as always, amicably bobbing a quick curtsy and a brisk bow before heading in different directions, back to their separate lives.

Elizabeth wondered then if perhaps Robert would soon, too, witness a similar occurrence as she; where a lady cried continuously over the child in her bulging belly.

Was what Mary was experiencing normal? Was this what childbirth was supposed to look like up close?

Elizabeth had no idea.

After six full days and nights had gone by where Mary had not uttered a single word and her face had become red and swollen from the constant crying, her ladies decided that it was time to fetch the midwives, for not even they knew what else was left to do to console their hysterical queen.

The midwives fussed over Mary as she lay in her bed, and her ladies, Cecily and Frances, stood by the fireplace, watching with concerned faces as the midwives did little more than they had already done themselves.

Elizabeth approached them slowly from behind, eager to learn if the child would be born soon.

"What if she has miscarried?" Elizabeth heard the girl – Frances – whisper, and Elizabeth stopped dead in her tracks behind them.

"There would be blood," Cecily replied quietly, her voice completely emotionless.

"What if the baby is... dead?" Frances whispered back, fear hitching her voice up a decibel.

Elizabeth swallowed and took a step towards them, her brow furrowing as she remembered her sister curled up, her knees hugged against her chest in a most unnatural way for a woman great with child.

"What if there is no baby," Elizabeth said then, suggesting the only other possibility that made any sense.

The two ladies turned and bobbed a curtsy at her, "Your grace," Frances mumbled while Cecily remained silent.

Elizabeth turned her wide-eyed gaze from her sister to the ladies beside her, "There may not be a baby at all," Elizabeth repeated.

"Of course there is a baby," Cecily said monotonously, and Elizabeth could feel Cecily's dislike of her like a cold breeze, "The queen has all the signs."

Aware that she had said too much, and suddenly fearful that to utter such thoughts would not be advantageous, Elizabeth shrugged her shoulders.

"I am only making conversation," she said as she turned away, hoping with all her might that she had not sounded in any way in favour of her own opinion.

Elizabeth was embroidering yet another landscape onto a piece of cloth when her sister suddenly wailed like a wounded animal, and before Elizabeth could even stand from her seat by the window, all hell had broken loose.

Midwives were scurrying around the royal bed like flies on horse manure, flitting from one side to the other, seemingly busy with what seemed like a load of nothingness to Elizabeth.

Above the commotion, she heard the faint sound of her sister calling her name, and she instantly abandoned her embroidery and sped towards Mary.

"I am here," she said as she took her sister's hand in hers and offered her a small smile.

Within moments there was a loud gush followed by an exclamation from the midwives and Elizabeth was relieved to see Mary's face relax, believing the worst to be over.

How wrong she had been.

Elizabeth took a step back, dropping her sister's hand so that she may hold her long awaited baby in her arms.

But when the bundle was placed in the crook of Mary's arm and everyone watched bewildered as a mother met her child,

Elizabeth was horrified to see that what her sister held was not a child at all.

"What is this?" she heard the queen ask; her voice thick with horror.

Elizabeth looked from one midwife to the next, hoping to find an explanation in their eyes. But there was none, and when Mary placed the bundle on the bed beside her, Elizabeth caught a glimpse of its fleshy, veiny form.

She saw a clump of thick, wiry black hair sprouting from one side and a row of what looked like fully formed adult teeth on another.

There were no eyes and no mouth. And certainly, no sign of life.

Elizabeth could feel the bile rising in her throat, and before anyone could notice her, she turned away from the creature and her sister, her hand covering her mouth as she hurried to the far corner of the chambers and out of everyone's sight.

She swallowed the vomit that had threatened to spill and brushed the tears from her eyes before steeling herself.

Now, Elizabeth thought, *now my life is truly in danger*.

Following Mary's strange birth, Elizabeth was dismissed from the queen's birthing chambers but ordered to remain within Hampton Court Palace until the queen was recovered.

Kat did not ask for details, but she knew from Elizabeth's face when she entered her chambers that something terrible had taken place, for her eyes shone with unshed tears and her lips moved as she mumbled beneath her breath.

But when Kat approached, she heard the dangerous words Elizabeth was uttering.

"I do not want it, Kat," she whispered in a daze, her eyes wide and red with fear and tears, "I do not want the crown!"

"What?" Kat said, suddenly perplexed, "What is the meaning of this?"

"Mary's baby," Elizabeth replied quietly, "It – it's not…"
Kat raised her hand and shook her head, hoping to silence Elizabeth's ramblings.
But she continued, "And now I'm next in line again…" she concluded, "And I don't want it…"
Finally, Kat understood. Though she knew nothing of what had happened within the queen's birthing chamber, she understood, at least, that it had not ended with the birth of a live child.
And yet, Elizabeth's ramblings confused Kat. She had been Elizabeth's governess, confidant, and arguably her closest friend for most of her life. How could she not have known that Elizabeth had harboured an aversion to the possibility of attaining the throne?
Kat grabbed a hold of Elizabeth's wrists then, pulling her upright with a strength she did not know she had.
"You may die yet, Elizabeth!" Kat replied hotly, hoping to snap the young lady from her daze, "Stop this whimpering and stand!"
Elizabeth wiped her eyes with the back of her hand.
"I *would* rather die than become queen," Elizabeth replied, her throat cracking, "For to become queen only leads to death regardless. I would rather die by my own choosing than to be plotted against, poisoned, or thrown aside like my mother was."
There. She had said it.
Her long-kept secret. And yet she felt no better for having uttered it.
Kat grabbed her forcefully by her arms, "Elizabeth!" she called furiously, hoping her anger would shake the girl to her senses, "What has brought this on?"
Elizabeth met her governess' gaze uneasily, "It has always been within me, Kat," she shook her head violently, "I do not want it."

Kat let go of her, and her stern expression changed to one of pity.

She nodded her old head, "I understand your fears. It is only natural to fear the uncertainty of something which has seen to endless deaths. But listen to me, my sweet child. You speak of your mother as though you knew her. But the truth remains that you did not."

Elizabeth frowned, but the fear in her eyes remained.

Kat offered her a sad smile, "You do not know this," she said slowly, weighing each word carefully before she uttered it, "But it is said that your father offered your mother a choice, in secret. He is said to have visited her in the Tower in private, on the eve of her execution."

"He did?" Elizabeth asked, unable to understand, "Why?"

Kat licked her dry lips, "It is only what I heard rumoured at the time, Elizabeth, but they say the king offered her a choice: to die accused of high treason, or to accept an annulment as Katherine of Aragon had done, and to live out her days in exile with you."

Elizabeth stared, her heart racing to hear more though she already knew the ending to this sad tale.

"She refused of course," Kat continued, "But not before declaring that she would never choose her own life over her child's legitimacy, for to have chosen an annulment would have made you a bastard."

"She chose to die? She chose to die rather than to live out her days as my mother?" Elizabeth whispered, stunned by the revelation.

Kat took Elizabeth's face in her hands, "No, dear girl!" she answered, "Your mother chose *your* future over her own! She sacrificed her own life so that you may one day achieve the throne of England as the king's true and legitimate child."

Elizabeth's throat was tight, and she suddenly felt as though she could not breathe.

"You may never have wanted it, Elizabeth," Kat said quietly, "But your mother died in the hope that her blood would have been well spent. Do not allow her sacrifice to have been in vain."

Kat folded Elizabeth into her embrace then, to let the girl weep.

But Elizabeth did not weep.

Instead, she stared blankly ahead over Kat's shoulder, wishing she had never learned of this.

For now, it no longer mattered what she wanted.

She had to become Queen of England. For her mother.

January 1556
Hatfield House, Hertfordshire

After the queen's confinement, Elizabeth was relieved to be allowed leave from court, and for the following months she made sure to speak to no one but the two people she trusted most in the world, Kat Ashley and Robert Dudley.

Political matters were never discussed, for it was safer to no longer have an opinion on anything at all.

Elizabeth never once mentioned what she had witnessed during the queen's confinement, not only for her sister's sake but also for her own.

But even after almost a year, she could do nothing to erase it from her mind's eye, and it continued to haunt her dreams still.

One afternoon, as she, Robert and Kat sat at a wooden table by the fire playing cards, Elizabeth winning by two hands, there was a rap at the door and a guard strode in.

"There are horses approaching, my lady," he warned, and Elizabeth's eyes narrowed in thought.

She looked at Kat, who shook her head in confusion.

"Close the gates," Elizabeth ordered but the guard stood frozen.

"They are flying the Queen's banner, my lady," he replied sheepishly, "I cannot."

Elizabeth placed her cards face down upon the table, as though it still mattered that her hand remained a mystery to the other players. She looked at Robert, who met her gaze with fear in his eyes. His beautiful, dark eyes.

"The time has come," she said, knowing that if the queen had sent men to her without forewarning, that she was no doubt about to meet her doom, since she continued to ignore the queen's order to convert to Catholicism.

Moments later, the doors to her chambers burst open and the queen's guards entered the room, their hands wrapped around the hilts of their swords as if they assumed to be met with violence.

Elizabeth breathed a laugh at the notion, since she was nothing more than a mere woman.

"Lady Elizabeth," one of the guards boomed threateningly, "You and your household are hereby arrested under suspicion of treason!"

Elizabeth stood from her seat at the table.

"What treason, good sir?!" Elizabeth called back over the ruckus as her furniture was being tossed about.

The guard shook his head, "I have been entrusted to bring you before the queen, my lady," he said, "I know of nothing more."

"Very well then," she said, raising her chin defiantly and taking a step towards him, "Take me to my sister."

For the second time in her life, Elizabeth had been accused of treason against the monarch, and for the second time – by the grace of God – she had escaped a guilty conviction.

The plot that had spurred her arrest had been led by a Sir Henry Dudley, a cousin to Robert's own father, John Dudley.

As it turned out, Sir Henry Dudley had been directly financed by the King of France himself, in an effort to rally enough of an army to overthrow Queen Mary. But when the plot was discovered, he and his men fled in direction of France in an effort to save themselves from certain death.

His escape was not successful however, and on his way to France, the queen's men caught up with him and arrested him without hesitation.

He was racked for information before his execution, and in the hope of being spared more torture, he admitted that at the heart of their rebellion, had been the plan to replace Mary with her Protestant sister – Elizabeth.

The confession was what had led the queen to arrest her own sister, for since her confinement ended in tragedy, Mary had become increasingly paranoid, knowing that her people and the rest of Europe saw her as a failure.

Upon Elizabeth's arrest, she was immediately flung into the Tower, and though the queen's guards had searched her person and her home high and low, turning everything upside down and inside out, they had found nothing incriminating to suggest Elizabeth to have been involved.

She was released to return to her vandalised home a month later.

May 1557
Hatfield House, Hertfordshire

"It is an unsafe world we live in, Robert," Elizabeth mumbled as she placed her cards down on the table, showing her winning hand at their game of *primero*.

Robert leaned forward to check the cards and threw down his own in defeat, "Anything to do with you is unsafe," he said in frustration, "Even to play cards with you, I am made poor."
Elizabeth picked up the coins in the centre of the table, a smug smile on her face, "You ought to have learned your lesson last time you were here," she mocked, "I do not lose at *primero*."
Robert sat back in his seat and inhaled deeply as he watched her carefully.
She was a woman of twenty-four, and yet her mind was and always had been that of a much wiser woman. It was something he had always admired in her, and in the late hours of the night it was often the thing he lay awake thinking of – on the occasions that he was not envisioning the tops of her plump breasts or the creamy colour of her neck.
Her mind and how she thought was what Robert had fallen for, so many years ago. She was unlike any other woman he had ever known – and not even his own poor wife could compete with Elizabeth.
He shifted in his seat then as the thought of his wife brought on a bout of shame. It was not her fault that he felt no connection with her.
She was a good wife to him, in truth. She took care of him, and she undoubtedly loved him even when he so obviously did not return her feelings.
The guilt of it weighed on his conscience sometimes.
But then he would think of Elizabeth, and the way her fiery red locks never did quite stay hidden underneath her hood, and how she would often opt to simply let them tumble over her shoulders freely. It was his favourite image of her, in fact, when her red mane was bouncing wildly upon her beautiful head.
He crossed his legs then as his thoughts provoked a stirring in his trousers, and he adjusted his erection accordingly so that no one would see just how desperately he desired her.

"Another hand?" Elizabeth said then and he nodded as he watched her shuffle the deck.

There was nothing he could do to stop himself from loving her. He had tried year after year, and even the months in which he would not see her did little to quench the fire that burned within him.

He had often thought that perhaps she felt the same for him – there had been enough lingering glances that he had caught her out on, and many tense moments between them over the years that suggested at least a physical attraction.

But he had never acted upon it – not because he was a married man, for that, he knew, would not stop him for even a second if Elizabeth admitted her feelings for him.

No, he had not acted upon it for fear of losing the most important moments of his measly life in case he was wrong. It was simply safer to love her in secret, for that way, at least, he could be sure to be around her whenever their lives permitted.

"Don't you think so?" Elizabeth was saying then, and Robert was pulled out from his trance, as though he had emerged from underwater.

"What?" he said, his dark eyes wide.

"I said: I do not support the war on France and that it will only end badly for England. Don't you think so?" and she laid a card face down upon the wooden table before picking up another from the deck.

Robert picked up his cards and fanned them out, shaking his head free of his own thoughts and considering Elizabeth's question.

He cleared his throat, "I am no politician," he said in a bid to gain time.

He had not come to Hatfield to play cards with Elizabeth. Nor had he come to dream of them both lying naked on her bed, wrapped in each other's arms with nothing covering her body but her long, red locks –

"—But you must have an opinion," Elizabeth continued.
Robert shook his head to clear of the image in his mind and shrugged his shoulders, "Does my opinion matter?" he suggested, and then he gasped theatrically, "Will it change the queen's mind?"
Elizabeth laughed and the sound filled Robert's heart, "Robert…" she breathed then and shook her head lightly.
He looked up at her and their gaze lingered for a moment too long before they both returned their attention to their cards.
He had not come for lingering stares, or to hear the sweet sound of her laugh.
He had come to give her news which would break his heart.
Elizabeth lay down her hand yet again, cards facing up, and sat back triumphantly in her seat.
Robert glanced at the winning cards and tossed his own into the centre of the table, "It is useless," he remarked, and Elizabeth flashed him a smile.

"Elizabeth," he said as she counted her winnings gleefully. She did not look up, but perhaps that was for the best, "I have been summoned to take part in the Battle of St. Quentin."
Elizabeth's smile vanished and her pale blue eyes stared back at him, "What?" she mumbled.

"Under king Phillip," he said as though it were enough of an explanation.
Elizabeth blinked, dumbfounded, "I can speak to my sister," she said as she nodded, sure that her word counted for something, "I will get you out of it."
Robert sat slouched in his seat before her, his dark eyebrows furrowed together, "You cannot," he said, "My family's name is ruined since my father's attempt to stop queen Mary's accession and supporting Jane Grey's claim to the throne. Not to mention my father's cousin, Henry Dudley's, rebellion against the queen. One which almost led to your own end."

Elizabeth shook her head, "Their executions were punishment enough for that," she countered, though she knew it had not been enough to expunge the Dudley name from ruin.

"If I do not do this," he said quietly, "I will be condemned to death."

In truth, Robert had long wished for a way to prove himself worthy, even if it meant fighting in a war he did not believe in. As John Dudley's fifth son, Robert had been born without ceremony – a fifth son being of no great importance. And so, when the war in France called for any soldier England's disgraced and imprisoned could muster, Robert saw this as his way to clear his family name.

After all, what had all the years of harsh training from his father been for, if not to prove himself in battle to regain his reputation. Or, at least, to die trying.

"If you go to war," Elizabeth replied, her final attempt to get him to stay in England, "you will surely die."

But she knew he had no choice.

He breathed a laugh, an attempt at masking his fear, but he said nothing.

They remained in silence for a while, the only sound around them coming from the fire cracking in the hearth, and Robert wondered if perhaps now would be the time to tell her of his true feelings. How he had longed for her every day since their first meeting over fifteen years ago. How he looked into his wife's eyes every night and wished she was her.

But it was too risky. He would gain nothing from honesty. Especially now that he was headed for certain death.

But then Elizabeth slowly rose from her seat and walked around the table towards him.

He looked up as she approached, her snow-white skin illuminated by the fire light.

She knelt down beside him, and Robert followed her with his gaze until he was looking down at her, her eyes shining with unshed tears.

Then she reached up, cupped his stubbly cheek in her hand and stroked it lightly with her thumb, her eyes flickering from her hand on his face to his dark, intense stare. And then slowly, so slowly, she leaned forward and touched her lips to his. They remained there for a moment, breathing in each other's scents as their lips pressed together softly, and their hearts pounded madly in their chests.

Then Elizabeth pulled away, and Robert felt suddenly like a blind man who had just seen the sky. He blinked at her, waking from the daze.

He opened his mouth to speak but no words came out, and for a moment he thought that perhaps she had enchanted him.

Then Elizabeth's tears fell, and she inhaled deeply before whispering, "Promise you'll come back to me."

May 1558

Queen Mary was dying, and Elizabeth's greatest fear was coming true.

The war on France had not gone as planned, as Elizabeth had predicted, and England lost its only foothold in France – Calais – which had belonged to England for over two hundred years.

This defeat was the final loss in a long line of losses Mary had endured in her lifetime, and though she had tried her hardest to be a good queen, Elizabeth believed there would not be much her sister would be remembered for, other than perhaps the revival of the Heresy Act which saw nearly three hundred Protestants burned alive...

Over the years, Elizabeth and Mary had had a strained relationship to say the least, and though they loved one another as two similarly abandoned and lonely daughters of a king, the last few years had been filled with suspicion and fear.

All of which had stemmed from Mary's distinct dread of leaving the crown to the only person in England that did not want it. If only Elizabeth had been able to tell her sister that little truth.

It would have spared them both so much pain.

"I have faith that it will be safe to attend," Elizabeth told Kat as she pulled on her riding gloves.

A messenger had arrived with a letter from the queen, asking for Elizabeth to attend court for an audience.

"She is dying Elizabeth," Kat pointed out, "She may not even live past the night! Just wait some more days before you head straight into a trap."

"I cannot believe she wishes to trap me," Elizabeth replied, "She could have had me thrown into the Tower for all these years. She could have named any number of Catholic relatives as her heir, but she has not. If she wished to murder me or replace me as her heir, she could have done so any time in the last five years."

How Elizabeth wished Mary had named another as her heir…

But she knew that even if she had, Elizabeth had too much support from secret Protestant nobles, as well as the people, and another heir would only be overthrown as a usurper, leading to unnecessary deaths and end with the same outcome – with Elizabeth on the throne.

She had seen it happen with her cousin, Jane Grey.

Greenwich Palace, London

Elizabeth made her way through the throng of courtiers, and as she reached the end of the hall and saw her sister sitting slumped upon the throne, she was saddened to see that the rumours were indeed true, and that Mary I would not be long for this world.

She dipped her queen a curtsy, "Your majesty," she drawled, hoping to soften whatever Mary's current feelings were towards her.

"Lady Elizabeth," the queen replied icily, and Elizabeth swallowed, suddenly wishing she had heeded Kat's warning, "I have invited you here in the hope that we may speak plainly with one another."

Elizabeth met her sister's gaze intently and flashed her a smile, hoping to placate the hardened queen.

"I am but your humble servant, your majesty," she said, and though she meant every word, she knew, as soon as the words left her mouth, that Mary would undoubtedly assume them to be in mockery.

"You may not choose to be so insolent when you hear what I am about to say," Mary replied, to which Elizabeth flinched.

"I have summoned you here," the aged queen continued, "to *insist* that you relinquish your heretical faith in favour of the one true and Godly path of Catholicism. There will be no discussing it. You are here today to either accept or refuse. And your answer will lead you to your future," she paused, giving Elizabeth a moment to blink away the tears that had sprung to her eyes. Then Mary continued, "I urge you to choose wisely, Elizabeth. For today I make my ruling as your queen, and not your sister."

Elizabeth stared wide-eyed at Mary, whom she had loved all her life, and as she breathed erratically before her, she knew then that her judgement day had finally come.

She allowed herself one final thought of Robert, and how she now wished she had told him how she had always felt; and in the next instance she cursed Thomas Seymour for robbing her of what could have been a happy life until this moment, when he had forced himself on her, sullying her mind, body and soul with one unforgivable act.

Then she pushed all thoughts aside and straightened her back, her chest feeling tight with an anger she had never known. And she readied herself for battle.

"Do I have a moment to consider, or must I speak now?" she asked, though she knew the answer.

"Now," Mary replied, and Elizabeth saw just how tired her sister was with all this nonsensical back and forth on religion.

Elizabeth dropped her gaze, her cheeks blotching in anger.

For so long, she had not allowed herself to be angry – she had not wanted to be her father or indeed her sister.

She had pushed that emotion aside time after time again when she had been wronged first by her own father, then by Thomas Seymour, followed by so many who used her as a pawn in their rebellions. But now that her life was surely at an end – as so many others had gone to their end over the crown – she could no longer control her rage, and she raised her head and met Mary's gaze, her eyes blazingly furiously.

"I have made my choice, *sister*," she spat out.

"Speak it," Mary whispered, tears glistening in her eyes.

Elizabeth raised her chin defiantly, "I say nay," and the court behind her gasped, "You shall have to burn me alive for my sins."

June 1558
The Tower of London

As not only sister but also heir to the queen of England, Elizabeth was granted the best cell in the Tower of London – the very same one her mother had been imprisoned in years earlier, as she had awaited her own end. And the insult was not lost on Elizabeth, this final act of torture cementing the new hatred she now felt for her sister.

The psychological torture that derived from pacing the same stone floors that Anne Boleyn had paced, scorched any remaining familial feelings she had clung onto in the hopes of a sisterly reunion.

Despite receiving the most luxurious prison cell London had to offer, the thick stone walls were wet with damp each morning before the summer sun grew warm enough to heat the cold tower, and moist moss grew wildly in each corner of the room.

At night she would often wake to the sound of people crying or scratching their nails against stone, and night after night she was not sure which of the sounds unsettled her more.

Elizabeth was granted permission to have Kat attend her each morning, to help her dress and to bring her food, and though she received only one meal per day, it was not the bowl of gruel or stale bread that sustained her, but the news Kat would bring with her in secret.

"The Privy Council is now discussing your potential marriage to a foreign Catholic noble," Kat whispered hurriedly one morning once the cell door was closed behind them and the two women were alone, "It seems the queen is fighting her council in their pleas to have you executed."

Elizabeth sniffed; it was not enough. She would not forgive her sister.

"Have they chosen a suitor?" she asked, her pale eyebrows furrowing.

Kat shook her head, "Not yet," she said as she watched Elizabeth break apart the crust of bread and stuff some in her mouth hungrily, "Mary needs you here in England, and alive – she does not falter in her belief that you are her true heir as your father proclaimed in his will."

"She knows full well the people of England would not accept another instead of me," Elizabeth said, her newfound anger towards her sister still burning within her, "It is nothing to do with her love for me, but with her love for her people."

Kat blinked, "She is struggling with what she believes is best for her people, or with what is best for you."

Elizabeth looked up at her governess and noticed, again, how she had aged, and though she would always hold a special place in her heart for Kat as the mother she never had, Kat had begun to appear more and more haggard to Elizabeth. She wondered then if she had indeed always looked this way or if Elizabeth's newly acquired anger was causing her to have an uglier outlook on life.

Kat looked at the young woman before her, a sad expression in her eyes, "They may yet order your execution, Elizabeth," she whispered, her voice breaking with fear.

Elizabeth's eyes blazed, "She wouldn't dare…"

"It may not be by her command," Kat pointed out, "She is weak. Anyone from her Privy Council could trick her into signing your death warrant."

Elizabeth raised her chin, "Then so it shall be!" she proclaimed defiantly.

And Kat flinched, for in that moment, she looked just like her late father.

"Queen Mary is dead."

"My sister's ring."

Chapter 12

December 1558
Westminster Abbey, London

Queen Mary I's embalmed body, as requested in her will, was clothed as a nun, and buried at Westminster Abbey. Her final wish of having her mother's body exhumed and lain to rest with her however, had been ignored by Elizabeth and her new Privy Council, and the first Queen Regnant of England was buried and forgotten in death, much like she had been forgotten in life.

January 1559

The new queen's accession was such a grand occasion, that Italian ambassadors later compared it to their annual celebration in Venice where 'the city wed the sea'.
But she had never wanted it.
Elizabeth was carried along in an open litter, dressed magnificently in a robe of cloth of gold as a thousand riders escorted her through London.
But she had never wanted it.
The vast crowds cheered and waved from behind the barriers decorated with flowers, and Elizabeth was reminded of her sister's entrance into London just five years prior, when Mary had been adored by the people.
But Elizabeth had never wanted it.
This very day had been Elizabeth's most dreaded outcome for most of her life, and yet she knew now that she could have done nothing to stop it from happening.

Her sister had led a life of solitude in the hope of one day attaining the throne, while Elizabeth had done the same in the hope of avoiding it.

And yet, both paths of loneliness and sorrow had led them to the same dreaded fate.

At that thought she blinked the tears away quickly before anyone could accuse her of the truth – that this day was perhaps the worst of her life – and she shook her head free of her own troubling thoughts.

This was her reality now, and no amount of dislike for it would cause it to change. Just like her mother before her, Elizabeth would have to make the best out of a life she was being forced into. And as she moved slowly through the great crowd of people, she realised that the first step to finding happiness in this life was to accept the things she could not change.

Though she was this day being crowned before God as England's new queen, her great gold robe spread out behind her and her bright red locks flowing freely down her back, when she finally arrived at the Abbey, she had to admit she felt suddenly very small. All around and before her were thousands of onlookers, noble men and ladies, ambassadors to all the countries of Europe, princes and princesses of foreign lands – they had all come to witness the coronation of 'Henry VIII's bastard daughter' by the Great Whore, Anne Boleyn.

She inhaled a shallow breath in an effort to compose herself and then took her first step into the Abbey and towards the throne, where the bishop stood waiting.

The coronation went by in a blur, Elizabeth's heart thundering throughout.

When she was finally presented to her people in full majesty with her sceptre and orb, she forced a delighted smile, and the observers gave a huge shout, followed by the sound of

trumpets, drums and bells ringing so loudly that it sounded to Elizabeth as though the world was coming to an end.
Little did she and her people know that it had awakened a new beginning.

Though there was no disputing that Elizabeth was Henry VIII's heir as named in his final will, as well as Queen Mary's heir as named in her final will, there were those who did not support Elizabeth's claim to the throne.
And it soon became clear to Elizabeth that she had not been the only one who had dreaded her accension.
She knew that the country was bitterly divided between Catholics and Protestants, the people of England being torn to-and-fro for decades ever since her father had broken from the Catholic Church and the authority of the Pope.
During her sister's reign, however, the Catholic policies had been reinstated, and the England Elizabeth had now inherited was once again reunited with the Catholic Church.
As a Protestant daughter to the very woman who had instigated Henry VIII's need for reformation, Elizabeth could not allow England to continue within the clutches of Rome, and the very first thing she had to do to regain the country's independence from the Pope, was to establish a strong, Protestant Council.
During her coronation, as the people had called excitedly for their new queen, Elizabeth had felt a wave of panic engulf her.
She had never wanted this. Of that, she was sure.
But there was something in the back of her mind that kept troubling her ever since the crown had been placed upon her head.
All her life she had known that she had been her father's very last option, and that the chances of her inheriting the throne had been slim to none for the majority of her life.

And yet, despite all the odds, here she was today as Queen of England, with the people's love at her feet, and the power of no other in her hands.

Perhaps it mattered little what *she* wanted. God clearly had great things planned for her if He saw fit to remove every obstacle that stood in her way on this path to becoming queen.

And it had certainly been her mother's wish for Elizabeth when she gave up her own life for the slim possibility of this very moment.

And yet, as she sat facing the looking-glass in her new chambers – the queen's chambers – Elizabeth could tell by the fear in her eyes that she continued to dread the coming days and weeks in which she would regain her footing in this, her new life.

But the people's adoration, and the delight in their eyes, had given her a new viewpoint.

She was no longer just Elizabeth. She was suddenly a mother to all those people. They had watched her become anointed before God. They had cheered for her good fortune.

And though she did not wish for this herself, Elizabeth knew that it no longer mattered, for she held the sake of the people's – *her* people's – lives in her hands.

And she knew that, for them, and for her mother, she had to be strong.

March 1559
Greenwich Palace, London

William Cecil, former Secretary of State during the late Edward VI reign, had retired from his position when the Catholic Queen Mary I had attained the throne, with the knowledge that to remain at court with his opposing beliefs would only lead to death.

He had been right of course, and he thanked God and his good sense daily that his decision to retire to the country with his wife, Mildred, had spared them such a fate.

But it seemed God had not been prepared to leave England to rot under the shadows of Rome, for He had anointed yet another Protestant ruler to guide the people into the light of the reformation.

And so, with his wife's blessing, William Cecil returned to the public life he had previously left behind, in the hope of advising the new young queen as best as he could – if she would have him.

"Sir William Cecil, your majesty," the usher announced as a short, grey-haired man entered the great hall and strode confidently towards the queen, who sat straight-backed on her large throne.

As an unmarried monarch, the consort's smaller throne had been removed, leaving the fiery haired queen to sit at the far end of the great hall completely alone. And William Cecil smiled to think that hopefully soon there would be a great wedding between herself and a suitable candidate who would unite their strength with England.

"Your majesty," William said as he bowed, "I am honoured to be in your presence, finally, after having heard so much about you."

Elizabeth breathed a small laugh at the flattery, "What have you heard, Sir William?" she asked.

"Your lady, Blanche Parry," William replied, "Is my cousin."

At the mention of her lady, Elizabeth glanced beside her, to which Blanche smiled and nodded in confirmation.

"As well as that," William continued, "Your brother king Edward spoke often of you and your undeniable understanding of the world."

"My brother was too kind," Elizabeth replied modestly, "I am but a mere woman."

At the comment, William Cecil's eyes widened purposefully, and Elizabeth got the distinct impression that he was warning her not to continue with such public self-degradation.

"A woman with a man's mind, I have been told," William Cecil remarked, raising his grey eyebrows meaningfully.

Elizabeth only smiled in response, having understood his warning, and cursing herself for forgetting that she no longer had to play the witless, foolish woman to avoid ruin, but rather the exact opposite.

"What brings you here, my lord?" the queen asked then, hoping to move on from formalities.

"My queen," William replied, his voice clear and confident, "I would like to offer you my services," and he bowed again, "as I served your late brother as Secretary of State before his untimely death."

"I know who you used to be, Sir William," Elizabeth replied, "And I thank you for your services to my brother. But why should I consider reinstating you?"

William cleared his throat and took a step towards her, lowering his voice slightly in hopes of gaining some privacy in the public setting.

"Your majesty needs those who care for your safety to surround you," he said, his kind, green-eyed gaze speaking volumes.

Elizabeth stared back, "And why do you care for my safety, Sir William?"

The gentleman sniggered, "Oh, my most noble lady," he said as he shook his grey head, "Because you are the very light that will guide us to a brighter England."

❖

It had not been his words, but rather his conviction, which had given Elizabeth cause to reinstate William Cecil as Secretary of State in her Privy Council.

His subtle warning at her reckless comment alone had given her enough reason to believe him to be a loyal servant to the crown.

However, though Cecil was a devoted Protestant and supporter of the reformation, Elizabeth believed it would be in her best interest not to appoint only reformers as her advisors.

She had long ago realised that a person's differing belief did not warrant them a fool, and she believed wholeheartedly that to remove all Catholic advisors from her court would only end in rebellion and civil unrest, as it had done during Mary's reign. Elizabeth believed that to have a religiously mixed Privy Council was the key to understanding *all* of her subjects, and when it came to religion, she intended on walking a similarly cautious middle-way as her father had done. Never showing a preference for one religion or the other.

With that in mind she chose to allow William Herbert, Earl of Pembroke – a Catholic – to remain within the Privy Council, after having successfully served as councilman under Henry VIII, Edward VI and Mary I, all of which had had very differing religious outlooks.

His savvy and ability to serve under all three rulers before her suggested an impressive loyalty to the monarchy, which was exactly the characteristics she sought out in those who would advise her.

She also hoped a religiously mixed council would mark the beginning of a unified and peaceful England and set an example for a new act she desperately wished to present to Parliament.

"Gentlemen," Elizabeth said, raising her voice just enough to be heard over the men's low kerfuffle, "It is time we begin discussing the re-establishment of the Church of England, which my sister saw fit to tear down."

Most of the men before her nodded approvingly.

"I have decided," she said, looking down at her hands as they rested upon her lap when suddenly she heard someone clear their throat and she looked up to see William Cecil at the far end of the council table, raising his chin at her faintly.

Elizabeth, understanding his silent caution, straightened up and looked the men before her in the eyes.

"I have decided," she repeated, this time with more confidence, "That Parliament must revive the Act of Supremacy to regain England's independence from Rome."

There was chatter of agreement from most of her advisors.

"That is not all," Elizabeth continued, "It is not enough to simply reinstate previous laws and hope they remain in place."

"What do you propose, your majesty," the Earl of Pembroke asked, his dark eyebrows furrowed, and Elizabeth noticed, for the first time, a hint of a lisp in his speech.

Elizabeth cleared her throat, "I wish to end my country's religious turmoil," she declared passionately.

"Your highness –" one council member began as suddenly many others interjected.

"It is not a matter of –"

"You cannot simply wish for it –"

"What do you propose?"

The buzz that vibrated off so many frustrated men in such close quarters filled the queen's head, and she wondered briefly how anyone had ever made a thought-out decision with so much ruckus around them.

But Elizabeth grasped at the final question from among the frustrated uproar.

"My lords!" she called, "What I propose is simple."

And she watched them as they one by one stopped their confused ramblings.

"When England is once again freed from the Pope's control, we shall reintroduce the Book of Common Prayer as published during my brother Edward's reign, but it shall have some modifications… to appeal to the Catholics."

The men before her blinked their beady eyes at her, utterly shocked into silence.

"You wish to unify the two religions?" one asked, his face contorted into disgust.

"I wish to end all religious disputes!" the queen replied boldly as she stood from her throne and stared them all down.

"And I suggest you begin the necessary paperwork to present to Parliament, gentlemen," she said, "for many other issues need addressing. England's economic and military infrastructure need urgent attention! From what I have gathered, my father spent ruinously during his reign, and my poor brother and sister did not rule long enough for England to recover. We must put our religious disputes behind us and focus on rebuilding our strength."

The room fell silent for the first time that day, and the men looked around at one another, stunned by their young queen's understanding of matters of state.

William Cecil, however, smiled faintly at his queen.

"There is another pressing matter, your majesty," a voice braved from among the crowd of men then, "Your majesty's marriage."

Elizabeth swallowed and sat back down, "What of it?"

"You are twenty-five," he pointed out, "You are a queen. You must marry to form an alliance and produce an heir."

Elizabeth licked her lips in thought, "Marriage may wait."

"But your majesty –"

"I am your queen!" Elizabeth bellowed then, her father's anger finally emerging, "I am not a brood mare! I will decide when I shall marry, and with whom."

"Unfortunately, my queen," a bearded man said from among the crowd, speaking for the first time, "That is not how the world of kings and queens works."

His name was Francis Walsingham, and though Elizabeth knew of him by name, she had been able to learn only very little about him in the few months since her coronation.

"What do you know of it?" Elizabeth countered, raising her chin.

Walsingham did not immediately reply and simply gazed upon his young queen with knowing eyes, as if he were looking right into her soul, "Was there someone you had in mind for a husband, your majesty?"

Elizabeth's cheeks flushed bright red, but she remained silent, choosing instead to stare the man down and silently cursing him for his strangely astute remark.

"Send word for Lord Robert Dudley to return to England," queen Elizabeth ordered over her shoulder as she walked hastily through the candlelit hallways towards the queen's chambers.

"Yes, your majesty," Lettice whispered as she broke off from the group of women and took a right down a narrow passageway.

Lettice was not unaccustomed to summoning Robert Dudley for her mistress. And yet she knew that, now that Elizabeth was queen and her friend was away at war, it took more than a simple rider with a message to bring him before Elizabeth.

Lettice was no fool, though she was often perceived to be for she was the quieter of Elizabeth's ladies and did not like voicing her opinion aloud. But despite her timid nature, she was observant and wise beyond her years, much like Elizabeth herself, and she had long ago known that the relationship between her mistress and her friend was much more than either of them dared to admit to one another.

The queen's lady took a right into the great hall and hurried up the staircase to the Secretary of State's chambers. It would be William Cecil – as Secretary of State, and therefore in charge of all government correspondence – who would have to sign the formal document to allow Lord Robert leave from war. But Lettice did not think it would be too much of a scandal, for the war in France had unquestionably ended when the Spaniards left Calais defenceless for the French to siege during the end of Mary I's reign.

In fact, Lettice did not quite understand *why* English troops still lingered in St Quentin, when the peace treaty England and France had signed shortly after Elizabeth's coronation confirmed an end to the Anglo-French dispute.

The guards opened the doors to William Cecil's chambers, and she strode in to find the older man sitting hunched over at his writing desk.

"The queen wishes for Lord Robert to return from war," she said without introduction, for there was no need for small talk.

Cecil looked up from the paperwork before him.

"Lord Robert?" he asked.

"Dudley," Lettice replied, "Robert Dudley."

Cecil narrowed his eyes at the queen's lady, remembering the young queen's flushed cheeks at Walsingham's mention of a suitor for marriage earlier in the day.

"He is married. Is he not?" Cecil asked, recalling the union during Edward VI's reign, where the nobody Robert Dudley became Lord Robert through his marriage to a noble farmer's daughter.

Lettice nodded, "They are great friends."

Cecil raised his eyebrows and nodded slowly, "Ah yes," he said.

Then he sat forward and picked up his quill, "You may tell her majesty that the order for Lord Robert's return is being drawn up. You may go."

Lettice curtsied, "My lord," she mumbled and turned to leave, her heart skipping a beat at the prospect of the handsome Lord Dudley coming back into their lives.

May 1559
Greenwich Palace, London

Upon his return to England two months later, the most beautiful queen he had ever seen granted Robert the title of Master of Horse and gave him a position in her Privy Council as an advisor.
They had not seen each other in two years, their final moment together before he had gone off to war flashing in Elizabeth's mind as he stood gallantly before her as she bestowed his new titles onto him.
And the entire time, their eyes remained fixed on one another, the tension between them as clear as though it were a physical thing.
He looked different. His skin was darker, and his beard was longer than the stubble Elizabeth had always known him to done. But most clearly of all was the look in his eyes. They were eyes that had seen things she could not even imagine, eyes which were very visibly glad to be home and away from the fighting.
And dare she think it... glad to see her?
"With your new title as Master of Horse," the queen said, her voice as smooth as melted butter to Robert's ears, "You will be granted a place within my court, Lord Robert."
Robert bowed, "I am honoured, your majesty," he replied, flashing her a grin, "I look forward to spending a lot more time in your majesty's most gracious presence."
Elizabeth smiled excitedly and had to press her lips together to suppress her joy. Then she waved her pale hand, dismissing him to resume his place among the crowd.

Elizabeth could not help it, but she knew that she loved Robert. She was not sure when her feelings for him had started to form, but she had known it for a fact when he had told her of his departure to war two years ago.

In his absence, she had dreaded every messenger and every letter since that day, and even cried uninterruptedly when word had come that one of his brothers, Henry Dudley, had died in battle.

She had prayed to God to keep Robert safe. There had not been a day that had gone by when she had not prayed to Him.

But now Robert was back. He had safely returned to England – and to her – as he had promised he would. And the young queen's chest tightened with anticipation to spend more time with him again, to share stories, play cards and enjoy each other's company as they had always done.

Their kiss burst into Elizabeth's memory then. The recollection of that delicious moment causing her heart to hammer against her ribcage.

She was in love with Robert. She could no longer deny it.

The queen glanced at him standing among the crowd of courtiers then.

He stood tall and handsome beside his blonde wife, her arm resting in the crook of his elbow. And Elizabeth realised with a pang that she was living in a fool's land.

None of it mattered. Their connection. Their feelings. Their growing need for one another.

No matter her feelings. No matter his…

It was all irrelevant. They could never be together, never mind become betrothed.

For he was already married.

August 1559

Eight months after her coronation, Parliament passed the Act of Supremacy which saw England once again separated from the control of Rome and revived Henry VIII's original Act of Supremacy, issuing Queen Elizabeth I as Supreme Head of the Church of England.

Elizabeth's Act of Uniformity was also passed, with the small changes added which declared that while Protestantism would be the true faith of England, it allowed for leniency on certain Catholic doctrines.

Parliament joined these two Acts and formed one clear document – The Elizabethan Religious Settlement – which Elizabeth hoped would be the beginning of the end of religious conflict in her country.

But there were many who continued to plot against their new Protestant queen, and staunch Catholics awaited in the shadows for their moment to spit venom at the monarch they openly referred to as 'The Heretic Queen'.

"Let them boil in their own hatred," Robert Dudley told his queen and friend one evening as they strolled the gardens of Hampton Court Palace, where Elizabeth and her court had moved to shortly after her coronation.

"Why can't they just go on living their lives?" Elizabeth complained, "I have granted them all I can, and have upset many of my councillors in doing so! But I wanted an end to the religious disputes. It is barbaric!"

Robert nodded.

"We must look to the future," Elizabeth continued, "And not constantly be at war with each other over *how* we pray to the same God. There is only one Christ! All else is a dispute over trifles."

"Give it time," Robert said as he took Elizabeth's hand.

"Don't," she said then, pulling her hand away and looking over her shoulder at her ladies who walked some paces behind, "I do not wish for rumours."

"They would not be rumours if what they were to say were true," Robert replied teasingly.

Elizabeth blushed, "It cannot ever be true," she said, "You are married."

"I am," he said and then bit his lip pensively, his playful disposition gone.

Elizabeth glanced at him, "What is it?" she asked, knowing his expressions well enough to notice his change of mood.

Robert swallowed and met her gaze as they continued walking slowly through the hedgerows, the crunch of their feet upon the gravelled path masking their hushed conversation.

"She is not well," he said quietly, "Amy. She – she is likely to die."

Elizabeth's stomach dropped as she realised that the terrible news brought her nothing but joy. And she felt sick at herself for her selfishness.

"To die?" she repeated, her eyes wide with shock.

Robert nodded, then looked over his shoulder at her ladies.

"When she does die…" he whispered.

Elizabeth shook her head, "Don't say it," she warned, covering her ears dramatically.

Robert waited for her to regain her composure. Then, as she slowly dropped her hands from either side of her head, he steeled himself before he spoke.

"Would you?" was all he said.

It was the weighted question he had long wished to ask her.

The fair queen looked up into his dark eyes and inhaled slowly.

She had never wanted to marry.

Even as a child, the very prospect of it caused her stomach to churn. She had witnessed too many ruined by it.

Her mother.
So many stepmothers.
Mary.
Even Catherine Parr who had fortunately married for love – her *fourth* husband – had been betrayed by him and shortly thereafter died in childbed.

The memory of all the women she had seen fall at the concept of wedded bliss danced before her.

Robert continued to stare, hopefully, into her eyes, his question hanging between them.

Bile began to rise in her throat, but she knew she had to marry. One way or another, Elizabeth's duty was to conceive an heir for England.

And she loved him. Perhaps it would be enough...?

Elizabeth nodded then. A tiny, curt jut of her head.

But it was an answer.

It was *the* answer. The answer Robert had long been waiting for.

Chapter 13

October 1559
Hampton Court Palace, London

Queen Elizabeth stood by the window overlooking the freshly cut gardens of Hampton Court Palace as the members of her Privy Council behind her took their seats around the council table.

"My lords," she said, continuing to look out the window as she applied the newest mask she had been moulding for the past few months, a mask of confidence in her queenly duties, "I have news of a suitor which I forewarn you, I shall be rejecting."

There was low grumbling from some of the men, and Elizabeth turned around to face them, a small smile on her lips, her mask firmly in place, "You too shall be of the same opinion as I when you hear who it is from."

She took her seat at the head of the table and nodded her head at her Secretary of State, William Cecil, who sat on the opposite side of the long wooden table, facing his monarch.

He cleared his throat as he unfolded the letter he had been clutching and all eyes fell to him.

"Your most gracious majesty," he read aloud, "I offer you my hand in marriage, oh most beautiful queen, for I believe our countries should once again be unified as they were when your sister was alive."

Robert tore his eyes from Cecil and turned to look at Elizabeth, who sat straight-backed on her throne. She met his gaze, a small, amused smile twitching on her lips.

She raised her chin in direction of Cecil, coaxing Robert to continue listening.

"While I still grieve the death of my late wife, your sister," Cecil continued reading, "I am willing to set aside my personal turmoil for the sake of my people as well as England's. Signed King Filipe II of Spain."

"That snake –" Walsingham bellowed angrily, and Elizabeth raised her hand to silence him.

"Bring in the imperial ambassador," the queen called to her usher, who nodded and opened the door.

A tall, slender man walked in donning a thick head of dark curls upon his head and a bored, heavy-lidded expression.

He approached the council table to complete silence and took his seat to Elizabeth's right, caring little for the looks of distaste being thrown his way.

Elizabeth turned to the imperial ambassador once he was settled in his seat, breaking the tense silence, "*Senor,*" she said, the Spanish flowing easily off her tongue thanks to Kat's education, "What am I to make of your king's proposal?"

The dark-haired man sat forward in his seat, resting his forearms on the table and intertwining his fingers, "Your majesty," he replied in English, his accent heavy and his words slow, "It is a very noble offer."

"You cannot be serious, Feria!" Cecil boomed, matching Walsingham's distaste.

Count Feria turned to look at the elderly man, "His majesty King Filipe is *very* serious, my lord," he replied calmly, blinking slowly as though he were deliberately trying to provoke them, "A match with *Espana* is exactly what England needs to strengthen itself under a…new ruler."

He had not needed to say it, but the unuttered word hung in the air.

Female.

Elizabeth breathed a small laugh through her nose at the unspoken insult, grateful to have learned early on in life how to project an entirely different mindset to her true one. For while she exhibited amusement, inside she was burning with rage.

She rested her gaze onto her Secretary of State, "What say you, Sir William?" she asked, feigning to be considering the marriage proposal, when of course, it was utterly inconceivable. For not only was Filipe II of Spain her former brother-in-law, but he was also a staunch Catholic hell bent on returning England towards the darkness of Catholicism, as it had been under Mary and his ruling.

Cecil folded the letter in half, "We do not wish to insult Spain."

"Of course not," Elizabeth replied, too quickly.

He nodded his head, knowing of her decision, "We shall consider the proposal and write up a reply in due haste."

Elizabeth turned her pretty face to Count Feria, a tight smile on her lips, her mask slipping ever so slightly as she struggled to maintain a calm exterior, "You have your answer."

The imperial ambassador raised an eyebrow, "It is not an answer."

"It is the one you have, nonetheless," Robert replied hotly then, his first utterance at the topic.

Elizabeth, without breaking eye contact with the ambassador, reached a hand across the table and placed it over Lord Robert's, who sat to her left. She had hoped to dampen his outburst and to quash any assumptions that may be drawn from it. But instead, she saw in her peripheral vision, how some members of the council looked at each other uncomfortably at their easy touch.

"You may tell your master that a more solid answer shall be underway in due course," she said sweetly, hoping to put an end to the discussion.

"You cannot react in such a way!" Elizabeth raged later that same day as she and Robert Dudley quietly argued in the queen's chambers, her true self finally able to appear, none of her many masks ever having been necessary around Robert.

Her former governess and newly appointed First Lady of the Bedchamber, Kat, sat in silence in the corner as she embroidered, serving as a buffer to the queen who may never again be left alone, especially not in the company of a man.

"The Catholic king of Spain, your former brother-in-law," Robert replied disgustedly, "Asks for your hand in marriage… it is *insulting*!"

"I am the newly appointed queen of England! Of course I will be receiving proposals from suitors!" Elizabeth replied as she turned away from him, one hand pressed to her forehead, a headache beginning to take root between her eyes.

"Kat," she called, "remove my hood, it is too tight."

Kat approached, did as she was bid in silence and watched the two young people breathe angrily as they fought to control their passion for one another as it materialised itself in the form of fury.

Kat offered Elizabeth a warm smile and returned to the far corner of the queen's chambers to continue her activity.

"Sweet Robert," Elizabeth said lovingly then, her previous anger starting to subside as she began to understand his rage, "I will not accept any betrothal," then she took a step towards him and lowered her voice, "I know that I am already betrothed."

Robert breathed a sigh of relief, the jealousy melting from his eyes, "How I wish I had never given into my father's pressure to marry Amy."

Elizabeth frowned, the intimate moment suddenly dashed at the mention of his wife.

"Yes, well," she said as she turned from him, her heeled shoes clinking on the stone flooring as she walked away.

Robert furrowed his brows together and watched her distance herself, and the anger which had previously been directed at the King of Spain was suddenly focused on his queen.

"Can you even blame me?" he called after her.

She spun around, "What?"

"You made it clear, many times, that you were never to marry."

Elizabeth narrowed her eyes, then glanced at Kat in the corner, who pretended to be deaf to the goings on around her.

"Not now, Robert," the queen warned.

"Yes, now, Elizabeth," he replied daringly, his dark eyes blazing, "If only you had paid attention, you would have seen that my feelings for you have always been clear."

The queen flinched.

"You do not know what I have suffered through," Elizabeth replied in quiet anger.

Robert scoffed and shook his head, "I am not your father!" he said, "I would only have treated you as the princess I always believed you to be."

Elizabeth remained silent, her mouth drawn into a tight line as she fought with herself to keep her secret, her fury trying desperately to bubble it to the surface.

But she could never voice the truth: that her aversion to marriage stemmed not only from what had happened to her mother and stepmothers, but also from what had happened to *her*.

Thomas Seymour's violence against her had robbed her of a healthy and happy outlook on the physical side of love.

The idea of a wedding night turned her stomach in knots; and not even the prospect of Robert as her new husband could calm her terror of it.

She inhaled deeply then, straightening her back and, for the first time in all their years of friendship, Elizabeth became hardened towards him, and Robert could see one of her many masks beginning to take form.

"Lord Robert," she said formally then, causing him to frown in confusion at the icy tone of her voice, "It is of no concern to you how I, your queen, choose to address the issue of a suitor. I shall receive many proposals, I am sure, from those who wish to claim England for themselves through a union with me. Until you are free to have an opinion on the matter, you may not presume to speak to me so offhandedly."

Robert had come too close. Her guard was up. Her feelings were becoming too strong. And she had to protect herself before she admitted to the world that she was madly in love with a married man.

For it would be her ruin. Just as it had been her mother's.

Robert blinked, his handsome face twisted in pain, "Until I am *free* to have an opinion?"

Elizabeth breathed erratically as she continued to stare him down.

"You mean to say that I have no say in this, because I am married," he said matter-of-factly.

Elizabeth's heart hurt to see him in pain, but the fact remained: until his wife died of whatever ailment possessed her, the queen of England had to be seen to entertain the prospect of marriage with a foreign prince. Her country was too weak to insult half of Europe by openly fawning over one of her own *married* subjects.

"You may leave court, Lord Robert," his queen said coldly then, "I give you leave to spend time with your wife."

"Elizabeth –" he said, taking a step towards her, but she raised one hand to stop him.

"No," she said, "It is 'your majesty' to you."

November 1559

With Lord Robert gone from court, Elizabeth was able to focus solely on her country and the crucial political matters which still needed addressing. And, to begin with, she had been too busy to miss him.

She continued to receive many offers of betrothals from princes as well as nobles from all over Europe, and she gave them all the same answer: that she would consider them wholeheartedly before giving a direct response.

"Your majesty," William Cecil told her one morning as they sat by the roaring fire in the queen's chambers, "You cannot continue to reject all these offers."

"I am not rejecting," Elizabeth replied casually.

Cecil cocked his head to one side, "The whole world knows by now that your strategy is to keep them at arm's length until they give up."

Elizabeth shrugged, "If that is what they wish to believe."

The doors to her chambers opened then and her usher announced Francis Walsingham.

"My queen," he said as he bowed, "I bring news of the Catholic opposition to your majesty's Religious Settlement."

Elizabeth nodded for him to go on.

He smiled, flashing a mouthful of crooked teeth, "It is good news," he said, "The majority of the clergymen took the Oath of Supremacy, accepting your majesty as the Supreme Head of the Church of England. Of the nine-thousand Catholic priests, only two-hundred-and-fifty refused and have resigned. They are no threat to your reign as they are too few to form a strong opposition."

Elizabeth sighed, then laughed, "Excellent news, Walsingham."

The man bowed and turned to exit, leaving Elizabeth and her Secretary of State alone once more.

"How does he hear such news before you, Sir William?" Elizabeth asked curiously, the flames from the fire casting an orange glow over her pale skin.

"I am told he spends much of his own money to attain such information."

"He is loyal then," Elizabeth deduced.

"It would appear so," Cecil agreed, "However, there are those who are not so loyal who still remain on your council."

Elizabeth raised an eyebrow, "I had begun to consider removing some members," and she nodded her head pensively, "The Privy Council weighs more heavily towards Catholicism currently, and though this latest development was positive, I cannot risk its progression by appearing to favour the old faith."

"I admire your neutral approach to religion, your majesty," Cecil said, "It is something your father did well, though I believe his actions derived from indecisiveness, while you seem to be accepting of both?"

Elizabeth shrugged, "I am not accepting of Catholicism. I was raised a Protestant. But I acknowledge that not all my subjects were, and there will be those who wish to keep their Catholic traditions," she paused then as she thought, "But I am also aware that if I continue to inspire harmony among my people, that within two generations, Protestantism will prevail as long as it maintains the upper hand."

"So, you wish to let Catholic practices simply…die out?" Cecil asked.

"Precisely," Elizabeth said, "Is it not easier to allow it to run its course than to create martyrs in an effort to destroy it?"

Cecil narrowed his eyes at his young queen, a small, proud smile brightening his face, and he was suddenly convinced that England finally had a ruler who wanted nothing more than the very best for her country.

It would appear that the queen wished for a united England, one who was not constantly at war with itself as it had been under her sister, Mary's, rule, as well as her brother Edward's. Perhaps this too was why she could not decide on a betrothed? Did she wish to strengthen England from within and without a foreign power to surrender her authority to?

Cecil was not sure on that final point. It certainly would make sense since she so routinely dismissed any suitor's advances.

But he had been observing the young queen for many months now, and though he liked to believe her actions against marriage came from a political standpoint, he had to consider the possibility that perhaps a certain young lord had more to do with it.

And if this were indeed to be the case, Cecil would have to do all he could to make sure that that nobody Dudley did not become king consort of England.

For what would Dudley contribute towards England's advancement? Nothing. He came with no personal land, armies or notable monies.

In fact, all a union with him would achieve would be to lessen her majesty's own value, for a queen's choice of husband needed to strengthen her. And Elizabeth nor England would find strength in a match that were in any way beneath her.

January 1560

Elizabeth stood true to her decision that fewer Catholics within her Privy Council would be the next logical step to enforcing Protestantism as the principal faith of England.

She was no fool. She had been educated well enough to understand that men did not like to be dominated by a woman, especially in matters of policy.

She also knew that, if she wished to keep control over the men who advised her, she would have to maintain a much smaller group, while simultaneously giving those who remained more power to stroke their egos as they served below her.

"Gentlemen," she said once the three remaining members of the Privy Council – Walsingham, Cecil, and the Earl of Pembroke – entered the council chambers, after having been dramatically slimmed down from the former nineteen.

She waved her hand for them to take their seats and then sat down slowly in her throne.

"You have been chosen and will be charged to commit yourselves wholly to your queen and the realm," she said eloquently, "Your honesty will be praised! And I assure you that I want for you to always tell me *what you think*, and not what you think I wish to hear."

The three men nodded their heads at her, and she smiled in return.

"While I, of course, do not expect you all to agree all the time, either with me or with each other, I do demand honest advice and a commitment to give your best for me and for the country."

She fell silent and noticed Walsingham wiping a tear from his eye before meeting her gaze once more.

"Sir Robert Dudley, too, will be remaining on the Privy Council when he returns to court," Elizabeth continued, "And I will of course have the ambassadors attend the meetings as well. But otherwise, we are alone, gentlemen. I have carefully weeded out those who could not be trusted to guide me, and I am looking forward to building a strong England with you at my side."

August 1560

Though, as queen, Elizabeth would never again be alone, surrounded eternally by her ladies, as well as hundreds of servants and courtiers, she had never felt so lonely as she had done that past year, since sending Robert away.

Though her separation from him had originally proven successful, allowing her to focus solely on her kingdom; as the months passed by, she began to feel as though her duties were melding into one continuous, never-ending compilation of burdens. And slowly but surely, she no longer felt any joy or triumph in her achievements.

Though she knew that sending him away had been the right thing to do to, it had begun to feel as though a little hole had started to form in her heart, proof that while she knew she could not have him, she missed him desperately, nonetheless. And when the food had lost its flavour and the birdsong had lost its melody, she had allowed herself to consider summoning him back to court, under the pretence of needing his services as her advisor and Master of Horse.

But throughout the months that followed, her pride had never allowed her to give in to her gaping heart, for deep down she knew that as queen of England, she no longer had the privilege to give into selfish, earthly desires.

And so, she put her wishes of reconciliation aside, never giving into the loneliness that haunted her. Instead, she went to bed every night secretly conjuring up a memory of the sounds of his laughter from among the crowd, or of a glimpse of his lopsided smile meant only for her.

But in the morning, reality would wake her, and in the dewy light of dawn, the empty pillow beside her would mock her for a desolate fool.

7th September 1560 *('Into Your Arms' by Ava Max [no rap version])*

It was the dead of night.
Elizabeth was asleep in her royal bed, her long red curls plaited loosely over her shoulder, when there was a quiet

knock on the door. The sound woke her instantly, for she no longer slept deeply since having become queen.

She sat upright, her thick plait slipping off her shoulder like a snake, "Who is it?" she called, unable to see much of anything in the darkness.

"Your majesty?" her lady-in-waiting, Lettice, replied from the small bed in the corner.

"There is someone at the door," Elizabeth answered, and she heard Lettice scrambling from her small bed and padding over to the nightstand to light a candle.

She walked slowly towards the door but stopped as she reached for the handle and looked down at the floor instead, before bending over to pick something up.

"It is a note," Lettice said dreamily as she headed back to Elizabeth and handed her the folded parchment, stifling a yawn.

The queen took it and the candle, then waved Lettice away to give her privacy.

Upon unfolding the note, she knew instantly who had sent it from the handwriting – one she had known almost all her life, and one she had studied meticulously ever since she had been fooled by Thomas Seymour's falsified note beckoning her to meet him.

Elizabeth,
I know why you sent me away. And I understood it then.
But with each month that has passed, my longing for you overcame my understanding, and I can no longer breathe without you near.
Though you have not given me permission to return, I am here. And – if you will show me mercy – I will be awaiting you in the courtyard.
Forever if need be.

Elizabeth swallowed to quench her dry throat.

Despite their strained final encounter, it was not fear or worry she felt at the prospect of seeing Robert again after so many months apart. Instead, she felt wide awake, as though the sun had risen just for her.

"I am taking a walk," Elizabeth told Lettice quietly as she threw the covers off herself and wrapped her furs around her, but to Elizabeth's surprise, her lady-in-waiting was already fast asleep once again.

It was probably for the best, Elizabeth thought as she padded towards the doors, for she felt suddenly overcome with excitement to see him in secret.

There was something about the romantic letter.

A thrill about meeting in the darkness.

Whatever it was, her instincts were telling Elizabeth to meet him.

She slowly cracked opened the doors to her chambers and peered through to see her guard fast asleep as he stood upright, the long hours of security to the monarch proving an impossible task for only one man.

She frowned. She would have to appoint another to make sure one was always in attendance. But for tonight, this stroke of luck would do nicely.

She slipped outside easily and hurried quietly down the dark halls, the only light coming from the glow of the moon as it shone brightly through the windows. But she knew the way.

This was her palace.

When she eventually arrived at the courtyard to find it empty however, her stomach dropped with dread, and the memory of the empty field with the lonely Elm tree behind Chelsea Manor flashed before her like a lightning bolt.

She stumbled backwards, ready to retreat.

But then a shadow appeared from behind a pillar and Elizabeth knew in an instant that it was her Robert.

In that moment, relief and joy washed over her, and she did not care that she was queen, nor that he was married. She hurried towards him as though they were both free, for as they remained shrouded in the lonely darkness, it felt safe to pretend that they were.

Suddenly she was in his arms, and he held her face in his hands as they stared into each other's eyes, having a silent conversation through their gaze as only lovers could do.

And then his mouth found hers, hungrily at first as though his life would end if he did not take a bite of her – a forbidden apple – that very instant. But after a moment, his kiss grew slower, more tender, as if he were tracing a map of her lips.

Elizabeth melted into him, her body coming alive in a way she had never imagined possible at the touch of a man, and she pressed her hands against his strong chest, pushing him gently back against the wall and out of the light of the moon.

He raked his fingers through her hair, fidgeting with the plait to let her wild curls fall free, and once they did, he groaned. A deep throaty sound so filled with passion Elizabeth could not help but admit that she wanted him. She *needed* him.

In one fluid motion Robert carefully stepped out from against the wall and spun Elizabeth around, pressing her against it instead before pushing his thigh between her legs and feeling them separate willingly. And all the while they kissed, his tongue having now found its way to hers as their lust for one another grew uncontrollably.

He had never felt so alive in all his years. Not once had he felt so complete as he did right there in the arms of the woman he had always loved. Even in all the years that he had been married to his sweet, innocent wife, he had never known a craving so intense that it overpowered all other senses. And he knew then that this was exactly where he was supposed to be. Even if it was hidden in the shadows.

Elizabeth breathed heavily then as Robert slowly reached down to lift her nightshift, his fingertips brushing lightly against her thigh. But she did not stop him. In fact, Robert distinctly felt her legs parting further ever so slightly at his touch, and his hand continued to work its way upwards.
He was gentle. His fingers only just teasing.
But it felt good.
It felt so good.
And soon she was overwhelmed with pleasure, one which came again and again in waves of delight as her body shuddered against his. Her hands were in his hair, clinging on for dear life as she moaned quietly against his lips.
It was a feeling Elizabeth would never have associated with a sexual act, having previously only experienced pain, fear and humiliation at the touch of a man.
She did not know how long they had remained there, pressed so closely against the wall they may as well have become part of the palace's architecture.
But in that time Elizabeth had lived a thousand lives, for she had finally learned what it felt like to be touched by someone who loved her. And though she had vowed to never again allow a man to claim her fully, she believed she could live off this moment for the rest of her life.

8th September 1560

The following morning the queen awoke with a glow to her cheeks which gave Lettice and Blanche a moment of pause, for they had never before seen her quite so happy.
The reason for Elizabeth's joy – though no one would ever know the full extent of it – was made clear later that same day when Lettice spotted Lord Robert among the crowd in the great hall, and her own heart leapt to her throat as he locked

eyes with her briefly, his presence brightening Lettice's spirits as it had done the young queen's.

The crowd parted when the usher announced the arrival of their monarch, and as Elizabeth made her way towards her great throne, she could feel the people's energy, which – for a reason yet unknown to her – did not match her own elated spirit.

Something had happened.

She took her place upon her throne.

"My queen," a messenger called as he approached quickly, his eyes fixed on Elizabeth. He bowed before her, "I bring grave news. There has been a tragic accident involving the lady Amy Robsart."

Robert's wife.

All of a sudden there was a commotion from among the crowd as Robert Dudley began pushing people aside, "What's happened?" he demanded, his face ashen with worry.

The messenger looked from the agitated man beside him to his confused queen and back, unsure who to address with this sensitive matter.

"It appears she has fallen down a flight of stairs at her home in Cumnor Place," the messenger mumbled.

"How is she? Is she hurt?" Robert asked, his eyebrows creased as he tried to understand what he was hearing.

The messenger turned his attention back to the queen, "Amy Robsart was found dead, your majesty. Her neck was broken when her servants found her this mid-morning."

The great hall fell silent. There were no gasps of shock and no confused mutterings. There was only that judgemental buzz.

Only Robert and Elizabeth seemed utterly perplexed by the news. And it suddenly dawned on her that the people of the court must have already heard of it through the grapevine of slanderous gossip, and from the uncomfortable atmosphere reverberating from the crowd, it appeared they had already made up their minds as to *how* Amy Robsart had ended up on the bottom of those stairs.

Then the whispers began again, ladies covering their mouths as they snuck glances in Robert's direction, and Elizabeth's throat tightened with the words she wished to call to them.

That Robert Dudley could not have been involved, since he had been with her all night.

But she knew she could not, and she swallowed the words down like tiny shards of glass, slicing her throat open from within. And all the while Robert stared up at his queen, his face as pale as that of the moon the night before. And he knew that the world would judge him, for his only alibi involved the very woman he could not risk revealing.

Chapter 14

An investigation ensued in which Robert Dudley was questioned extensively as to the circumstances surrounding his wife's mysterious death.

Though he could not admit to having ridden off to Hampton Court Palace the night before for fear of involving Elizabeth in the scandal, he was able to state with complete truth that when he last saw his wife, she had been very much alive.

"We ate supper that night together," Robert testified, "Which was, frankly, very unlike her. She would usually take supper alone in her quarters and I in mine."

He looked up, and he was clearly grief-stricken.

"I didn't think much of it but only that she was perhaps feeling better, since she had been unwell for some time," he sniffed, "I then left in the early hours of the morning to return to court. I cannot explain how this has happened, but I can say with all honesty that I did *not* hurt my wife."

The men of the jury sighed, and one shook his head before he spoke, "Her relatives are crying 'murder', Lord Robert."

"I did not *murder* Amy!" Robert protested, his eyes bloodshot.

The men then leaned closer to one another and mumbled amongst themselves, while Robert could do nothing but watch them with wide eyes.

"Her servants saw her that morning, well and happy, they have testified," the man at the centre of the jury said, "She is said to have sent them away to the market, quite adamantly in fact. And that when they returned, they found her dead."

Robert exhaled and hung his head, "Amy…" he mumbled, guilt overcoming him as he realised the sad reality – that she had likely awoken that morning to find him gone, and undoubtedly knew where – or who – he had gone to.

The jury continued their quiet deliberation. Then, as they all sat back in their seats nodding to one another, one spoke, "We see your distress, Lord Robert, and while your account fits the servant's testimony, we can come to no other conclusion but that you are not involved. Amy Robsart's death is a mystery. But whether it was a terrible accident, or a purposeful act of melancholy, the fact remains that we do not believe you associated."

Robert looked up at the old men's faces as tears streamed down his face, the guilt he felt for his wife's tragic ending breaking his heart in two.

For though the jury concluded that he had not been to blame for her death, he knew the truth: that while he had not committed the crime itself, his actions over the years had undeniably been what had given his poor wife the push she had needed to plummet to her grave.

November 1560

"Your majesty," William Cecil said as he, Walsingham, Lord Robert, and the Earl of Pembroke all sat at the council table, watching their queen pacing up and down the length of the room, "You must give Spain an answer for their marriage proposal. King Filipe is becoming insistent that you join with him and allow for more leniency to the Catholic faith."

Elizabeth shook her head as she continued to pace.

Cecil sighed, "The threat of religious rebellion is on our doorstep, my queen. If Spain, as a Catholic nation, is out of the question for a marital union, then choose any other of your proposed suitors… If you do not marry and strengthen England with a foreign force and an heir, then…"

"What?" Elizabeth snapped abruptly, "Then what? Hmm? I may be a woman, sir, but there is more to me than conceiving heirs!"

Robert hung his head. He knew that the queen's recent anger had stemmed from the gossip which now surrounded him.

His wife was dead. And though it was something he and Elizabeth had been waiting for so that they could be married, the scandal that derived from her mysterious death now made Robert and impossible candidate for the queen's husband. And though no one else knew of their plans, it had been promised to one another again and again the night they had given themselves to each other.

Robert's name had been cleared of any crime. The coroner's jury had utterly denied any possibility of foul play surrounding his wife's death; and on paper, Lord Robert was innocent.

But gossip continued to surround him even two months later, and anywhere he went, people whispered behind their hands and shook their heads at him in disgust.

And the reality of their situation had started to weigh heavily on them, made so much heavier by the constant discussion of the queen's marriage to another.

"Your highness, you must marry," the Earl of Pembroke said then, his deep voice adding a sense of calm over the queen, who stopped pacing abruptly and inhaled deeply through her nose.

She turned to her small, intimate council then with her hands upon her hips, "You may write back to Spain that I continue to be unsure on the matter."

"Oh, your majesty!" Cecil called frustratedly, throwing his hands in the air, "The king of Spain will not wait forever. Look," he said, then riffled through his documents before pulling out a letter, "He has this morning written that he is also considering a Valois alliance. If he creates a union with the Catholic royal house of France, the two most powerful Catholic countries in Europe will be united against us. They will seek to overthrow you, Elizabeth."

Cecil's informal use of the queen's name softened the information he was giving her into wise, fatherly advice. But it rattled Elizabeth's senses, nonetheless.

To use a threat of potential invasion to put pressure onto her to form an alliance she did not want, stirred something within her she could not control.

And suddenly her father's characteristics took life in his daughter as she raged angrily at her council.

"You tell that slimy Spaniard," Elizabeth spat out, "that he may have succeeded in controlling my desperate sister, Mary, into doing as he pleased. But I am not my sister. I will not be told what to do and certainly not at the threat of my people! You tell Spain that I have made up my mind – I have his final answer. My answer is nay!" she exclaimed, her eyes blazing angrily, "Let him form his Valois alliance, and we shall see what they dare to do with it when it is done."

February 1561

Months had passed since Amy Robsart's mysterious death and, since the Christmas festivities, the people of the court had begun to forget.

King Filipe's threat to unite Spain with France had not yet come to pass and as the weeks went by, Elizabeth's informant, Francis Walsingham, kept his queen updated that there seemed to be no preparations for it.

It seemed that England was safe for now.

But that did not stop her advisors from continuing to press Elizabeth to marry and produce an heir for the continuation of the Tudor line, and England's stability.

"The people need an heir," Cecil told his queen as she walked hastily through the hallways, the great skirts of her riding gown flapping at her sides as she attempted to hurry away from him, but somehow his short legs kept up.

"Your majesty!" he continued, "You cannot escape this. It is your duty!"

He watched bewildered as she did not reply but merely raised an eyebrow, as if in disagreement.

She continued ahead and emerged into the courtyard, her ladies following closely behind.

Though it was not yet Spring, the sun was shining, and Elizabeth had requested to go out hunting, suggesting to Cecil that she would likely be gone for most of the day.

They continued on in silence, the weight of their disagreement hanging heavily between them, but Cecil knew there was not much more he could do but to continue insisting. And he cursed the Tudors' persistent talent for stubbornness.

As the queen, her ladies and her advisor exited through Hampton Court Palace's gate, they were met by the queen's steed and another, both saddled and awaiting their riders.

Between them, holding onto their reins, was none other than Lord Robert; and Cecil's shoulders sagged at the sight of him.

By now, Cecil was convinced that the queen's resistance towards the prospect of marriage was directly linked with her feelings for that young man. After all, given the not-so-discreet looks shared between the two of them at the council table, and the queen's rejection of all her other suitors, there was absolutely no denying it any further.

"Your grace," Robert greeted his queen with a bow and a lopsided smile.

"Lord Robert," she replied as she took her horse's reins from him, smiling to herself as she noticed the crossbows and firearms hanging off her guards' saddles, knowing that they would never use them. Then she turned her attention back to Cecil.

"You may stop your fretting, Sir William," she said, "I am but twenty-seven and healthy. England must not fuss too much about a future without me in it."

Cecil watched as the stable boys helped their queen into her side saddle, and she looked down at her advisor with a smug smile on her face.

"Your majesty may yet fall from the horse this very day and leave the country in ruin," Cecil replied brazenly then, to which Elizabeth's smile disappeared in an instant.

She looked sheepishly from Robert on his horse beside her, to her ladies who hung their heads, pretending they had not heard.

"You forget yourself, Sir William," she warned, but her cheeks were burning, and the truth of his words brought on a deep red blotching to her neck and face.

Cecil bowed grandly before her and stepped back three paces. Then the queen and her favourite clicked their tongues to spur their horses on, and they rode off into the woods, the queen's three guards following closely behind, their horses saddlebags filled with hunting gear they would never use.

They rode along leisurely through the woods, the pretence of a hunt forgotten once Elizabeth and Robert were away from prying eyes and engulfed by nature.

Their knees were almost touching as they rode side by side, the heat that radiated from Robert's proximity causing Elizabeth's heart to beat faster.

The queen's guards remained at a distance to allow the queen some privacy, but close enough to jump to action if the need arose.

She and Robert had not been alone once since that night in the courtyard five months prior. The tragedy of his wife's death, his connection to it, and their emotions running high ever since, having given neither of them the opportunity for selfish thoughts.

But since the new year festivities, something had changed.

Elizabeth had observed from her throne, as Robert had circulated the crowd, that women could not stop stealing glances at the newly widowed, handsome young lord.

She had watched them with a smirk playing on her lips, taking small sips from her cup of sweetened wine to hide her thoughts.

But the amusement of it had dissipated swiftly and jealousy had taken over like a tidal wave, causing her to envision all kinds of different ways that she could cause those gawking ladies harm.

But instead of resorting to violence, Elizabeth had decided that enough time had been wasted grieving Amy Robsart, and the ladies' interest in her Robert had spurred her on to steal him away for herself.

The first step of leaving the castle grounds having been successfully achieved...

After some minutes, Elizabeth, believing to be deeply enough in the woods to attempt to rid herself of her guards, glanced over her shoulder briefly before whispering to Robert.

"Race me?" she said, her pale blue eyes glinting with mischief.

Robert read her thoughts, her body language that morning having given him more than enough signs to know that she was burning for him, and he nodded his head once, his eyes darkening with desire.

Elizabeth firmly spurred her horse on, and but a split second later, Robert followed suit, whipping his reins into his steed's neck.

The guards, having been conversing quietly among themselves at a generous distance behind, did not react for a few seconds, causing the couple to be almost out of sight when they too pressed the heels of their boots into their horses' sides.

Elizabeth and Robert rode their horses hard, dodging and weaving beneath the branches of trees expertly, the adrenaline in their veins revealing a newfound agility as they attempted to lose sight of their chaperones.

When they could no longer see the queen's guards, they took a swift turn off the path and into the depths of the woods, hoping to watch from the darkness as they rode past them, none the wiser.

And just moments later, they did exactly that.

When the sound of the guards' horses dissipated far enough away, Elizabeth let out the breath she was holding, and the pair looked at one another before bursting out in a fit of laughter.

"Shhh," Elizabeth insisted after a moment, "They may yet hear us."

They fell silent and Robert dismounted before pulling the reins over his horses' head and holding them in his hand.

Elizabeth followed suit and they slowly stepped deeper into the wilderness, their horses walking behind them lazily.

After only a short while, Robert stopped and tied his horse's reins to the branch of a tree.

"Do you think this far enough, your grace?" he asked.

"We're in private, Robert," Elizabeth said as she turned to tie up her own horse, "You don't have to call me that."

They faced each other, suddenly feeling awkward. Then Robert looked around, "Is this what you had in mind when you hatched this elaborate plan?" he teased.

Elizabeth smiled, her eyes never straying from him.

And then, as his gaze returned to his queen and he saw the fire in her eyes, Robert swiftly closed the space between them, and with his hand on the back of her neck he pulled her to him.

Their lips crashed into each other's eagerly, both of them fully aware that they had but a moment together before they would be found.

And they must not be found.

"You don't know how long I've waited for you," Robert mumbled against her neck then as he traced kisses along her skin.

Elizabeth took his face in her hands, "We will be wed soon," she promised, though her stomach churned with anxiety at the words.

She kissed him to drown her fears, hoping to draw courage from him.

She *wanted* to marry Robert.

In fact, she knew that if she were ever to marry anyone, it would always be Robert.

She felt safe around him. He had a way of calming her troubled soul that even Elizabeth could not comprehend.

And yet the prospect of consummating a marriage – no matter with who – turned her stomach in knots.

Robert pulled away from her and began to kiss a length down her neck again, kissing the tops of her breasts before pulling her down slowly onto the leafy ground below.

She would have to overcome her fears. It was detrimental to the production of an heir. It was detrimental to the future of England. And she knew that, above all else, it was detrimental to her healing.

As they sat upon the ground, their arms and legs tangled around each other, Robert began to hitch her skirts up over her thighs.

Then, as he returned his lips to hers gently, she could feel his hands working to open his trousers, when suddenly Elizabeth froze up and pulled away, yanking her skirts back over her knees in one fell swoop.

"No," she mumbled, "I –"

That was when they heard it. The unmistakeable sounds of urgent horses galloping nearer at a deafening speed.

Robert's head snapped toward the sound, then he scrambled up, tucking his dishevelled shirt into his hose and running a hand through his dark hair.

"We must get to the road before they find us," he said, and turned to untie the horses from the branches.

Elizabeth grabbed the reins of her horse from his outstretched hand and pulled her steed along, pushing past the shrubbery quickly as the sound of thundering horse hooves was almost upon them.

As they caught a glimpse of the path between the trees, they quickly swung themselves into their saddles and trotted towards it, emerging sheepishly as they looked from side to side.

They had just about enough time to right themselves onto the path when suddenly the riders were upon them and the guard at the head called, "Halt!" the two other guards behind him pulling their horses' reins to stop them in their tracks.

"Your majesty!" the guard said, his tone heavy with relief, "Are you hurt?" and his eyes darted to the top of Elizabeth's head.

Her hand shot up self-consciously to where he was looking and pulled a small leaf and twig from her hair, her heart racing as she suddenly feared being caught.

"Her majesty was thrown from her horse," Robert replied from beside her, "She is well, it was not a hard fall."

Elizabeth nodded and threw the twig aside, "All is well, gentlemen. Let us return."

As they trotted back to the palace in silence, Elizabeth chastised herself for her stupidity, her naivety dawning on her.

How could she have allowed her carnal lust for Robert to cloud her judgement?

Had she not vowed to maintain an aura of virtuousness and purity to the outside world?

She had been foolish to think she could continue on unmarried, stealing kisses with Robert, and thinking herself above suspicion.

Though she was the daughter of King Henry VIII, she was also the daughter of the proclaimed Great Whore.

She *had* to be careful that she would not be painted with the same brush as her mother. And to do that, she had to remain above reproach.

There was no more avoiding the issue.

She could not afford to be caught out scandalously.

It was time to grab her fears by the throat and squeeze the life out of them.

She would marry Robert.

She would consummate their marriage.

And she would give England an heir.

Elizabeth could tell that her Secretary of State, William Cecil, was most displeased with her.

By now, just one hour since their return, news of the queen's alleged fall from her horse had caused a hubbub of worry to vibrate throughout the court, and Elizabeth thought it was only fitting that she put her people's worries to rest with her new decision.

"My lords," she called as she sat upon her throne in the great hall, her four advisors staring up at her as they awaited to hear why she had summoned them and the rest of the court before her.

"You may put your minds at ease," she said slowly, the magnitude of the announcement weighing heavily upon each word, "For I have made my choice of groom."

The Earl of Pembroke exhaled and smiled broadly, slapping Walsingham beside him on the shoulder in triumph.

But Cecil and Robert continued to stare up at her, both of them knowing who she would name, and both of them awaiting the announcement with two very different kinds of anticipation.

Robert's of hope, and Cecil's of dread.

Elizabeth rose from her throne and extended her hand to Robert, who smiled and swiftly ascended the three steps to the throne, taking her hand and pressing it to his lips.

He took a place beside the queen.

"My lords," Elizabeth announced, "I present to you my betrothed, Lord Robert Dudley."

The advisors blinked uneasily up at the pair, but Elizabeth would not be deterred. Was this not exactly what they had wanted?

"We do not need a foreign alliance to heal this broken land," she continued, "but a domestic one! Through our union, England will gain an English heir to the English throne. The country will unite as one, and it will become stronger for it!"

Chapter 15

March 1561
Hampton Court Palace, London

William Cecil was outraged.
With the country at its weakest in the first few years of a new monarch's reign, it was imperative that said monarch created a stable path before them during that time.
In the case of a female ruler, it was only logical that marriage be at the forefront of her mind – the former queen, Mary I, had known this to be true at least, though she had sadly been blinded by the promises Spain had made through reconciliation with her mother's homeland.
And yet, after months of leading on numerous suitors, all from noble backgrounds, only to discard them all for a low-born alleged murderer…Cecil could not understand the woman's thinking.
But then, she was just that – a woman.

"She cannot marry him," Cecil mumbled pensively, staring into the flames as they danced hypnotically in the fireplace, his wife, Mildred, beside him.
She shrugged, "She is the queen," she said without looking up from the bible perched on her plump lap.

"And a queen needs deviating from bad decision just as a king would," Cecil replied, "But this is a sensitive subject for our young queen."

"She is in love," Mildred pointed out.

"Precisely," Cecil agreed, and he fell silent as he thought.
It would be a dangerous path to tread, but Cecil had to put a stop to it.
He understood that Elizabeth loved the young Lord. From what he had observed, Robert was a good man with much

potential to establish himself. And Cecil had no *personal* dislike of him.

But he could not allow his queen to marry beneath her. To do so would be taking a step down from royalty.

Many continued to refer to Elizabeth as king Henry's bastard. Many continued to call her the Heretic Queen. And many Catholics were said to be plotting to replace her with her Catholic cousin, Mary Queen of Scots.

No, this was not the time to marry a gentleman of her own country.

Elizabeth would have to join forces with a foreign power, there was no doubt about it. Perhaps even a Catholic union to appease the Catholic people – if not Filipe II of Spain, then another?

But the question of *who* the queen ought to marry was for another day.

For in this moment, the matter at hand was to make sure this current betrothal did not go ahead.

There was no other way, Cecil realised. He would have to break her majesty's heart, to ensure the preservation of her reign.

('Minefields' by Faouzia & John Legend)

The rumours that had surrounded Robert in connection with his wife's tragic death, resurfaced shortly after the queen's public announcement of her engagement to him, and though they were but whispers, they resounded in Elizabeth's ears like warning bells.

"We cannot marry, Robert," Elizabeth told him bluntly one evening as soon as he had entered her chambers upon her request.

He blinked, then turned to look over his shoulder, waited for the guard to close the door behind them, then returned his gaze to his queen.

"According to who?" he asked, clipped.

Elizabeth cocked her head to one side, the pain she was inflicting upon him causing her the same hurt.

"Everyone…" she whispered, and her heart broke to see his shoulders sag in defeat.

He hung his head.

"You pay attention to idle gossip then, your majesty?" he said, suddenly angered.

Elizabeth breathed a laugh, "When it affects me then of course I must! I must be above reproach. Always, Robert!"

He nodded, "I have been proven innocent by Parliament."

"But talk persists."

Robert stared at her, his dark eyes shining like two lost ships in dark waters, "You know I am innocent," he said, his words' meaning weighing heavily upon Elizabeth's guilty conscience.

She nodded, "I know. But only because I met you that night. Alone," her cheeks blushed to think of his hands on her bare skin, "I should never have been alone with you – or any man. My virtue cannot come into question. My name cannot be sullied."

"Mine has been sullied!" Robert burst out then, thumping his fist onto his chest, the shine from his eyes replaced with fire, "As we speak, my name is being dragged through the mud as a murderer! And I say nothing in my defence for I understand your innocence is worth protecting even above my own! I have stood beside you, Elizabeth, through everything you have endured. And now that I need you to stand up for me and prove to the world that you CAN marry me because I AM innocent, you cannot do it. You cannot do it because you must protect *yourself*."

He stared at her as his chest rose and fell with the fury that raged inside him, "You cannot do this one thing for me," he concluded.

A silence ensued in which Elizabeth swallowed and raised her chin before speaking softly, a whisper of a promise.

"Robert," she said, her voice heavy with emotion, "Until the day I die, you shall always be the one who I *would have* married."

Robert looked away, his forehead creased as he tried to contain his rage and sorrow.

"But I can promise you this," Elizabeth continued, "my undying, unchanging love for you. I vow that my heart will always belong to you, and that my final breath will be for you."

He looked back at her, and they stared at each other for a moment, the only sound that of the crackling fire in the hearth in the adjoining room, where Kat bustled about soundlessly.

"But," Elizabeth continued, breaking the heavy silence once more, "I must listen to my people and my council when making a decision that shall affect my kingdom. And though it breaks my very soul to have to utter the words, I must be clear that you and I…shall never be husband and wife."

"Am I being foolish, Kat?" she asked her First Lady of the Bedchamber later that day.

Kat, now a woman of fifty-nine years of age, donning a shock of white hair that peaked through the front of her hood, only sighed.

She did not have to answer, for she knew that Elizabeth understood the reality: that to marry for love was not an option for a queen of England. Especially when that man was accused of murdering his former wife.

"He is innocent…I know he is innocent," Elizabeth mumbled weakly, exhausted from the heartache.

She was silent for a while as she sat before her mirror, Kat standing behind her as she brushed her long, bright red curls.

"My father married for love," the queen said, as though love were enough to wipe someone's reputation clean, "More than once if accounts are to be believed."

"Men are different creatures, Elizabeth," Kat said, breaking her silence, "You know that."

Elizabeth shook her head lightly and looked down at her hands on her lap.

She did know.

Men *were* above reproach. They could marry whomever they pleased.

Had it not been her own great-grandfather, Edward IV, who had been the first ever English king to marry a widowed, common woman?

They had reigned gloriously until his death, and that widow had given him many children. One of which had become queen of England herself, and Henry VIII's mother, Elizabeth of York – one of her name sakes.

Yet, nearly a hundred years later, it seemed women would not be given such equal rights.

But then again, Edward IV's chosen widow, Elizabeth Woodville, had not been accused of murdering her former spouse...

The reality of her impossible situation overcame her, washing over her like a tidal wave and sinking her deeper into despair.

And – not for the first time in her life – she cursed men for making the rules of the world.

Where not even a *Queen* could argue against them.

August 1561

Since Elizabeth had been forced to withdraw her betrothal to her favourite, Lord Robert Dudley, she had become a much more hardened version of herself.

Her advisors noticed it in the way she no longer cared to listen to their concerns, and her courtiers noticed by the way she no longer smiled – unless she and Robert shared a dance at court events.

Their formerly joyful and lively queen was now quite clearly a shell of her former self, but she was not one to be pushed over either, the ordeal having steeled her significantly to any and all aspects of her queenly duties.

"What news?" she snapped as she entered the council chamber one morning.

The four advisors rose from their seats at her entrance and bowed as she glided past them and took her seat at the head of the table.

"My queen," the Earl of Pembroke said, his aged face creased with worry, "Your cousin, Mary Queen of Scots, has returned to Scotland upon her husband, the French King's, death. She has been away many years and though she is Scotland's queen she has never ruled there directly. Her own country has become largely Protestant in her absence and they are not pleased with their Catholic queen's return."

Elizabeth looked from one advisor to another, "What does this matter to me?" she asked, her eyes resting on Cecil.

"It matters because while her country does not favour her return, there are many Catholics here in England who support her claim to the English throne," Cecil said matter-of-factly.

Elizabeth scoffed, "If she cannot even gain support from her own people, then what threat is she to me?"

"None at this moment, your highness," Walsingham interjected, his bushy eyebrows raised, "But she is once again free to marry. And if she were to marry into a favourable alliance, she may claim support in that way."

Elizabeth waved his comment aside, "Until the time comes, I have nothing to fear from her."

Cecil shook his head.

"Do you wish to say something, Sir William?" Elizabeth called, sensing her Secretary of State's disapproval.

"Your majesty must forgive me," he said, "But is it not safer to quash a potential threat than to await an actual one?"

"How do you wish me to quash her?" Elizabeth asked, her mouth pulled into a sarcastic smile, "Send her a fruit basket laced with poison?"

"You jest, madam," Walsingham said tactfully, a sly smile playing upon his lips, "But that is precisely how monarchs are assassinated."

"Monarchs have tasters for that," Robert said then.

"Tasters can be bribed," Walsingham replied swiftly, his sharp eyes glancing sideways at Robert.

Elizabeth listened intently, then nodded her head, "Are you suggesting she may attempt such a thing towards me?"

Cecil leaned back into his chair and interlaced his fingers together on his lap while Walsingham looked directly at his queen.

"I can assure you that would never come to pass," Walsingham declared passionately.

Elizabeth raised her chin, "How so?"

He flashed her a smile of his crooked teeth, "What your majesty does not know cannot be blamed on you," he said cunningly, "But let me assure you that my network of spies are all well paid and taken good care of. They are loyal to your majesty through their loyalty to me as their financier."

Elizabeth inhaled deeply, then nodded once, "Your services are greatly appreciated, Walsingham," and he replied with a bow of his head.

Elizabeth continued, "In regard to my cousin, the Queen of Scots. I do not wish her harmed. Until she directly threatens my life or my reign, I am not inclined to wage war, however discreetly, under the basis of suspicion of a potential attack on me in the future."

Cecil raised his eyebrow but said nothing.

And Elizabeth pretended not to notice.

Chapter 16

10th October 1562
Hampton Court Palace, London

Queen Elizabeth, unmarried and childless at the age of twenty-nine, was suddenly struck down with a violent fever – and the country was on tenterhooks.
It had begun as nothing more than a cold just three days prior, when out of nowhere the queen had fainted and been taken to bed in her chambers.
There the physicians observed her and declared that the cause for her fever was that she had contracted smallpox, and that she would likely die within the week.
Cecil and her other advisors scurried about the Palace like frantic ants caught in the rain, each carrying important documents in the crook of their elbows and meeting with nobles in dark corners to try and figure out a way to keep the Catholic Mary Queen of Scots from claiming her rightful throne, if Elizabeth were to die.
And all the while the poor queen lay helpless in her great royal bed, with only one lady in attendance to avoid the spread of the disease.
Blanche Parry did all in her power to make the queen comfortable in what were said to be her final days, caring little for her own safety as she sat beside the royal bed day and night to mop Elizabeth's sweaty brow or to read the bible to her quietly.
The physicians attended the queen twice each day, from a safe distance at the threshold, peering onto her with craned necks.

"Her majesty must be wrapped tightly with these red linens," the physicians told Blanche on the fifth day of the queen's unbroken fever.

They handed Blanche the red linens sheepishly, their arms extended awkwardly to avoid any direct contact with the queen's lady.

"What will they do?" the lady asked, her pretty face creasing in confusion.

"The colour red will draw the heat and fever out of her majesty," one of them replied, "It is hopefully in time to cure her…"

Blanche nodded and watched them as they left, crossing themselves and mumbling to each other.

The queen's lady inhaled deeply and returned to Elizabeth, who lay shivering on her back, her eyes closed, and her cheeks flushed.

Despite the intense fever and fatigue, Elizabeth only had three small clusters of lesions on her face, and very few on the rest of her body.

Blanche had prayed to God that this would surely mean the queen may yet recover… but the physicians continued to tell her there was little hope.

It took some time and a lot of effort but, after a while, Blanche fell into her chair beside the queen's bed, breathing heavily as she watched Elizabeth's teeth chattering despite being wrapped up tightly in the red linens the physicians had brought.

Blanche marvelled at her handywork, and when her breathing had returned to normal, she sat upright and clasped her hands together before quietly asking God – yet again – to spare England's most gracious queen.

Seven days had passed since the queen had been taken to bed, and on the morning of the seventh day she awoke from her slumber as if miraculously recovered.

The clusters of blisters remained, glowing angrily against her normally smooth, pale skin. But the fever had suddenly broken and when news reached her council of an inexplicable recovery, the men all released a great sigh of relief.

The queen remained abed for two more weeks to ensure a full recovery, and all the while Blanche tended to her day and night, caring little for her own respite.

It came as no surprise then when just one day after the queen emerged from her chambers, that Blanche Parry herself fell ill to the terrible disease, her body too exhausted to fight off the contagion.

She was taken to the country to recover or to die, and – unlike when Elizabeth had been struck down by the same ailment – not a single soul in England worried about whichever outcome would affect the queen's lady. After all, she was a mere nobody, and her death would mean nothing to anyone else.

And Elizabeth was reminded, yet again, of just how disconnected from one another her subjects really were, despite her hard work to try to unify them.

November 1562

Elizabeth's smallpox rash had finally ebbed, leaving behind only one small scar above her eyebrow as proof that it had even happened at all.

Her devoted lady-in-waiting, Blanche, however, had not been so lucky.

Though she too had survived – the queen having sent her, once washed and dried, the very same red linens she had been cured by – Blanche's rash had not been so kind as Elizabeth's. And when the lady returned to resume her duties to the queen, her pretty face was left permanently disfigured.

"Your majesty," she said as she bobbed before the queen, "I see you have recovered well."

Elizabeth forced a smile, "And you, my dear friend," she replied, her chest swelling with appreciation for the kind soul who had risked her own life to make Elizabeth comfortable as she had lingered at death's door.

Blanche laughed unenthusiastically, "There is no need for politeness," she replied, "My husband tells me himself that my beauty has faded. But I am glad to be alive. God is good. And so is your majesty," and she offered her queen a deep curtsy in thanks.

Her close brush with death had not altered Elizabeth's feelings about marriage, much to her council's frustration.

"If you are adamant that you shall not marry," the Catholic Earl of Pembroke said, his lisp prominent with exasperation, "Your majesty must at the very least name a successor so that the country is not left in ruin should you –"

"Should I what?" Elizabeth countered, "As you can see, I am well. I am healthy. And I shall not be dying any time soon! God is clearly not ready to call me to Him."

"Nevertheless, your highness," Cecil said calmly as he scratched at his grey beard, "It is the least you can do to put your subjects' minds at ease."

Elizabeth sat back in her throne and exhaled sharply through her nose, "I shall not name my cousin Mary," she said, "I would have thought that was obvious."

The members of her council nodded their heads, "The only other possible candidate is the late Jane Grey's sisters however," Cecil commented, "and they remain under house arrest at your command, your grace. The eldest, Katherine Grey, has also recently married quite scandalously without your majesty's permission. She is of course therefore out of the question."

Elizabeth sighed, waiting for an alternative to be suggested, but when no one spoke, she looked from one to another, "Well?" she asked, her eyebrows shooting up, "Is there no other?"

The members of her council remained silent, only Robert daring to look at her.

Elizabeth risked a glance at him, but swiftly tore her eyes away as the pain of his loss still stung her heart.

As Cecil riffled through the papers before him in search of an answer for his queen, Elizabeth steepled her fingers pensively, an idea suddenly coming to her.

"What if," she said, speaking slowly, the thought still taking form in her mind, "What if I named Mary my successor after all?"

"My queen!" Walsingham gasped, chocking on his own spit in shock at the comment.

"My lords," Elizabeth called, "Hear my thoughts," and they all stared at her, "I could name Mary as my heir…under one condition. A condition in which she would be controllable: through a union with someone completely devoted to the continuation of a Protestant England. Someone I would trust with my life."

The councillors looked at one another, dumbfounded.

Only Robert stared at Elizabeth, his dark eyes wide as he understood her way of thinking.

Elizabeth felt his eyes on her, imploring her not to speak the words, but she pretended not to notice. Instead, she turned her head towards Pembroke who sat to her left, knowing that she would not have the strength to utter the words if she held Robert in her sight.

"Tell our ambassadors in Scotland to convey a message: That if Mary Queen of Scots agrees to marry my most loyal and trusted subject then I shall gladly name her as my heir."

"Who shall I name as her suitor?" Pembroke asked.

Elizabeth swallowed, "Lord Robert Dudley."

('I'm loving me' by Janine)

"Lord Dudley, your majesty," her guard announced as he opened the door to the queen's chambers but an hour later.

"Robert?" Elizabeth said as she turned to face him, "I did not ask for you," and she raised her chin, steeling herself for the outburst she knew was to come.

"I will not marry her," Robert said, his face hard as stone.

Elizabeth glared at him, breathing angrily. Then she cleared her throat, "Leave us," she called to her ladies.

Blanche and Lettice looked at each other, "But your majesty cannot be alone –"

"Leave us!" Elizabeth yelled, snapping her head round to glower at her ladies, "Now!" she added when they had not immediately begun exiting.

Robert and Elizabeth resumed staring at each other as her ladies left hurriedly, their dresses rustling loudly as they scurried past their angry monarch and her former betrothed.

As soon as the door clicked shut behind them, Elizabeth turned away from him, "You will do as I ask, Lord Robert," she said casually, as though they were discussing something trivial.

Robert breathed a laugh and took a step forward, running a hand through his thick chestnut hair, "You cannot do this to me, Elizabeth," he mumbled as he shook his head, "Is it not enough that I must live here as your advisor, be near you every day, and not be allowed to touch you? To even *look* at you, without you flinching!"

Elizabeth turned around to face him, the sorrow in his voice pulling on her heartstrings.

But before she could allow her queenly mask to slip, she re-applied it with a sharp intake of breath. Robert noticed her eyes shining briefly with sadness for him before they once again hardened. The beautiful frozen lakes of her eyes turning to lifeless puddles.

"The queen of Scots may yet decline the offer, Sir," she said formally, a shell of the girl Robert once knew.

Robert continued to watch her; his face crumpled in despair.

Then he straightened up as if in battle formation, strode towards her and reached out to touch her face.

Elizabeth froze, her eyes wide, "You dare to touch your queen?" she whispered, and his hand paused midair.

She was just inches away from him, and yet she felt so far.

Elizabeth searched his pained face, still as handsome as she remembered, but creased with lines of grief that she knew had been inflicted by her.

Her heart pinched, and she willed herself to look away, but his dark gaze held her prisoner.

"I would dare to touch my Elizabeth," he finally replied quietly, his voice a saw, serrated with sorrow.

And then he saw her hard mask slip, and the girl he had known and loved for so many years was suddenly standing before him.

Elizabeth pressed her lips together as the tears pricked her eyes, and then she took a step towards him, leaning her cheek into his outstretched hand.

Suddenly they were folded in each other's embrace, kissing fervently as though their air supply derived from one another.

"You must do this for me," Elizabeth mumbled against his lips as she felt his hands reaching to undo her hood.

Her hair spilled over her shoulders.

"I'll do anything," he replied, but she knew he was no longer thinking clearly.

He pulled away from her and began kissing and biting her along her jawline and down her neck.

Elizabeth gasped as he tugged on her corset, desperately hoping to gain access to her breasts. But to no avail.

Instead, he led her urgently backwards until the backs of her knees pressed against the foot of her bed, then he guided her down onto the mattress.

And all the while, she was complicit.

She sat down, her hand at the back of his neck, pulling him down with her as they kissed aggressively.

Then she bit his lip. He drew away, stunned, but Elizabeth showed no sign of remorse, her eyes glinting with desire as she looked up at him.

He pressed his fingers against his lip before licking away the blood.

Then he closed the space between them once more, and she fell back onto the mattress, the weight of his body above her sending a shock wave of excitement through her.

He kissed her once more, one long desperate kiss, before breaking away.

Elizabeth licked her lips, tasting his blood on her tongue, and all the while she watched him moving lower down her body, then hiking up her skirts.

She did not know what he was about to do, but she did not stop him when he sank down between her legs, for nothing had ever felt so natural.

He snaked his strong arms under her thighs, and she lay her head back as the waves of pleasure darkened the corners of her mind. She covered her mouth with her hand to muffle the moans she could not control.

But after a while, she no longer worried about being heard.

Whatever power he held over her had engulfed her, and she was drowning in their lust.

She suddenly no longer cared that she was queen, or whether her virtue would come into question; only that this moment would never end.

Damn the country to Hell, she thought, as her body tensed with pleasure.

Damn them all to Hell.

March 1563

"Mary, Queen of Scots, has refused the offer of Lord Dudley's hand in marriage," Cecil told Elizabeth one cold Spring morning, four months after the offer was made.
Elizabeth was standing by a window in her chambers, looking out into the distance and completely unaware of the thick curtain of rain hammering down onto the glass.

"Refused?" she asked monotonously, unable to decide if she felt relieved or frustrated at the news.

"Refused," Cecil echoed.
Elizabeth tore her eyes from the window and turned to look at her advisor, "Her reasons?"
Cecil inhaled and licked his lips before stretching his short stature to as tall as he could muster. He produced a document and held it out before him, "She has but one," he said, raising his grey eyebrows disparagingly at Elizabeth, as a father would to a misbehaving child, "She writes: 'I, Mary Queen of Scots and Dowager Queen of France, would never subject myself so low as to consider marriage with a nobody such as Queen Elizabeth's own lover."
Elizabeth froze, her breath catching in her throat, and she stared at Cecil.

"My lover?" she repeated, trying and failing to sound confused.
Cecil tossed the letter into the roaring fire beside him.

"Do not play coy with me, madam!" he whispered harshly, looking over his shoulder at Kat who sat in the far corner of the room, her nose buried deeply into her bible.

"The whole court is whispering that Lord Robert visits your bedchamber at night!" he accused.

"My lord!" Elizabeth bellowed then, her pale face suddenly red with rage, "How dare you throw such wild accusations onto me, your sovereign Queen!?"

Cecil had the good grace to look ashamed. But Elizabeth continued, "I remain as much a virgin as I did the day of my coronation! Of *that* I can assure you! Let the rumours of bedding travel far and wide if they must but believe me when I tell you that I have not and would not *ever* allow a man to lie with me until I am lawfully married before God!"

Elizabeth felt no shame at the furious outburst, for her words were not entirely untruthful.

Since that lustful day some months prior, Robert had visited Elizabeth's bedchambers in secret once a week. Some nights they did nothing but stay up all night, talking and playing cards by the fire.

But other nights there would be no words, and they would explore each other's bodies in the quiet darkness, where she had discovered Robert had not been entirely unscathed by the war in St. Quentin, a cross-like scar glowing angrily on his shoulder, where an arrow had shot him down.

"It seems my father had been right to be disappointed in my fighting skills," he had said, and Elizabeth had lain her head on the scar gently, loving him even more for it, and wishing she could erase his all his past's pains – both from the war and from his father's cruelty.

Their moments of passion had never again been as hostile as before, the secrecy of their encounters allowing for a slower and more gentle approach.

But Elizabeth never allowed Robert to take her fully, though she had often been very close to permitting him to.

And he had never asked her of her reasons, being satisfied with the knowledge that she could not risk conceiving out of wedlock.

But in the stillness of those nights, while the rest of the Palace slept, there had been times when Elizabeth had wanted to confide in him about the encounter at Chelsea Manor which had altered her life. Where she had been raped when she had been nothing more than a child.

Each time, however, she had buried the truth, telling herself that some things should be left unsaid. For to breathe life into it, when all other who had known about it were already dead, would cause it to no longer remain simply what had happened to her; but what would define her. And she did not want Robert to look at her as though she were a victim.

In fact, she had begun to believe that if she continued to never speak of it... had it ever even happened at all?

With a clap of thunder, Elizabeth returned her mind to the present and directed her full attention back to what her Secretary of State had just told her.

Her Scottish cousin had not accepted the betrothal.

Whether she be relieved or frustrated – the manner in which Elizabeth felt about it was not relevant.

Mary's public snub and her reasons, however, they were entirely relevant, despite Elizabeth's angry remark that rumours were nothing more than that.

Elizabeth waved her hand, dismissing Cecil, before turning to resume staring out the window pensively.

"Your majesty," Cecil mumbled, then he bowed and exited the queen's chambers.

If all of Europe already speculated that she and Robert were secret lovers, there was nothing she could do to deny it – other than perhaps banishing him from her court, and she was not prepared to do that. She would not give him up.

But it was also Robert's low rank that had given her cousin cause not to wed him, Elizabeth thought as she continued to stare blindly out the window.

What had she called him? A nobody?

Perhaps it was time to gift her favourite with a new title and lands. After all, he had very nearly become King Consort of England not long ago. And after all the years of faithful service to his queen, it seemed only right that she grant him an Earldom.

Perhaps then her cousin would reconsider Elizabeth's generous proposition of allowing her to marry the best man England had to offer.

Chapter 17

May 1565
Hampton Court Palace, London

Two years had passed since the Scottish queen's initial refusal to marry Elizabeth's chosen suitor in exchange for the title of successor to the English throne. Two years in which England had continued to thrive under the constant state of peace.

"What news?" Elizabeth asked over her shoulder to the four advisors behind her as she walked leisurely through the hedgerows of the Palace gardens.

"The Elizabeth College in Guernsey is beginning construction later this month," the Earl of Pembroke said.

"Good," the queen replied with a nod of her head.

"Mary Queen of Scots continues to reject the betrothal between herself and the newly appointed Earl of Leicester," Cecil added, "And so the matter of a successor for England is still to be resolved."

Elizabeth sighed irritably and looked into the sky above her, squinting at the bright sun in her eyes.

"What else?" she said after a moment, ignoring Cecil's mention of her heir.

"That is all, your majesty," Cecil concluded.

"Excellent," she said, clapping her hands together once and then waving them all away.

As all four turned to leave, she grabbed Robert by his sleeve, pulling him back, "Not you, Earl of Leicester," she said, a playful smile on her lips.

July 1565

"She has what?!" Elizabeth screeched, her invisible brows furrowed in anger.

"She has married a Protestant Englishman, as you had yourself suggested she do," Walsingham repeated, "Just not the one you had chosen for her."

"Who?" the queen fired back.

Walsingham pursed his lips, showing disapproval at the Scottish queen's blatant mockery of his queen, "Her cousin, Henry Stuart, Lord Darnley."

Elizabeth's face drained of colour, "Lord Darnley?" she asked, stunned.

Walsingham nodded and Pembroke beside him dropped his head in his hands and groaned, shaking his head in despair.

"With this union she has strengthened her right to the English throne," Cecil said, his tone monotonous as he spoke of facts, "Lord Darnley being an English descendant of Margaret Tudor – your majesty's aunt – he has a claim to the throne of England. With Mary's union to him they could both lay claim to your throne if they so wished."

Elizabeth was seeing red. Her chest heaved and her neck blotched as she tried to control her fury.

There was nothing she could do about it. The queen of Scots had married before God. To one of her own subjects. But he had not needed Elizabeth's permission for the union, since Mary herself was not Elizabeth's to control.

It was lawful.

It was undisputable.

It meant Mary Queen of Scots could try to take England by force with the backing of an English nobleman and his supporters.

And it was yet another great inconvenience to Elizabeth, who continued to stand by her decision not to marry for the sake of her own future as queen.

All she could hope for now was that her Scottish cousin would not rear her ugly head towards the English throne.

The following day, Elizabeth sat leisurely on a blanket in the Palace gardens to soothe her troubled mind from the previous day's grave news, when a messenger arrived and handed her a note.

She passed the note to Lettice as she took a large gulp of her favourite honey mead, ordering her lady to read the news aloud to her with a flick of her hand.

Lettice opened the parchment and cleared her throat, "I bring news of my lady's sudden ill health," she read, and Elizabeth's head snapped round to look at her questioningly, "The lady went to bed feeling lightheaded last night and continued unwell throughout the small hours of the morning. I regret to inform your majesty, that the lady Katherine Ashley has this mid-morning passed in her sleep. I hope it brings you some comfort to know that she died peacefully and without pain."

Lettice looked up at her queen with tears in her eyes and flinched to find Elizabeth staring bewilderedly back at her, her own eyes wide in alarm.

"Kat..." Elizabeth mumbled, "She is dead?"

Lettice inhaled and swallowed her tears, "She is with God, your grace," she whispered.

At the confirmation that she had understood correctly, Elizabeth slowly set her cup of honey mead down, then nodded her head, the news still sinking in.

Kat had been feeling more tired than usual in the last few weeks. She had asked Elizabeth to return to her home for a few days, in the hope of regaining her strength through some well-deserved rest.

Elizabeth had granted it, thinking nothing of it, for though she was a woman of sixty-three, Kat had always been...well, she had always been *there.*

She had been Elizabeth's one constant throughout the years.

The idea that she would never again be in the corner of the room embroidering or sitting with Elizabeth by the fire to offer wise advice, had never even crossed her mind.

And while she knew that Kat was not to blame for leaving her, her heart wept nonetheless at the familiar feeling of abandonment.

Her beloved Kat was gone. Just like that. And Elizabeth had had no forewarning.

Just like with mother.

The thought crushed down on Elizabeth, her heart feeling heavy with sorrow though it was utterly drained.

She was an orphan now – and yet, she had been one for many years already. But Kat had been her family.

Now she was gone.

And Elizabeth had not even had a chance to say goodbye.

Just like with mother.

September 1566

"What is it?" Elizabeth asked Blanche the following year as her lady stood before her opening a small tin, her face and neck painted entirely white.

"It is ceruse, your grace. It is for the face. To cover my scars," she admitted, "See?" and she held the opened tin up for Elizabeth to inspect.

"It's white," the queen pointed out.

Blanche nodded, "The whiter, the better," she said, "My husband is finally coming to my bed again. He says I look more youthful than I have in years."

Elizabeth turned to look at her own aging face in the mirror. At thirty-three, her youth was beginning to slip away from her, the grief over Kat's loss having etched deep lines on her face. Wrinkles formed of despair. Lines carved from a miserable hurt.

As if Kat's death had not been enough misery for one year, another brutal reminder of her misfortune had come shortly thereafter when it had been announced that Mary Queen of Scots was with child.

"An heir for her country," Cecil had pointed out, as if Elizabeth needed reminding that she had so far failed to give her country an heir of its own.

"Youthful?" Elizabeth repeated then, drawn out of her thoughts and back into the present. She was pulling the skin of her forehead up a little, stretching it smooth, "What is it made of?"

Blanche shrugged, "The ladies in Europe wear it," she said as if in explanation, "It is considered very fashionable."

Elizabeth laughed bitterly, but it did not reach her empty eyes, "You continue to wear it if it reignites your husband's love," she said, "I do not need it. For fashion's sake I think we women suffer enough already."

Cecil was deeply troubled.

As Secretary of State to the Queen of England, he had a front row seat to all her thoughts, feelings, and fears. He knew that Elizabeth wanted to maintain peace among her country and to strengthen it from within, despite her councillor's advice that she should marry and strengthen it through a foreign alliance.

Through marriage, the queen would be killing two birds with one stone. England would be stronger through a union with another land, and through consummation an heir would surely be underway.

Cecil knew that Elizabeth had the potential to be a highly intelligent and logical woman. He had known it since the moment he had met her. And yet, she could not seem to understand – or want to admit – that by denying the country a marriage and an heir, that she was causing it great unrest.

Her Elizabethan Settlement Act, passed near ten years ago, had proven that she wished for a unified and peaceful people. And yet, there was nothing anyone could tell her that seemed to change her mind about discarding her lover for a more suitable match.

"There is threat of civil unrest, your majesty," Cecil said one evening as he arrived within the queen's chambers at her order.

She was sitting at her table by the fireplace, with a plate of pheasant and a cup of her favourite sweet honey mead before her. She had been eating it delicately, small pieces of meat speared onto her two-pronged fork, when the news he announced stopped her in her tracks.

"Civil unrest?" she repeated, her eyes widening for a fraction of a second.

"Indeed," Cecil replied.

She placed her fork down slowly, "Elaborate," she ordered as she picked up her cup and sipped the honey mead.

Cecil took a step towards her and produced a document, which he lay down on the table before his queen.

She leaned forward and skimmed it, its contents showing a long list of names.

"What is this?" she asked.

Cecil raised his brows and sighed, exhausted of the topic he was to broach yet again.

"Madam," he said, "Your continuous deflecting of naming your successor, as well as your lack of interest in marital union, has left the country brewing in fear. If your majesty were to perish – God forbid – you must realise that the country would be left to tear itself apart. Without a clear line of succession there is only the people's own wants. And they all want something, or someone, different."

Elizabeth stared up at her Secretary of State, aware that he had not answered her question. She picked up her fork and continued eating.

After a while she swallowed, sat back in her chair and nodded at the seat beside her.

Cecil slowly pulled the chair back, watching his queen as he sat down, his expression one of disappointment.

Elizabeth stared him down, her lips slightly pursed as though she cared little for his opinions.

But she did care.

She cared a lot.

Cecil did not have ill-intent in the way he spoke and advised Elizabeth, she knew that. And she always took heed in his words, even if she later chose to disagree with him.

But he was a headstrong character. And he was a man.

And so, in his presence, Elizabeth applied her most indifferent mask, so that she may seem majestic before him, and not wilt like a trampled flower.

She jerked her chin in direction of the document that lay on the table between them, "What is this?" she asked again.

"It is a list of lords who plan to meet with you to urge the question of your marriage and succession," Cecil stated.

Elizabeth frowned, her jaw clenching in anger at the news that she would be asked so outrightly about such matters as though she were a commoner.

Cecil, noticing her growing rage, breathed a laugh, "Your highness," he said, "If you do not wish to continue having these discussions, I urge you to reconsider your choices," he said, "Your love for Robert is blinding you, my queen," he said gently, "It has been eight years since your reign began. The people are rightly concerned. Don't let one man go before all others. As queen you must consider the wellbeing of the many, before your own."

Elizabeth, sensing her queenly mask slipping at the gentle tone in the older man's voice, sat up straight in her chair and cleared her throat.

"I have sacrificed a lot for my position, Sir William," she stated, aware that he would never know just how much, since she had never wanted the crown in the first place, "I will not let the common people and the lords presume to tell me what else I should be forced to lose for it."

She looked at him, her eyes shining with the threat of tears, but her expression was as hard as stone, "For until I give you or anyone else reason to doubt my judgement, I shall continue to rule as I see fit."

November 1566

As Cecil had forewarned his queen, Parliament presented a petition from the House of Commons and the House of Lords that Queen Elizabeth either marry or name her successor to avoid a civil war.

She received this petition as she sat upon her throne in the great hall, her courtiers, lords, ladies, and Privy Council all standing before her and listening intently as Cecil read out the appeal.

The great hall, though it was filled with near five-hundred people, had grown silent, and once Cecil had concluded reading the petition aloud, all eyes fell to their queen.

The colour had drained completely from her face, but within moments it returned, red forming on her chest and cheeks bright enough to match the flaming hair coiffed upon her head.

She had known this would come, and yet she had not been prepared for the nausea and rage she felt at the words spoken aloud to her – their queen.

How dared they tell *her* what she ought to do?

The prospect of forcing her to wed against her will brought back the memory of Thomas Seymour, and his failed attempt of locking her into a marriage with him.

The fact she was now queen and men were, yet again, trying to force her into a situation she did not want…well it was maddening.

Though she had not been prepared for the onslaught of anger she felt in that moment, she had, however, prepared her reply.

As the court continued on in silence, Elizabeth stood up slowly from her throne, her great red and white gown ballooning at her sides and her hands clasped elegantly before her.

She looked from Cecil, to the lords behind him, to the courtiers all around, allowing the silence to drag on for a moment longer, so that she could be sure that all would listen closely to her speech.

Then she cleared her throat and smiled sweetly, before opening her mouth to speak.

"I give you all my hearty thanks for the loving care you seem to have towards me and the whole state of the country! Though, since it is I who am Queen – and therefore responsible in governing the kingdom – it would seem a folly to draw attention from my people in pursuit of a marriage."

A murmur had begun emerging from among the crowd, but Elizabeth continued.

"I remind you all," she called, "of the rites of my coronation, where I was symbolically married to the kingdom with the receiving of my coronation ring," she looked around the room slowly, then rested her gaze upon Cecil who stared up at her,

"And therefore: *England*…is my husband. And my subjects are my children."

Cecil continued to stare, shaking his head slightly in disbelief. Even when presented with an ultimatum, the queen somehow managed to sidestep the country's great issue.

Elizabeth smiled, looking out into the crowd once again, "I do not rule out marriage altogether, and I can assure you good people that when the time comes, I will only choose someone who, like myself, has the common good in mind. But if the day does not come where I find someone suitable, it will have been enough for me to have remained married only to England. And upon my death you shall engrave on my tomb that: Elizabeth I was a virgin pure until her death."

And as she knew there would be, an explosion of protests erupted from the crowd, and as the nobles called out their discontent, Cecil glanced disapprovingly at Robert, who stared up at the queen, pale-faced and bewildered.

Chapter 18

1567
Hampton Court Palace, London

It had been a year since Elizabeth proclaimed to the country that she was likely never to wed and declared herself married to England.

And in that year, England had continued to thrive in a state of peace, despite the threat of civil unrest persisting. The topic continued to be broached occasionally at Privy Council meetings, its possibility always at the forefront of their minds. But, by the grace of God, there was never true cause for concern, the few whispers of disgruntled Catholics never amounting to enough to fear a rebellion.

Mary, Queen of Scots, had birthed a healthy baby boy and heir for her country. A fact Cecil did not hesitate to mention whenever possible.

But Elizabeth paid him no heed.

She and Robert continued to meet in secret, though by now almost the entire country knew that the queen and her favourite were indisputably devoted to one another. And yet – despite this common knowledge – since her speech, Queen Elizabeth had become widely related to by the people of England as the Virgin Queen.

One afternoon, the two lovebirds were walking lazily upon the manicured lawn of the Palace gardens, their arms interlocked and with Robert leaning into Elizabeth as he whispered sweet nothings into her ear, when Walsingham emerged from the Palace gates.

He stood there for moment, looking from side to side before spotting the queen and her entourage. Then he made a swift beeline towards her.

As he approached, he pushed past the queen's ladies and cut in front of his queen and her lover.

"Walsingham!" Elizabeth yelped, frightened by his sudden arrival.

He bowed quickly, "Forgive me, your highness," he said breathlessly, "But I bring urgent news. The Scottish Queen has been forced to abdicate her throne."

"Forced?" Elizabeth repeated, frowning as she pulled her arm free of Robert's grasp.

"Following her husband's suspicious murder," Walsingham explained, "she has since married the man who is said to have been responsible for Lord Darnley's death. Her Parliament holds her accountable for the murder. At least in part."

Elizabeth's mind was racing, and she began biting on her thumbnail as she tried to process the news.

"There is more," Walsingham said, looking over the queen's shoulder.

Elizabeth followed his gaze and spotted a messenger running towards them, who then handed Walsingham a note at his arrival. He skimmed it quickly and then nodded his head.

"My suspicions have been confirmed," Walsingham told Elizabeth, "The Scottish Queen has fled her land. To seek sanctuary."

Elizabeth's eyes widened, "Seek sanctuary with who?" she asked.

Her spymaster handed Elizabeth the note, "With you."

"It is an outrage!" Cecil thundered, "To have your Catholic cousin seek refuge here in England while the Catholics await their moment to supplant you, your majesty! This would be their time to do so. If she is rallying forces as she travels south, her numbers would be vast once she reaches London!"

Elizabeth was silent as she sat at the head of the council table, her head in her hand as she sat awkwardly on her throne. She stared blindly ahead, her fingers repeatedly running back and forth over the pox scar above her eyebrow.

"What say you, Pembroke," Cecil asked in his queen's stead. Pembroke glanced at Elizabeth, but following no objection to Cecil's question, he replied, "As a Catholic myself," he said carefully, "I understand Sir William's concerns. There are many who would see this as an opportunity."

Elizabeth sighed deeply but continued to stare ahead in silence.

"Walsingham," Cecil said, an order to speak.

He cleared his throat, "My spies will send word from every town she passes," he assured, "We will know if she is raising an army."

Cecil nodded, "My queen," he said finally.

Elizabeth looked up and met Cecil's hardened face, "What say you?" he said, pressing her for a verdict as to her own cousin's fate.

For a brief second Elizabeth considered allowing her cousin to take her throne.

In that one second, she imagined the happy life she could lead as a noble lady, free to marry the man she loved above all others...

She glanced at Robert beside her.

But then she shook her head, clearing it of those delicious images. Abdicating would not safeguard her from assassination.

As Queen or no, Elizabeth would always be in danger, so she may as well continue on her path to clearing her mother's name. She had already given up enough of her life for it...and the task was not yet complete.

Elizabeth sat up straight and cleared her throat, "What makes her believe I would offer her sanctuary? She is a threat to my rule."

No one replied. They all knew the details. Just as Elizabeth knew them.

She looked from one man to another. She knew what she had to do.

And yet – despite never even having met her cousin – she was reluctant to utter the words.

But then she did.

"If she makes way towards London," she said, licking her dry lips, "With an army or no…she must be arrested."

It had not been difficult to capture the former queen of Scotland on her way to London, since she had not been hiding. In fact, Mary had hoped that Elizabeth would find her, with the expectation that her cousin would support her cause in regaining her title as Queen of Scots.

"She has been seized, your majesty," Walsingham reported as he entered the council chambers.

The queen and the other members of the council were already seated, Walsingham's absence having been the main topic of discussion as they had awaited news.

Now that he entered with triumphant information, there was a loud sigh from all around the table, as if they had all been holding their breaths in unison.

"What is to be done with her?" Robert Dudley asked as Walsingham continued to stride proudly towards the council table.

"There is no need –"

"Send her back –"

"This is no –"

Elizabeth raised her hands, "My lords," she called, "It is clear what I must do! Her presence in my country brings an immediate threat to the peace I have worked hard to maintain in England. Her presence ignites passion in the hearts of Catholics to replace me."

The Earl of Pembroke hung his head in shame for those who shared his faith but lacked his loyalty to the crown.

"But I cannot simply send her back, for she will only return, and that time perhaps with more support against me," Elizabeth went on, "And I cannot order her executed when there has been no crime."

Walsingham exhaled and shook his head, a small smile playing upon his lips, "Your grace," he mumbled in disagreement, ready to kill for his queen's safety.

"There has been no crime, sir!" Elizabeth replied hotly, "I shall not send my cousin to her death if there is no cause! Not only for the preservation of my good conscience but also for the fact that to execute her could provoke foreign attacks for killing a queen – it would be regicide."

"She is no longer a queen," Cecil pointed out, "She was forced to abdicate."

"She is still a queen in the hearts of many," Pembroke mumbled.

Elizabeth raised her eyebrows briefly at Cecil, as if to say, *see?*

"There is no need for concern," Elizabeth said then, "I am certain we will have a solution to this dilemma in due course. Until then she shall be allowed to live at Carlisle Castle, as a closely guarded *guest*. That way we reduce the risk of Mary gathering more support, and it allows us control over her."

"Unlawful imprisonment of the former Scottish queen will not be taken lightly," Walsingham added wisely, "Whatever your majesty does, your Catholic cousin being here…it will cause you much trouble."

November 1569

Walsingham had been right.

And just weeks later, her once peaceful country was rocked by a rebellion.

Though the people of England had been content living under Elizabeth's Protestant rule with a generous leniency on Catholics, it seemed that once an alternative option was presented to them, the Catholic people suddenly wished for change.

The Northern Rebellion – as it became known quickly throughout the country – was led by Charles Neville and Thomas Percy, two noble lords with a large Catholic following. And it was not long before seven-hundred mercenaries joined their cause to replace Elizabeth with Mary.

"They have taken Barnard Castle in the north," Walsingham informed his queen, "And are proceeding south to Clifford Moor as we speak."

Elizabeth was pacing up and down in her chambers, "What of our army? Have we succeeded in raising enough to defeat them?"

Walsingham swallowed, uncomfortable, "Not yet, your highness," he admitted, "The Earl of Sussex is raising a force, but we are yet to receive word as to how large it is."

Elizabeth pressed the palms of her hands against her forehead, "I'm going to be sick," she muttered to herself as she continued to pace.

Walsingham frowned, "You must remain composed, your grace!"

Elizabeth only breathed in and out deeply, her eyes shut tightly as though she could block him out.

"My queen!" Walsingham whispered rashly, "Think of how your father would present himself!"

At that, Elizabeth stopped in her tracks and pried her eyes open, "My father?" she mumbled.

Walsingham only stared at her, as if to will the strength of a man into her.

"My father would have executed Mary on the spot and caused a war with Scotland," Elizabeth snapped, "My feminine attributes may be perceived as weakness, sir! But do not be fooled to believe a man would be doing a better job that I!"

Then she stormed away from him, her silk gown swishing loudly as she put distance between herself and her advisor.

Then, as she continued to stomp away, she turned her head and called over her shoulder, "Spread the word that the Earl of Sussex has raised an army large enough to defeat Spain itself!" she ordered, "Send out all your spies with the message that Queen Elizabeth has an army so vast, those rebels have no chance of survival if they dare to come up against her!"

Her bluff had worked, and the rebels – which had grown from seven hundred to six thousand on their way through England – began to disperse, retreating northward and fleeing to Scotland.

"We were lucky," Cecil said as he met Elizabeth some days later.

She and her ladies were sitting underneath a canopy, wrapped in furs as they watched a play being enacted before them.

"We were," Elizabeth agreed over her shoulder, the actors never breaking from their role at their queen's quiet interruption.

"Madam," Cecil replied, "Forgive me for ruining your fun. But there is more to your luck that what you are aware of."

Elizabeth turned in her seat, her frown prompting him to continue.

"The leaders of the Northern Rebellion were in cahoots with your former brother-in-law."

"Filipe…?" Elizabeth breathed angrily.

"He had sent promises of Spanish troops to the rebel leaders to support the uprising in their cause to remove you from the throne."

Elizabeth fell silent, her anger rendering her speechless.

"The rebels dispersed before his promise of Spanish soldiers was fulfilled. But his intent to support your overthrowal was there all the same. As you know, king Filipe has wanted to reclaim England and return it to its Catholic roots ever since your sister died, your majesty," Cecil summarised, "It must not come as a surprise to you that he would seek to support a Catholic uprising against England's Protestant queen after you rejected his marriage proposal."

"Enough!" Elizabeth snapped, but the play continued in the background, though the queen was no longer enthralled in its story, "I know full well who our enemies are."

"Do you?" Cecil countered, "It seems you have been rather blinded of political relations of late."

Elizabeth knew of what – or rather of *who* – Cecil was speaking. She glanced sideways at her ladies, who quickly looked away as though they had not heard a word.

Then Elizabeth returned her gaze to her advisor and inhaled, "Call a meeting of the council," she ordered as she stood, "And summon the imperial ambassador. He will have a lot of explaining to do for his master."

"We must keep the Scottish Queen from lingering too long in one place," Cecil muttered quietly.

He was leaning over Elizabeth's shoulder, whispering into her ear as she sat upon her cushioned seat at the head of the council table.

"The rebels had planned to spring her from her prison in Carlisle Castle," he continued, "If we move her often, future rebellions may be avoided if they do not know of her whereabouts."

Elizabeth nodded her approval of Cecil's plan.

Just then, the door to the council chamber opened and the imperial ambassador, Count Feria, entered.

Cecil straightened up behind his queen and stared the bearded Spaniard down, knowing that Elizabeth before him would be doing the same.

"Ambassador Feria," Elizabeth said in greeting.

The ambassador bowed and awaited her invitation to sit at the table.

She did not give him one.

"The Northern Rebellion," Elizabeth stated casually, her chin raised as she addressed him, "What do you know of it?"

Feria smiled but it did not reach his eyes, "I believe I know as much – if not more – than perhaps your majesty knows," he said arrogantly.

"Speak plainly!" Walsingham thundered, his dislike of the ambassador and his underhanded king quite clear from the anger in his voice.

Feria turned his beady eyes to Walsingham and the two men stared at one another for a moment before Feria opened his mouth and – while still looking at Walsingham – addressed the queen.

"It is no secret that my master," he said, "wishes for a return to Catholicism in England."

"You admit to involvement then!" Walsingham bellowed as he stood up abruptly from his seat.

"I admit only to my master's wishes on the matter of religion!" Feria fired back.

"This means war!" Walsingham replied hotly, waving his fist in the air, and suddenly all the men were standing and shouting, pointing fingers in each other's red faces.

Elizabeth sat perfectly still, watching from her throne as the five men argued, her mind reeling at the word which had stood out from all the rest.

War.

Spain was the wealthiest and most powerful nation in all of Europe, and perhaps the world.

How had it become just that? Elizabeth wondered briefly, instantly knowing the answer.

To wage war upon Spain would not only be reckless, it would be suicide.

Elizabeth looked around at the hot-headed men as they quarrelled aggressively, spittle flying through the air with the passion of their words.

What a strange thing to witness, she thought. *Such noble and intelligent men threatening war on a country so powerful it could crush England between its finger and thumb...*

It seemed to Elizabeth as though it were more a matter of honour and ego than plain and simple logic.

But if war was a threat so easily thrown around at the failed prospect of betrayal from a fellow monarch, then it was no wonder to Elizabeth why countries continuously warred with one another.

Their leaders were men.

And from the looks of things, men acted more irrationally than women when it came to defending their bruised self-esteems.

But she was no man. And she would not amount to war. Not while her country was not yet strong enough to even have a chance of winning.

No, she would have to consider other means by which to retaliate to this act of betrayal.

She would beat them at their own game.

"Leave, Feria," she said, abruptly enough to slice through the men's continuous arguing.

Silence befell the council chamber before the imperial ambassador bowed, turned, and left. And as soon as the door closed behind him, Elizabeth sat back in her throne and folded her hands upon her lap.

"Fetch me the pirate Francis Drake."

Francis Drake and John Hawkins, pirates known among the English court for attacking Spanish slave ships in the Atlantic and selling the slaves for their own profit, had a highly negative reputation within England.
They had gained this reputation for breaking into the Spanish dominated slave trade of West Africans some years prior, successfully making a sizeable profit through the transportation and selling of humans as though they were no more than livestock. And although slavery itself was not illegal, it was against English Law to capture and transport people, as Hawkins and Drake were doing.
Though queen Elizabeth had not been naïve to these occurrences, she had looked the other way with the belief that their knowledge of Spain's naval weaknesses would one day be of use to her.
That day had finally come.
And she now saw Drake and Hawkin's activities not as a stain on England's society, but rather as the perfect way to strike back against Spain's betrayal, without directly instigating a war England could not win.
But pettiness was not Elizabeth's only reason for arranging a meeting with the pirates. Despite their bad reputation, the queen knew that their attacks on Spanish ships over the years had enriched them greatly – not only through the profit made from slave trade, but also through gold and silver – and she knew the benefits such riches would have for the advancement of England. Advancements that would work in England's favour to one day becoming a power to be reckoned with.

"You cannot be serious!" Cecil gasped as he looked up at his queen on her throne in the great hall, his grey beard quivering with anger, "You would support these...these...*pirates*!?"

Francis Drake turned his tanned face from Cecil to the queen, an amused smile on his lips, "He spits the word as though it's an insult t' us," Drake commented, shrugging his shoulders at John Hawkins beside him.

Elizabeth raised an eyebrow at the pirates, ignoring her Secretary of State's outburst.

"I have a proposition for you," she said, "One you will hopefully accept since it will largely benefit not only you but also England."

Hawkins and Drake exchanged a look, eagerness and greed reading clearly on Hawkins' face, while Drake's was a little harder to read.

"I bid you to persist with your plundering of Spanish ships," Elizabeth continued, "I bid you to cause chaos whenever possible within the Atlantic, and I bid you to do so now…with my most fervent support. In exchange for you to continue doing what you have already been doing, I offer you one of my very own royal ships."

Hawkins' mouth fell open, while Drakes' expression softened to one of admiration.

"I give you the Jesus of Lubeck," Elizabeth clarified, "One of my largest ships. All I ask from you in return, is that the crown benefits, in part, from your profits."

Silence befell the great hall then as the two pirates and William Cecil stared up at the queen.

"You do, then, give us the *legal* right…t' capture and transport those people?" Hawkins asked, hoping to obtain more from Elizabeth than she could give.

Elizabeth smiled, having already known that her offer would be pushed further. After all, she was dealing with pirates.

"My aim is to plunder Spanish ships, and to gain maritime dominance over trade passages," she spoke slowly and clearly, "My *ultimate* goal is to strengthen England. If you wish for *legality,* I cannot give you it. But I *can* continue to look the other way in regard to your kidnappings, if these people are non-protestants, or criminals perhaps?" she raised an eyebrow meaningfully.

Hawkins looked at Drake. They had understood her suggestion of a loophole. And then they both nodded at their queen before huddling together to mumble underneath their breaths, occasionally stealing glances up at the queen before them.

They continued their secret whispers for a minute too long in which Cecil grew more flustered, and suddenly he could no longer wait.

He waves his hands in the air, "Take your whispering and colluding outside!"

The two men did just that, neither of them stopping to ask the queen's permission to quit her presence. But Elizabeth allowed them their leave, knowing they would accept her generous offer, the Jesus of Lubeck being a fantastic naval asset to their pirating.

Once they were out of the great hall, Cecil began his inquiry.

"What are you thinking, my queen?"

Elizabeth stood from her throne in one fluid motion, "Do not ever question me in front of others, Cecil!" she hissed, referring to his earlier interruption.

Cecil bowed, "Forgive me, your majesty," he begged, "But help me to understand how this will not enrage not only Spain but also your own people!"

"My aim as queen is to enrich my country," Elizabeth replied as she walked down the three steps from her throne, "I will use any means at my disposal. Spain and Portugal have long benefitted from this. I want part of it."

Cecil searched Elizabeth's face for a scrap of remorse, while she searched his face for understanding. But when she found none, she felt compelled to explain further.

"It shall be a feudal relationship: their security through their sovereign's permission, in return for a cut of the fruits of their labours for the advancement of England," a comparison sprung to mind, "Like beekeeping!"

Cecil's brows twitched, thrown by her strange way of seeing the inhumane act of kidnapping and selling of innocent people.

"It is not honey we would be taking without consent," he replied, using her own analogy against her, "You will be dealing with pirates and aggravating Spain…If you insert your hand into the beehive, it might come out covered in honey, or it might become covered in beestings. Is the potential of one worth the risk of the other?"

Elizabeth smiled sweetly, flashing her teeth, and Cecil noticed suddenly that they had begun to yellow, no doubt due to her love of rich and sugary foods.

Or perhaps due to her darkening soul.

"Yes," she replied.

February 1570

Elizabeth was scared.

The very thing she had feared would happen upon becoming England's monarch was taking form right before her very eyes, plots and assassination attempts brewing in what seemed like every corner of her realm.

"I have been a fool to believe the Catholic people would be accepting of me as their queen," Elizabeth seethed as she paced up and down in her private chamber, the aftershocks of the Northern Rebellion still weighing heavily on her mind even three months later.

"You were no fool," Blanche disagreed, sitting by the fire beside Robert as they watched Elizabeth, "You were hopeful. Naïve perhaps. But no fool."

Elizabeth waved the comment aside, wishing not for the first time that Kat were still alive to give her solace.

"It's all the same," Elizabeth argued, "They will never be content with me. The plots will continue as long as there is a Catholic heir waiting in the shadows."

"You have moved Mary Stuart three times since the Northern Rebellion," Robert said, his voice taking on a soothing tone in hopes of relieving Elizabeth of her fears, "If they cannot find her and have no figurehead, then the Catholics cannot plot against you."

Elizabeth shook her head, her heeled shoes clinking loudly as she continued to pace, "I have enemies all around me," she mumbled, more to herself than anyone else, as she chewed on her thumb nail, "Spain is against me, and with Spain, all the Holy Roman Emperor's countries. The Pope..."

"The Pope has always been *against* you, as a reformed monarch," Blanche said, confused.

"It has gone further than that, Blanche," Elizabeth stated, "There is great support for my Catholic cousin now that she is in England. Walsingham's spies know more is coming. There is even talk of *excommunication*."

Robert and Blanche glanced at each other, "Why do you fear it?" Blanche asked, "You are Supreme Head of the Church of England. You do not answer to Rome," and after a brief pause, "Your own father was excommunicated."

Elizabeth pressed the balls of her hands into her forehead and groaned in frustration. It seemed *no one* – not even those closest to her – understood the immense pressures she was under as a female ruler without a clear successor.

"My father was an established *male* ruler!" she explained carefully, as though she were talking to a small child, "He had heirs and security. He had formed alliances. I am, and have, none of those things. This is but the beginning, Blanche. Mark my words."

❖

As it turned out, she had been right to fear the coming news from Rome, for as well as issuing an official proclamation which excommunicated Elizabeth, Pope Pius V also passed a Papal Bull, releasing all her Catholic subjects from any requirements to obey her as Queen, as well as calling upon them to remove her from the throne.

"It is essentially a kill order," Walsingham pointed out.

"What can be done?" Elizabeth asked her council members as they all sat sour-faced around the council table.

"The people will be struggling internally with who to obey, my queen," the Catholic Earl of Pembroke admitted, his lisp irking Elizabeth suddenly, "Whether to listen to their religious master, the Pope, or their monarch, you."

"Are you?" Elizabeth asked, "Struggling internally?"

Pembroke shook his head and straightened his back.

"I may be a Catholic, my queen," he said proudly, "But I voted for Royal Supremacy when your father presented it. I do not wish for papal authority within England."

"Do you believe others see it as you do, sir?" the queen asked.

He hung his head, "I cannot presume to know how others of my faith choose to act in these uncertain times. But since Henry VIII's reformation there are few who live to remember the old days when the Pope ruled on religious matters even above the king."

Elizabeth nodded once. She wanted to believe there were others as loyal to the crown as Pembroke.

"You give me hope, sir," she said to him with a small smile.

"We should bring in new tasters and increase the security around your majesty," Walsingham added.

Elizabeth inhaled deeply, the hope Pembroke had ignited within her, suddenly snuffed out by Walsingham's opposing opinion that her Catholic subjects would go so far as to attempt to assassinate her.

"Walsingham is right," Robert agreed, to which Walsingham nodded his head, "The threat is real, my queen."

Elizabeth saw the concern in Robert's eyes.

She nodded, "Increase security, Walsingham," she ordered, "Until we know how the people feel about this order from the Pope, we must not be reckless."

January 1571

It seemed the Pope had miscalculated the English people's loyalty to their peace, and in the year that followed the Queen of England's excommunication and the Pope's order to remove her from power, there was not even a whisper of an uprising.

And yet, Elizabeth could not help but fear for her life.

"It appears the Pope has overestimated his power over the English Catholics," Robert said quietly as he ran a finger up and down Elizabeth's arm.

They were sitting side by side underneath a tree on the manicured lawn of the palace gardens, a pile of cushions beneath them for comfort.

The queen's ladies sat behind them, and there were people all around, walking leisurely through the gardens or sitting by the fountain as they conversed.

Despite the time of year, the sunshine had proven a glorious day, and after so many months of tension and worry, Robert had suggested a moment in the open air, in the hopes of regaining some of Elizabeth's former serenity.

"Walsingham's spies did uncover one attempt," she mumbled as she stared straight ahead at the fountain, recalling the gruesome death of one of her newly appointed tasters.

How his eyes had rolled back inside his head as his body had twitched and foam had spilled out his mouth –

Robert *tsked,* "That was months ago," he said, interrupting Elizabeth's vivid memory, "and nothing has happened since."

He was trying his best to thaw some of her unease, but Elizabeth only glanced at him.

"Do you have no fear for me?" she asked quietly, looking at him accusingly.

His brows furrowed, and Elizabeth saw his almost-black eyes flash, "You know the answer to that question," he said, "Your safety is at the forefront of my mind. Daily."

Elizabeth's mouth twitched, and then she turned her face away once again, hoping to hide the fact that, underneath her composed mask, her fear was overwhelming her.

"Then do not speak so coolly," she said, "My life shall always be in danger. I was unwise to believe otherwise for so long," she returned her attention to nothing in particular in the distance, "I had hoped my people, Protestant or Catholic, could live together harmoniously."

Robert ran a hand over his face and expelled an exasperated breath.

"They do!" he said, "They are. This papal bull – it was the Catholic's perfect excuse to revolt against you. But they did not. They still do not. They value their peace more than that. A peace *you* gave them when you passed The Elizabethan Religious Settlement. You are an accepting queen. They know that. They love and respect that."

Elizabeth forced a small smile, "Your passion is admirable," she said, "And I so wish I could go on knowing that my people's love and respect was enough."

Robert frowned. It seemed the fresh air and lazy sunshine had done nothing to melt the icy exterior she had donned of late.

"But nevertheless," she sighed, "I need to protect myself. I have asked Parliament to pass a new Treason Act. It will deem it illegal to write, or even to *say,* that I am not the true Queen of England," she turned to face Robert, "And it will be an instant death penalty to anyone promoting conversion to Catholicism. I cannot live and rule in fear, Robert. I am Queen. And I must know that I am secure in my position. I cannot rule if I am worrying that one misstep would incite rebellion. My father understood the balance between being loved and being feared. And if I wish to continue ruling England for as many years as he did, I must show that I am not to be underestimated."

Robert searched her eyes for a glimpse of the compassionate Elizabeth he once knew, but she was buried underneath too many layers of distrust, though she was trying her best to hide it.

"You would have your people live in terror? As they did under your sister's reign?" Robert asked.

Elizabeth nodded; her mind made up.

Better *they* fear *her*.

"They need to cower before me, Robert," she whispered as she stared, unseeingly, into the distance, "They need to fear me."

September 1572

In the year that followed, dozens of missionary priests were executed under the new Treason Act for continuing to promote Catholicism in England. Some were hung, drawn, and quartered until Elizabeth decided that to have them burned at the stake for their heretical crimes against the crown was much more fitting.

For some time afterwards, England settled back into a state of tranquillity.

But it did not last long. For only a few months later, Elizabeth's own second cousin, the nobleman Thomas

Howard Duke of Norfolk, had been caught at the centre of a new plot to murder and overthrow his queen. He had been tracked down and arrested on the spot.

"I can understand my sister's actions now! There are traitors everywhere!" the queen seethed through gritted teeth, her eyes narrowed in anger, "Will this scheming never end!?"

Cecil watched her calmly, "No, your majesty," he said matter-of-factly, though he knew the queen's question had been rhetorical.

"Until you set a secure foundation to your rule through marriage and an heir, your reign will always be in question," he said.

Elizabeth continued to breath erratically, "How goes the trial?" she asked.

Thomas Howard Duke of Norfolk was this day being put on trial for treason.

"It is still ongoing," Cecil said, "It is not every day a duke is accused of high treason."

The Duke of Norfolk – while encouraged by the former Scottish Queen's advisor and bishop – had been caught secretly hatching a plan to murder Elizabeth and to place Mary Stuart on the English throne instead.

Supported by the Pope and King Filipe II of Spain, Norfolk had planned to marry Mary before taking the throne by force, rallying their Catholic supporters with their union.

"Do we know of her involvement in this?" Elizabeth asked, knowing that her councillors would know whom she meant.

"There is proof she wrote to Spain soliciting their aid," Walsingham said, "She did, however, profess her friendship and loyalty to your majesty…"

Elizabeth scoffed and rolled her eyes.

"But," Cecil interjected, "It is likely she added that in specifically in case the letter was discovered. All she has done that could be used to link her to this plot is her consent to marrying the Duke of Norfolk."

It was not enough.

Elizabeth inhaled deeply and closed her eyes, pressing her hands into her corseted stomach as it lurched, her body completely overwhelmed with the stressors of her daily life.

"What of Norfolk's servants and messengers?" she asked.

"Arrested, tortured, interrogated," Cecil stated.

Elizabeth nodded approvingly. Then she sighed.

"When will we hear of the verdict?" she asked, exacerbated by the wait, "The man committed high treason. An assassination attempt on his queen! Surely there is not much to deliberate."

Cecil opened his mouth to speak, but then the doors to the queen's chambers opened and her guard announced Robert Dudley.

"Your majesty!" Robert called, "He has been convicted."

Elizabeth's face beamed at the news.

Robert hesitated for just one moment as he looked upon her ecstatic expression at the mention of her own second cousin's certain death, "Norfolk has been convicted of three counts of high treason and is to be beheaded for his crime on Tower Hill."

Elizabeth's face broke out in a slow, wide grin at the news, like a wolf who had just cornered its prey.

Between her sudden support for Francis Drake's involvement in the slave trade, and her hunger for fatal revenge, Robert was struggling to recognise the woman who stood before him.

He could only hope, with this latest threat quashed, that she would return to her former self – the exuberant, forgiving young woman he had always known.

For though she looked like his Elizabeth, her new, ruthless persona had begun to often send a shiver down Robert's spine.

Chapter 19

January 1577

In the five years that followed, England prospered.
The queen had passed a series of Acts, one of which introduced severe actions against vagrants in the hope of removing them from within cities across the country. The Act had begun as a simple way of eliminating beggars from the streets to avoid the spread of disease. Three forms of punishment had been put forth to anyone being caught begging: holes being drilled into their ear lobes being but one of the penalties, as well as death. But with this Act, the common folk had begun offering the poor beggars easy labour for a small profit, in the hopes of sparing them their gruesome fate. And in the years that followed, Elizabeth's wish for fewer vagabonds was fulfilled – although not in the way she had planned – and employment rose greatly.
The queen's Scottish cousin continued under house arrest, her involvement in the plot to marry Norfolk and overthrow Elizabeth having been the final straw to break the queen's faint sliver of pity she had previously felt for Mary Stuart.
Let her rot away as she awaits aid from countries that no longer want her, Elizabeth had declared.
England had relaxed into peace once more, like a blanket of calm settling over a sleeping child. And in that time of peace and prosperity, England became stronger from within, just as Elizabeth had long hoped it would.
Thanks to the vast riches brought back by Drake and Hawkins' plundering of Spanish ships and their selling of slaves in the Spanish Indies, many schools were established in the Queen's name throughout the country. As well as this,

Elizabeth commissioned for England's very first permanent theatre to be built in London, so that her love for plays and performances might be shared with her people.

And so, Elizabeth's support for the immoral acts of slave trade continued, if only for the fact that it funded England's development.

But, in truth, Elizabeth had developed a taste for power, and her dominance over Spain in this one small matter brought the queen immense pleasure.

Yet, it was not enough for Elizabeth, for she then authorised an ambitious expedition consisting of five large ships – led by Francis Drake – to set sail across the Atlantic, with the Americas as their destination.

The queen and her council publicly dubbed this expedition as 'Francis Drake's Circumnavigation' and declared its cause to be to uncover new foreign knowledge of the world.

But behind closed doors, they referred to it as 'Drake's Raiding Expedition' and had informed the pirates that their true mission was to aggressively escalate England's raids on the Spanish ships.

The risk of aggravating Spain further being outweighed by Elizabeth's intention of building a stronger England.

July 1577
Kenilworth Castle, Warwickshire

Despite all England's recent successes, development and continuous tranquillity, there were still those who wished for more.

Elizabeth, now a woman of forty-three and yet to be married, had begun hoping that the issue of her unwed status would cease to be a topic of discussion among her Privy Council.

Cecil, to his credit, had given up hounding her about an alliance for some time, ever since her speech declaring herself married to England.

But Robert, it seemed, would not be deterred, and he spent months organising a lavish event of courtly entertainments in the hope of impressing his beloved.

The queen and her entire court had been invited to Kenilworth Castle, which Elizabeth had gifted him a decade earlier upon becoming Earl of Leicester.

She had been forewarned that the events were to take place for nineteen days, but she had been left speechless upon her arrival nonetheless, for the castle had been illuminated magnificently with thousands of torches and candles. The draw bridge to the entrance of the castle had been beautifully decorated with fruits, vines and even instruments. Music was playing as she and her large household made its way into the castle and shown to their personal wing, which Robert had had built especially for this occasion – large enough to accommodate Elizabeth's entourage of several hundreds.

Each day that passed was more astonishing than the next as firework displays burst through the dark skies at night, while during the days the court was entertained with lavish masques and balls.

One morning Elizabeth had been surprised with a specially built twenty-foot model dolphin, which she had admired breathlessly, even before musicians began playing beautiful music from *inside* it.

Unfortunately, on the final day of this lavish show of love by her favourite, the heavens opened up a floodgate of torrential rain, causing Robert's final surprise of an extravagant outdoor proposal, to be put off.

Instead, they enjoyed a great banquet where dozens of rows of tables were set with a thousand pieces of glass and silver. The banquet – according to many who attended – had been fit for a king, with over three hundred mouthwatering dishes presented to the queen's court.

The following day, Elizabeth had declared that she and her household would be departing to return to Hampton Court Palace, and Robert – who had failed to do the one thing he had planned to achieve during the entire nineteen-day event – was left with no other choice than to corner his queen as she made her way to leave.

"I do hope you have enjoyed your stay," Robert spoke softly to her as they walked through the halls of Kenilworth Castle, "I hope I was successful in showing you that I would do anything to see you happy, Elizabeth."

The queen glanced quickly at Robert beside her and frowned; she knew what he was wanting to say. Yet she continued to hope that he would not.

He had aged well, Elizabeth noted then, though she saw him every day.

His formerly chestnut brown hair was now peppered lightly with greys, yet his short beard remained dark throughout. His skin had become slightly more tanned with his continuous exposure to the sun, his love for outdoor activities remaining throughout the years. It had also kept his figure strong and toned, which she continued to appreciate during their once-weekly secret rendezvous.

His dark eyes remained unchanged, warm, and loving whenever he looked at her, although creases had developed around them, visible only when he laughed. Though his aging – and hers – irked her at times, those laughter lines put their lives into perspective for Elizabeth.

She had given up much to walk this path her mother had wanted for her – though there had been times she had wished she could go back and choose a different route; a route where she and Robert could have built a future together.

The image of her mother flashed before her mind's eye then, and she flinched at its intensity, as though her mother's ghost were reminding her to stay on track.

She raised her chin, hardening herself against her own thoughts. That path was long closed to her. She knew that.

Surely Robert knew that too.

But then... perhaps he did not. This extravagant show proved just the opposite.

Perhaps their secret encounters were no longer enough for him.

Perhaps their affair was becoming tedious for him after years of touching and teasing but never allowing him to fully have her.

Let me have you, Elizabeth, he had whispered to her yet again the night before as they had lain intertwined on her bed while the rest of the castle had slept, his fingers grazing lightly on the inside of her thigh.

Elizabeth had shoved him off her with all her might.

You know I can't, she had replied, *I am the Virgin Queen,* the same statement she always made.

Robert had exhaled sharply, covering his hands with his face.

Exhausted by their love.

Exhausted by her.

But he looked at her with nothing but adoration now as they walked out through Kenilworth's castle gates, her most recent rejection forgotten like all the others before.

Elizabeth's stomach tightened with guilt.

He deserved to be cherished by a woman who could love him fully. And yet, at the same time, her heart ached to imagine him in another woman's embrace.

She exhaled sharply then and shook her head to clear it from such thoughts.

"Have I riled you, my queen?" Robert asked, formal now that they had reached the riding party and were surrounded by onlookers.

Elizabeth suddenly turned to face him, her expression sour as she hissed at him quietly, "You know I cannot marry you, Robert!"

Robert flinched, caught off guard by her cruelty.

But he breathed a laugh, a smile pulling at the corners of his lips – still hopeful, "That does not mean I may not continue to try to change your mind."

"I wish you wouldn't," Elizabeth replied as she walked further away from him and towards her carriage, her ladies following closely behind.

As they hurried past Robert, Lettice offered him a small smile. But Robert hardly noticed.

He sighed and followed Elizabeth, as though she had some kind of magnetic pull over him. He caught up to her quickly, his long legs allowing for strides she could not compete with.

"Why do you treat me so?" he asked, his voice quiet though his temper was rising.

"Because of you, and *this*," Elizabeth said accusingly as she waved her hand at Kenilworth Castle, "Cecil has begun wanting to discuss alliances again. He is suggesting suitors as though I were still a young woman."

"You can simple refuse them," Robert replied with a jealous frown, "As you have all the others."

Elizabeth stopped in her tracks and stared at her favourite, "I should refuse them? And yet you offer yourself to me?"

Robert looked over his shoulder at her ladies who stood nearby.

"You know this was all for you," he said, "As a way of proposal."

Elizabeth did not reply.

Robert inhaled deeply, steeling himself, "My proposal may not grant you anything in return in form of land or glory," he said, "But I offer you my heart, Elizabeth. I would give you all that I have in the hope that it would be enough."

Elizabeth stared into his eyes. His beautiful, black eyes. Eyes she could drown in.

She had known this day would come. She had been prepared for it.

Though she had hoped their secret trysts would be enough to satisfy him, she knew a man would always want a wife who could give him heirs.

After all, was that not precisely what her father had wanted all his six wives for? Was it not precisely what he had killed her mother for failing to give him? A *male* heir?

"I cannot give you what you want, Robert," Elizabeth stated coldly, and began walking away again.

This time Robert did not follow, and he watched her, broken, as she walked up the small steps of her carriage and folded herself into it, her ladies entering after her.

And just before Lettice stepped inside, she turned once again to look upon Robert.

He caught her gaze this time, and her lips twitched once more into a small, reassuring smile.

The events at Kenilworth had been nothing if not eye-opening, Elizabeth would give Robert that much.

In his grand show of love, Elizabeth had realised that she had allowed herself to become distracted from her true goal: namely to correct her mother's memory.

She had spent too long a time blinded by the warm comfort of Robert's love; when they both knew that nothing could ever come of it.

It was irrelevant. Elizabeth had not embarked on this queenly journey – one she had not even wanted – to live happily ever after. She had accepted her birthright with the sole purpose of achieving glory for her mother's sake, so that Anne Boleyn would not be erased throughout the ages simply as Henry VIII's mistress.

Upon her return to Hampton Court Palace, the queen decided that she would like a constant reminder of her life's true purpose, one she would be sure to keep on her for the remainder of her life.

And so, she secretly commissioned to have her coronation ring altered to add a hidden compartment, one which would enclose a miniature portrait of her late mother, in the hope that her image would cease to haunt Elizabeth's subconscious.

January 1578

Months later, Elizabeth, having recently turned forty-four years old, sat before her looking glass as she reluctantly observed her aged face.
Elizabeth's beauty was quickly fading.
Much like Robert, she too had developed lines around her eyes, symbols of their secret moments of joy and laughter together.
But as well as those lines, deep creases had become etched between her eyebrows – anger and worry having created a chasm of ugliness upon her face which she could never reverse.
The lines certainly did not aid in her representation of a young woman.
Or that of a Virgin Queen…
Her ladies hovered behind her as they carefully made her bed, and Elizabeth caught a glimpse of Blanche's white face, covered with the 'fashionable' ceruse to hide her pox scars.
"Blanche," the queen called then, to which the lady looked up from her task and headed towards Elizabeth.

"Your highness?" she asked before bobbing a quick curtsy.

"Your paint," Elizabeth said, unsure of how best to word her need to look young again, "It is still fashionable."

It wasn't a question, but Blanche knew to answer, nonetheless.

"It is, my queen," she replied.

Robert had been paying her less attention of late and failing to meet for their secret nights together since her public rejection at Kenilworth Castle. She had not broached the subject to him for fear of appearing desperate and attached.

But the question of *why* flashed within her mind more often than she cared to admit. Perhaps a new, more youthful, look would ignite his passion for her once more.

"Do you wish to try it?" Blanche asked, to which Lettice turned from folding linens by the bed to observe the queen. Elizabeth cocked her head to one side as if to consider it, when in truth she had already decided she would be making use of it.

She nodded and Blanche left to retrieve the tin.

Moments later, with both her ladies before her as they applied the finishing touches, Elizabeth opened her eyes to see Blanche and Lettice smiling broadly at her.

"Your majesty looks –" Lettice began, but Blanche cut her off, knowing precisely what Elizabeth needed to hear.

"—very youthful."

Elizabeth turned to look at her reflection then.

Her face and neck were covered in the white concoction, two shades lighter than her own already-pale skin.

At first glance Elizabeth giggled like a young girl, but after another second's look, she realised that not only did she look younger than her forty-four years, but it also made an impressive contrast to the fiery red of her hair.

She turned her head from one side to another, "If I was not already queen," she stated, a small smile on her lips, "I would say I look rather majestic."

Lettice smiled, "It suits your majesty very well," she agreed, "Your skin has never looked better."

"You look..." Robert began, searching for the correct word in his mind, "Different."
Elizabeth smiled, her teeth looking suddenly more yellow in contrast with her white skin, "Better," she stated, "Younger?"
Robert nodded, though his eyes did not hide his confusion, "You did this for my sake?"
Elizabeth's smile vanished, "You do not like it?" she asked, her hand flying subconsciously to her cheek.
Robert shrugged one shoulder, turning his mouth downward, indifferent of her new look.

"Well," Elizabeth replied, feeling embarrassed by his lack of enthusiasm, "It was not for your sake, in any case," she lied, and then turned to walk away from him.
Robert leaned forward quickly and grabbed her gently by the hand – her whitewashed hand.
Was this stuff all over her? Robert wondered.

"Do not sulk, Elizabeth," he said with a smile, teasing.

"Sulk?" Elizabeth replied, "I could not care less what you think of this, Robert. I look younger than I have in years. I look regal and virginal, just as I ought to look as the *unmarried* Queen of England."
Robert let go of her hand and frowned, "I have asked for your hand," he said, misunderstanding her comment as a jibe, "There is only so often a man can be rejected."
Elizabeth exhaled through her nose angrily, suddenly frustrated by his inability to comprehend her difficult situation.

"You will never understand!" she snapped, "I am *willingly* unmarried. Love is not enough! Marriage is nothing but a death sentence," and she started listing things off on her fingers, "Childbirth – death sentence. Failure to conceive –

death sentence. Production of an heir – replacement and therefore, death sentence. No matter how much we wish it, no matter how much *I* wish it… I cannot marry you. I cannot marry anyone. This change was not for your benefit, Robert," she said, though her chest tightened at the lie, "It is to continue to appear strong and youthful to the outside world. As long as I have my youth and my looks, I continue to have power in the possibility that I *might* marry."

Robert scoffed, "So you would toy with men's hearts?"

Elizabeth flinched, "I have not toyed with anyone's heart. No foreign alliance proposals that I receive are incited due to a man's love for me."

"No," Robert agreed, "No foreign alliance perhaps. But my heart. With that, you have toyed with for far too long."

Elizabeth's anger melted away in an instant and she searched his eyes for a scrap of sympathy to the impossible position she found herself in.

But it seemed, after years of having had a front row seat to Elizabeth's life, that not even Robert could see that there was no future with her.

Had she not been clear enough? Had she not made it painfully obvious?

Her life was not for love and tradition.

She had been born into fire, a critical disappointment which had led to endless deaths – most significantly, her mother's death.

To fix that one failure – to have been born a girl – Elizabeth *had* to commit herself to proving that Anne Boleyn's child would have been enough.

She had sworn long ago that she would give up anything to attain that goal, to prove all those who had condemned her and her mother useless, as wrong.

She had sworn to be the one to lead England into its golden age, where it would be strong enough to rely on itself and to take orders from no one.

She could not risk the glory of England under her rule for the simple pleasures of life.

Even if it meant the breaking of her heart.

Even… if it meant the breaking of Robert's.

Chapter 20

August 1578

Lettice doubled over suddenly, her hand pressed against her mouth as she tried desperately to keep the vomit from rising.
Elizabeth and Blanche were in the other room, carefully applying the finishing touches to the queen's white face. But the queen's chambers were silent, and Lettice knew that if she were to spew into the queen's chamber pot, her condition would be discovered.
Tears sprung to the lady's eyes as she tried her hardest to swallow the lumpy bile in her throat, but before she could stop it, her stomach tensed, and the vomit ejected itself forcefully against the palm of her hand and onto the wooden floor.
"Lettice?" Blanche's concerned voice called.
Lettice only groaned. Then, as she heard footsteps approaching, her fear took over and she began to frantically search for something to mop up the mess, her eyes stinging with the tears brought on by the acid in her mouth.
Or perhaps it was for the fear of being found out.
Elizabeth's great silhouette appeared at the doorway to her bedchamber, her eyebrows creased to see her lady on her hands and knees, wiping up the mess she had created.
Lettice looked over her shoulder at her queen, "Forgive me, your grace," she whimpered, "I am not well."
"I can see that," Elizabeth replied icily, then she turned to Blanche, "What is wrong with her?" she asked, as though Lettice were unable to hear.
Blanche's cheeks reddened, visible even through the thick layer of milk-white ceruse.
Elizabeth's pale blue eyes narrowed suspiciously, then she snapped her head towards Lettice again.

The lady straightened up off the floor, wiping her chin with the back of her hand before smoothing down her dress. And it was then that Elizabeth saw it: the tiny, rounded belly that protruded ever so slightly beneath her lady's loosened corset.

"You are with child?" Elizabeth asked, her eyes remaining narrowed as she thought, "But you are a widow. Your husband is dead."

Lettice looked down at the ground before her, "Yes, your majesty," she mumbled.

Elizabeth stared at her for a moment. Just a moment.

But in that instant, all the pieces fit together in her mind.

She had always known her lady to have found Robert attractive, she had seen it in the blushing of her cheeks when he would walk past, in the hidden smiles she would flash him when she thought Elizabeth wasn't looking.

But she also knew that Robert had never paid her any attention, for he had only ever had eyes for her...

You have toyed with my heart for far too long.

Was that what he had said? Elizabeth could hardly remember. It had seemed so trivial at the time. Just another one of their many disagreements about marriage.

Had that been his warning?

A warning that if Elizabeth would not give him an heir, that he would attain one through...one of her own ladies?

The pang of realisation punched a hole in Elizabeth's chest, and she found it suddenly hard to breathe.

"Is...Is it –" she stammered.

Lettice looked up at her queen, red-faced and trembling, her hands fumbling shakingly before her. She opened her mouth to speak.

"I – Ah."

But nothing coherent came out.

Elizabeth clamped her mouth shut, her jaw clenching tightly before turning on her heels and storming out of her chambers.

"Robert!" she shrieked as she stormed through the halls of the palace, her shoes clinking sharply upon the stone floor, "Robert Dudley! Find me Sir Dudley!" she ordered as she raced manically past guards and courtiers alike, all of which stared bewildered at their ruffled queen.

"He is in the lower gardens practicing his archery," a voice called from behind her, and Elizabeth – without even looking back – turned sharply around a corner, heading straight in direction of her treacherous lover.

Upon emerging out into the sunlight, Elizabeth scanned the great lawn, swiftly spotting her target among a small group of his friends.

She zeroed in on him and, with her fists clenching at her sides, strode towards him hastily. As she approached, she could hear the men laughing at an inside joke while Robert let an arrow loose and one of the men clapped him on the shoulder in appreciation for the shot. She saw him flinch slightly at the friendly pat, the old war wound on his shoulder continuing to cause him pain even after all these years.

Robert looked around when he noticed Elizabeth approaching, and his smile vanished at the sight of her troubled expression. He shoved his bow into his friend's hands beside him, hurrying towards Elizabeth. And as the two fateful lovers reached each other, Elizabeth slapped Robert's face with all her might.

Later, people would say the *crack* had been heard all over London.

Robert's head had snapped sideways, and when he righted himself, he searched her face for understanding.

But he did not see Elizabeth looking back at him. Instead, he saw the icy queen he had begun to loathe.

Behind her, her two ladies finally caught up, and Robert looked at them over Elizabeth's shoulder as if to draw answers from them.

It was the wrong thing to do, for as soon as he averted his gaze from her to Lettice, Elizabeth saw red.

Without a word, Elizabeth turned and grabbed a fistful of Lettice's hair through her hood, pulling her head back sharply. Lettice squealed while Blanche gasped in horror.

"Elizabeth!" Robert called, raising a hand as if to stop her.

The queen stared at Robert, then blinked slowly when no one made a move to help her lady.

"Won't you come to your lover's aid, Sir Robert?" Elizabeth asked, her voice raspy from screeching.

Robert had the audacity to frown in confusion, "My lover?" he scoffed.

Lettice whimpered beside her queen, her head and back bent awkwardly in Elizabeth's grasp.

Elizabeth's lip curled up in disgust, then she threw the lady aside roughly, causing her to fall onto the soft lawn. Blanche knelt beside Lettice, whispering words of encouragement to her friend. But Elizabeth paid them no attention, for her gaze was fixed onto Robert.

"Do you not know?" the queen asked then, realising he had not rushed to Lettice's side.

Robert frowned and shrugged his shoulders heavily, "Know what, Elizabeth? What is the meaning of this?"

The queen took a step towards him, pressed her white face inches from his.

"Your whore," she hissed, "is with child!"

Immediately, Robert's eyes widened, his need for denial gone with the wind. He tore his eyes from the woman he loved more than any other, to the woman carrying his child. And for a split second, he did not know who to go to.

He swallowed, pushing away his need to aid Lettice up from the ground, and fighting every fibre of his being to stand before his queen – the love of his life – and explain himself.

"You gave me no choice."

Immediately, he regretted the words. Had he even meant to utter them?
He had hoped to soothe her, to tell her it was a mistake, that he was hers and no one else's.
But it would have been a lie.
Though he did not love Lettice the way he loved Elizabeth, she had been there for him in ways Elizabeth would never be. Lettice had listened to his troubles, been eager to lessen his strain. She had been sweet. She had reminded him of the Elizabeth he had once known, the one who laughed loudly and without smugness, the one who asked how *he* felt after a difficult day.
At first, Lettice had been nothing more than a distraction, and – though he was ashamed to admit it even to himself – he would often close his eyes and think of Elizabeth as he thrusted insistently inside her. But after some time, he had begun looking at her during those moments of pleasure, and he had been surprised to have seen a glimmer of something in her eyes. Something Elizabeth would never be able to give him.
A future.
As his words sunk in, Elizabeth staggered backwards as though she had been shoved. And then she lunged at Robert, her small fists hammering repeatedly on his hard chest.
"How could you do this to me!" she wailed, "How *dare* you betray me like this!" and her face crumpled in agony as she continued to painlessly strike him. Her tears streaked her white face, dozens of little rivers forming on the plains of her cheeks. And all the while Robert gazed down at her, his own tears threating to spill over the loss he knew was to come due to his betrayal.
Elizabeth slumped into him, exhausted from her outburst. And all that was left to do was for Robert to wrap his arms around

his beloved and soothe her – as he had always done – while she struggled to regain her queenly composure.

After spending the remainder of the day in bed, fighting a fitful sleep, Elizabeth awoke early the following morning feeling as though she hadn't slept in years.

The sun had not yet risen, and yet she could hear birdsong outside her window. She begrudged the carefree animals their easy life, and with a grumble she tore her sheets aside and leapt out of bed, her rage fuelling her forward.

She stopped suddenly then, when she spotted Lettice sleeping soundly in her small single bed in the corner.

Was she mad?

Had the babe in her belly drained her completely of common sense?

The thought of Robert's child dulled her anger momentarily, but when Lettice shifted slightly in her sleep, Elizabeth's hatred of her re-emerged.

She walked over to her lady's bed and, grabbing a fistful of the sheet, pulled it off Lettice in one fell swoop.

"Up, up, up!" Elizabeth called loudly, to which Lettice's eyes snapped open and she gasped in terror.

"Your majesty!" the lady called in fear, "I did not know you had awoken already."

"Get dressed, Lettice," Elizabeth ordered as she turned her back on her, "And then get out of my sight."

Lettice wasted no time in doing exactly as she was told, hurrying out of the queen's chambers before she had even managed to properly lace her corset. But Elizabeth did not care. Let the whole court see her for the sinful she-wolf that she truly was.

This would be the end of Lettice Knollys. That woman could no longer be her lady-in-waiting. The Virgin Queen could not have a *whore* attending her daily.

And so, the first order of business the queen would attend to this day, would be to discharge Lettice from her services and her palace, in the hopes of never having to see her treacherous face again.

September 1578

On the eve of the 19th September, Robert Dudley saddled his horse in secret – much like he had done almost twenty years prior when he had left his then-wife, Amy, behind to see his true love Elizabeth.

This time however, he was readying his horse to ride *away* from Elizabeth, and into another woman's arms. And Robert could not shake the paradox of this very moment.

With one last look over his shoulder at the Palace, Robert clicked his tongue to spur his steed ahead, eager to meet his lover as she awaited him at his home, Wanstead House.

He had waited long enough for Elizabeth's heart to thaw. But with each year that passed she had become less and less the person he had fallen in love with all those years ago.

Queenship had hardened his Elizabeth, and it was only rarely now that he saw her without, not only her white-washed mask, but also one of her many others. He had long hoped she would remove all her armour and simply *be* again. Especially when there had been no more assassination attempts on her for many years.

But the Elizabeth he had loved was gone. He admitted that now as he galloped away from her.

And there was no amount of love he could lay upon Elizabeth which would save her from herself.

"Married!?" Queen Elizabeth screeched at the news.

The only man she had ever loved, stood before her, his dark gaze fixed defiantly on her as his new wife stood beside him, her pretty head hanging in shame.

"You cannot marry without your queen's permission!" she continued, suddenly remembering her own sister's rage at their stepmother, Catherine Parr's, secret marriage without the late king's consent. And though she had thought Mary heartless at the time, Elizabeth could finally understand her fury at the blatant disrespect for the monarch's authority.

"Please forgive us, your majesty," Lettice said, raising her head to meet Elizabeth's angry gaze, her voice as small and unsure as that of a child.

Elizabeth stared at her, her eyes fixed on her former lady-in-waiting, the hatred she felt for her visible to even those in the far back of the great hall.

It was the wrong thing to say, however, for in one swift motion, the queen was on her feet and hurrying towards Lettice. And before anyone could even guess what Elizabeth's intention was, she raised her hand high and repeatedly boxed the lady on the side of the head.

"Elizabeth!" Robert shouted as Lettice cried out in pain and fear beside him, cowering away from Elizabeth.

"You are not forgiven, you she-wolf!" Elizabeth shrieked as she continued to pummel the pregnant lady with the palms of her hands.

Robert grabbed the queen by the wrists then and forcefully turned her to face him, "Enough!" he hissed at her under his breath, and the court behind them gasped in horror to see their queen manhandled before their very eyes.

Four guards instantly assumed a combat stance, their hands on the hilts of their swords as they approached their queen.

Robert glanced around at the guards surrounding them and let go of the queen, who then shoved him wordlessly away from her, her eyes speaking in volumes of disappointment and heartache.

"I am alright," Elizabeth said, waving her guards away to resume their positions. Then she raised her chin and turned to walk the three steps back to her throne.

Once seated she watched sourly as Robert helped his new wife to recover herself and then whisper something into her ear.

And the anger continued to bubble inside her.

"Lord Robert!" she boomed, her angry voice echoing through the high ceilings of the great hall, "I cannot reverse a union which has been witnessed in the sight of God. Though your betrayal to the crown is indisputable, I do need you here as member of the Privy Council," Robert's jaw tightened, but Elizabeth went on, "but I cannot allow for such actions to go unpunished!"

She sighed deeply in an attempt to soothe her thundering heart, but there was nothing for it, and she believed this hatred would likely be a part of her until her final day.

She tore her eyes from Robert to his new, pretty thing beside him.

"You are hereby banished from court, *Lady Dudley*!" she ordered, "Never to return again under pain of death!"

October 1578

With Lettice banished from court, Elizabeth selected a new lady to replace her treacherous one, in the hope of erasing Lettice from her mind entirely.

As first lady to the queen, Blanche took the new lady under her wing, teaching her all she needed to know of the queen's routine.

"Come, ladies," Elizabeth said, more for Bess' benefit than anything else, since Blanche already knew simply to follow, "Meeting of the council."

They made their way through the candle-lit halls in silence, Elizabeth looking over her shoulder occasionally to smile encouragingly at the new, young lady.

Elizabeth Throckmorton – to be styled Bess while at the queen's court – was a pretty, young lady with golden blonde hair and a bright, easy smile. She was of slim build and short stature, yet – to Elizabeth's surprise – she did seem to be keeping up with her quick stride well enough.

They entered the council chamber to find the advisors awaiting their queen's arrival. Those who had been seated, Walsingham and Cecil, rose from their seats and all four men bowed their heads in greeting.

Elizabeth took her seat on her throne, her two ladies standing behind her in the shadows.

"News," Elizabeth demanded bluntly, and the men took their seats.

"Francis, the Duke of Anjou," Cecil said, "he has set sail to visit your majesty."

"Whatever for?" she asked.

"To ask for your hand in marriage," he said, glimpsing briefly at Robert.

Cecil was hopeful for the first time in years.

Though the queen was past her childbearing years, the chance for a marital union with a foreign land to strengthen England was still a possibility. And now that her former lover was no longer available – or even in her favour – Cecil hoped Elizabeth would have a change of heart on marriage with another. Even if it were powered by the sheer force of jealous retaliation.

The queen jerked up her chin, "I shall look forward to his arrival," she said, turning ever so slightly away from Robert.

Giving him, quite literally, the cold shoulder.

February 1579

When the Duke of Anjou arrived at Elizabeth's court four months later, she was momentarily taken aback at how young he was, never having given it a second's thought to have asked beforehand.

The young duke, though handsome and tall, was yet, it seemed, quite unable to grow a full beard, his fair hair growing in patches on his cheeks and chin.

He was twenty-four, Elizabeth soon learned, and though she knew in her heart that it did not matter – for she would never go so far as to *actually* marry – she was flattered that he was undeniably keen to court her, despite being twenty-two years his senior.

"Most beautiful queen," he said in greeting as he bowed at the waist, his feather cap in his hand, "I am honoured to be in your glorious presence."

His French accent was thick, his grin was wide and cheery. And even though he was a Catholic, her councillors – with the exception of Robert who had remained stum at the topic – were very much for this union.

Elizabeth and the duke spent every day together for the following month, quite openly enjoying each other's company, the queen even flirtatiously referring to him as 'her frog'.

And all the while Robert was forced to watch, the queen having disallowed him to leave court even when news had arrived that his wife had borne him a healthy son.

But not all were in favour of this union, the duke's religion being a widely unpopular subject among her people.

"The country is not as overjoyed as you seem to be," Cecil pointed out one afternoon as he and the queen sat on opposite sides of the long wooden table in the queen's chambers.

Elizabeth put down her fork and wiped her mouth on a silk napkin, "What do they say?"

Cecil sighed without looking up from his plate of roasted pig, "They speak of their hatred of the French and of the Pope," he said.

Elizabeth shook her head pensively, remembering her sister's marriage to Filipe, back when he had been just a Spanish prince, and the rebellion that had ensued upon the announcement of their betrothal.

"If my people are against the union, perhaps it would be unwise to allow it to proceed," she said, looking directly at Cecil.

"Don't let the people control you," he said casually, as though the people's acceptance was not precisely what kept her safely on the throne.

"A union they do not approve of may cause great havoc in the future," the queen said, picking up her cup of wine and taking a sip, "I shouldn't like to marry someone England does not approve of."

Cecil practically slammed his fork down in shock, "Your majesty," he gasped, "After so many years of rejections…we are so close to attaining a wedded union. They duke is young, and he is keen. Your majesty is keen – are you not?"

Elizabeth shrugged one shoulder, "I only wish to avoid civil unrest," she said innocently.

Cecil shook his head and rubbed a hand over his old face, "At least sleep on it, my queen," he begged, "The people will come around if you wish to marry the duke. England will thank you for this in the future."

Elizabeth smiled sweetly, though she had already decided to use this exact reason as her scapegoat.

But for now, she would continue to make promises to her councillors and to her suitor. After all, at the age of forty-six, she was well aware that the likelihood of any more interested

suitors in her future to be slim, and she did indeed enjoy the young man's energy and enthusiasm.
It reminded her of simpler times.
And in the furthest crease of her mind was a whisper, *He reminds me of Robert.*

But it was not to be, and after another month of heavy flirtation, Elizabeth broke the young duke's heart under the guise that her people would never forgive her if she were to follow her own.
The Duke of Anjou took it well, though he was visibly defeated as he and his household departed Hampton Court Palace.
And with the duke's departure – and the charade at an end – Robert was finally allowed to go meet his newborn son.

Chapter 21

September 1580

Francis Drake, after having spent three years sailing across the oceans, returned to England with nothing but good news for his queen.

"Spain ain't best pleased," he said, his grin wide with pride at his part in aggravating the Spanish, "I crossed t' ocean an' laid claim to a land. I named it Nova Albion. We plundered t' coastal towns for treasure as we went. I also discovered that the Tierra del Fuego is a group of islands, y' majesty, not another continent at all, like we thought! Ships can sail between t' Atlantic an' Pacific Ocean through 'em!" and he flashed her another black-toothed grin.

"Fascinating," Elizabeth breathed, her eyes wide with wonder as she listened intently.

Francis Drake's Circumnavigation had been a great success, as expected.

The value of treasure he had brought back from his raiding of coastal towns of the Americas, as well as those plundered off Spanish ships, was exceptional. And England became increasingly richer for it.

This outcome gave Elizabeth a burst of delight, knowing that she was single-handedly catapulting England towards a greatness not even her father had achieved.

And all without even a single wedded union.

"Spain is outraged," Cecil reported as soon as Elizabeth entered the council chambers one morning, "Drake's continued attacks on Spanish ships during his circumnavigation has angered King Filipe."

Elizabeth took her seat when suddenly the door to the council chambers banged open, the imperial ambassador entering boldly and Elizabeth's guards following closely behind in case he posed a threat to their queen.

"Your majesty," ambassador Feria called with a hint of distaste, "your *pirata* has returned to your lands."

It was not a question, and so Elizabeth offered him no reply.

Feria looked from one council member to another as they all stared back at him in silence. Then he scoffed and narrowed his eyes at the queen.

"My master wishes to know how you plan to...punish your subject, who so blatantly sinned against our country repeatedly since his *circumnavigation*."

"Punish?" Elizabeth parroted, feigning confusion.

"*Si!*" he replied sharply, "Punished! How?"

Elizabeth blinked at her Privy Council members, "How does one punish a man who has not offended another?"

"Ha!" Feria barked, "He has offended. He has offended greatly. And my master, Filipe II of Spain, awaits your word on how he shall be dealt with."

With that he turned, pushed past the two guards who had followed him in, and marched out the door.

Elizabeth raised her eyebrows and grinned, "Well gentlemen," she said, addressing the advisors before her, but blatantly snubbing Robert, "I personally think instead of punishment, Francis Drake deserves a knighthood. Don't you?"

Cecil exhaled loudly as he rubbed a hand over his tired face.

"Something on your mind, Sir William?" Elizabeth accused.

He sat forward in his seat, "You cannot be seen to approve of Drake's tactics. To aggravate the Spanish king further will not lead to anything good."

Elizabeth waved his comment aside, "Do not fret, Sir William!" she said casually, "I am no fool! Drake's achievements shall be honoured. Though I shall not do it myself, and it shall not be the only honour given."

Cecil frowned, "Your grace?"

"Sir William, Walsingham," she said, looking at each in turn, "Stand."

The two old men did as they were bid, looking confusedly at Pembroke and Robert when their names were not mentioned, but they only shrugged.

"Francis Drake will be given a knighthood," Elizabeth proclaimed as she stood at the head of the table, her hands clasped elegantly before her, "He shall receive his title not at my hands but by the Marquis de Marchaumont, to avoid drawing attention to Drake's achievements and my approval of them. As well as that, Walsingham, you too shall receive a new title of Secretary of State."

Walsingham's bushy eyebrows shot up, and he bowed in gratitude.

"Sir William," Elizabeth said, turning her pale-blue eyes to him, "For your unfaltering loyalty and continued devotion to the crown, I create you: Baron Burghley."

Cecil blinked at his queen, dumbfounded by her generosity.

"With the new titles and riches I bestow onto you," Elizabeth said, her yellow teeth bare in a great smile, "No one can claim that the Queen of England favoured Francis Drake's slave trade and pirating of foreign ships. And in the years to come, when you are all dead and buried, there will be no one alive to tell the tale."

March 1581

"King Filipe is not stupid," Walsingham said as he and the queen walked leisurely through the Palace gardens.

Elizabeth sighed and stopped to admire a rose, hoping her lack of a reply would dwindle the topic at hand. She was tired of the mention of Spain. So much so that she sometimes thought back to times when she had been bothered by something else, anything else really. Even by the tedious topic of marriage.

England was strong. Through the continued peace and vast riches brought in by Drake over the years, Elizabeth had been able to reinforce the countries military and economic sectors that had been so terribly damaged during her father's reign.

Her naval capacity was vast in comparison to what either of her siblings had achieved too, new warships being commissioned as often as she ordered new dresses to be made. Elizabeth was confident in her position at last. And she no longer paid any heed as to whether king Filipe was being taunted by her actions or not.

Walsingham continued, "He is well aware that your majesty supports Sir Francis Drake and his antics."

Elizabeth continued walking then, each step slow and deliberate, "Let him think whatever he wishes," she said, "Drake is my subject, to do with as I see fit."

Walsingham licked his dry lips and nodded his head.

"What other news?" she asked, looking at Walsingham.

He cleared his throat, "There have been some more arrests of Catholic priests of late."

"Yes, the Catholic seminary priests," Elizabeth replied, "I am aware of their cause."

"Well, your grace," Walsingham said, "Their cause is quite literally to overthrow you."

"I am aware," then Elizabeth exhaled slowly, bored, "Will they not ask for pardon?"

Walsingham snickered, shaking his old head lightly, "They were openly mocking your grace by preaching the old ways. They have rejected their right to conversion and the jury has returned the verdict of guilty through the Treason Acts. They will be burned at the stake like all the others before them."

Elizabeth raised an eyebrow, "How many this time?"

"Two priests and eight laymen," Walsingham replied proudly, glad to serve his queen, "But they won't stop coming. Spain and France send more of their Catholic martyrs every year in an attempt to poison your people against you."

Elizabeth shrugged, indifferent, "Those martyrs are not my people, I cannot control what they choose to do with their lives. But I can control how I deal with them if they go against me in my own country."

Walsingham nodded approvingly, a silence befalling them as Elizabeth stopped once again to observe a rose. She bent down as if to caress it then, but instead snapped its stem clean off and held it to her nose.

"I don't care if we end up executing hundreds of them."

May 1581

"Lord Robert, your majesty," Elizabeth's guard announced as he opened the door.

The queen tensed for a moment before nodding her head and allowing him to enter.

They had not been alone together or even spoken past formalities since Elizabeth had allowed him to leave court to meet his son, whom Lettice had named Robert, two years prior.

In that time, the queen had made sure to punish him in any way she could, her open flirtations with the Duke of Anjou having been only the beginning of her tantalizing.

During banquets she would dance with any man that would offer, but if Robert were so much as to look in her direction, she would snub him instantly. She made him sit beside her at council meetings, where she would wear dresses that she knew shaped her small breasts appealingly with the corset.

Once, a year since his son's birth, Robert had quite brazenly leaned down at a banquet as though to retrieve a dropped utensil and traced the back of his finger over the bare skin of her leg underneath the table. No doubt as an attempt at reconciliation.

Remembering what he could do with those fingers had sent a shiver down her spine. But a second later, she had reapplied her icy mask, and had stared daggers at him when he had righted himself once again on his seat beside her.

She taunted him in any way she could, hoping to make him long for something that was now – through his own actions – unattainable to him, all the while knowing that he loved her still.

"Your majesty," he said now as the door closed slowly behind him.

Her ladies, Blanche and Bess, sat at the far window of the chambers, embroidering.

Elizabeth stood before Robert, unsure of the purpose of his unannounced visit.

He shifted from one foot to another and licked his lips. *Uncomfortable*, Elizabeth noted, and the sorrow of that truth stabbed her heart.

How could two people who had once meant everything to one another, suddenly feel like two total strangers? Like two passing ships in the night?

Because he betrayed me.

The thought burst into her mind like a cannon, and she straightened her back rigidly.

"What is it you want, Robert?" she asked finally, cracking the frozen ice between them slightly.

Robert could not help himself, but he breathed a small laugh, and Elizabeth stomach flipped to see those crinkles around his eyes. Crinkles she had so often traced with her fingertips.

"I miss you," he said then, quietly enough that only she would hear.

Elizabeth jerked up her chin but did not reply.

They stared at one another for another moment, his dark eyes heavy with guilt. Her pale eyes hard and unfeeling.

He knew it was not entirely her fault who she had become, and though an ice queen stood before him, he held onto the hope that there was yet a chance of melting her frozen exterior.

But then he turned and left, for there was nothing more to say. His words may have been few, but they were true. And they were all he could bring himself to admit, without opening a chasm of guilt inside him for the betrayal he was inflicting on his wife.

September 1581

"There is much conflict in Ireland, your majesty," the Earl of Pembroke informed Elizabeth one evening as she sat by the fire, embroidering with her ladies.

Elizabeth looked up, "Desmond?" she asked knowingly.

Some years prior, the Earl of Desmond and his followers, the Geraldines, had led an armed rebellion within Ireland in protest against the English. Their aim had been to maintain independence from Elizabeth as their monarch, the Earl of Desmond having been against the Protestant queen's new policies that were being implemented within Ireland. A battle had ensued near the city of Cork, which was quashed by Elizabeth's forces.

Over seven-hundred Irish men were executed in the aftermath of the uprising, their leaders being pardoned shortly thereafter, in the hope that the many Irish deaths would be enough to deter another rebellion.

It would seem it had not.

Pembroke nodded in reply and Elizabeth rose from her seat, discarding her embroidery, "Call a meeting," she ordered, and Pembroke hurried out the door ahead of her.

Once all members were gathered in the council chamber, Elizabeth nodded for Pembroke to speak.

"Desmond has landed back in Ireland with a force of Spanish and Italian troops, backed by the Pope and with more papal forces to come," Pembroke explained, "Many more Irish followers have joined this new rebellion. We must act before they do."

"What can be done?" Elizabeth asked the room.

"Send an army," Walsingham suggested, "Squash them like we did the first time they dared to defy your majesty."

"They only want independence from our policies, your grace," Robert Dudley pointed out, "They do not wish you harm."

Elizabeth narrowed her eyes at him, "They are acting defiantly against their monarch," she said, "They ensued violence before and clearly wish to do so again. Why else enlist *Spanish* troops to their cause. The pope too! I ask again," she said, looking away from Robert, "What can be done?"

Cecil leaned forward then, gently stroking his white beard in thought, "We send troops. We hold them off."

"There will be much bloodshed," Robert interjected.

Elizabeth ignored him, "Send the troops," she declared, "We cannot allow these rebellions against me to continue."

"Is there an arrest order, your grace?" Pembroke asked.

"No," the queen replied sharply, "Kill anyone who stands against us. I will take no prisoners and I will give no pardons this time."

The men bowed their heads and rose, only Robert remained seated, his brows furrowed in disbelief at her instructions.

He rose from his seat a moment later and glanced quickly at Elizabeth beside him as she watched the old men nearing the door. She was like a statue of stone, frozen solid as if by that white paint she now insisted on wearing.

The Virgin Queen.

That was what she had said it made her look like. And yet, to Robert, it made her look not like the innocent virgin she professed to be, but like a sculpture of ice, a queen whose body and mind was disconnected from other people's turmoil. He had often wondered just when one of her many masks would take hold of her completely one day. And it seemed now that her callous mask was the one to stay.

"Gentlemen," Elizabeth called then unexpectedly, a thought having come to her suddenly, and her Privy Council stopped in their tracks to quitting the room, "There is more we can do to make sure this never happens again."

The men all turned to look at her.

"Instruct our troops to kill anything in its path."

Cecil frowned, confused, "You have already said that, your grace."

"No," Elizabeth said, a small, unnerving smile playing on her thin lips, "It is not enough to kill just their armies."

Robert's shoulders stiffened. What more could she possibly mean to do to them?

"We must implement more ruthless tactics than the simple retaliation to their uprising. We must weaken their lands beyond recognition so that Ireland is forced to their knees for all the years to come."

"Your majesty?" Walsingham asked, not even he understanding how far his queen was willing to go on her quest for revenge.

"Kill all their livestock," the queen commanded, "Destroy their crops and burn down their homes. We must deprive the Irish of food and shelter. Hunt down anyone who stands in our way. Only then will your queen rest easily, knowing that Ireland has submitted to my power."

November 1583

In England's retaliation against the second Desmond rebellion, another two-thousand and six-hundred Irish men were massacred, supporters and their leaders alike.

In the two years that followed, the south of Ireland was racked by famine, Elizabeth's order to scorch the lands having caused turmoil on the harvests. What followed was another thirty-thousand people's deaths – innocent men, women, and children, all of which had starved to death.

And yet it was not enough for Elizabeth, who would only be satisfied to retreat her armies from Ireland when Desmond's severed head had been sent to her.

Chapter 22

September 1584

The months went by much the same as ever.
Elizabeth wore the best gowns and attended the most extravagant masques. But beneath the jewellery and the grandeur, her body decayed more and more each year.
While her beauty faded, however, her country flourished, and England continued to thrive under her rule. Schools began their teachings of the discoveries of America through the findings of Sir Francis Drake and his crew.
Soon after, Elizabeth sent two voyagers, Humphrey Gilbert and Walter Raleigh, to set sail to North America and to establish a colony there, which they did with great success, claiming a nearby island on behalf of England and naming it 'Newfoundland'. This created a base for Francis Drake and his pirates to continue attacking Spanish vessels, as well as beginning Elizabeth's plan to interfere with Spanish dominance over the New World by taking regions as England's own.
Soon, Walter Raleigh joined in Drake's attacks of Spanish ships in the Pacific, gaining him the attention of the queen as another useful pawn on her quest for power.
But the Spanish king Filipe II was too distracted by bigger problems to even notice, for his hold over the Netherlands – which had been an unofficial part of the Spanish sphere of influence – was sudden beginning to slip away.

"The Dutch Protestants in the Netherlands have taken up arms against their Spanish ruler," Cecil informed Elizabeth one morning at their daily council meeting, "The rebels are campaigning for independence from Catholic Spain."

"The Dutch Revolt," Walsingham added.

Elizabeth nodded thoughtfully; her forehead creased so deeply not even the four layers of the white ceruse she applied daily could hide her age of fifty-one years old.

"The Netherlands are a vital place of trade for us," Robert said, "Perhaps England should show their support."

"England is militarily strong enough now to send aid," Pembroke lisped, "If your majesty should choose to intervene."

Elizabeth exhaled. This was the moment she had been preparing England for her entire reign.

Since attaining the throne from her sister, England had gone from strength to strength. She had pulled it out of its military, economic and financial ruin her father had put it in during his rule. She had strengthened her country as she had promised she would.

And now her greatest enemy – Spain – was finally in a weakened state as it faced opposition from another Protestant country.

Elizabeth nodded; her advisors were right.

If she wished to finally put an end to Catholic Spain's upper hand to every other country in Europe, England should strike it at its weakest.

Another chance like this might not present itself during her reign again.

And if she were to aid in the defeat of the most powerful country in the world...then her reign would surely be remembered as glorious.

Her mother's name would be absolved; remembered no longer as Henry VIII's whore, but as the mother of the greatest monarch England had ever seen.

November 1584

"Your majesty's army has arrived in the Netherlands to aid the Dutch rebels," Cecil informed the queen in her chambers just two months later.

"Excellent, Sir William," Elizabeth replied, "We shall –"

Just then, the doors to her chambers burst open and Robert stumbled inside. He fell to his knees, his face in his hands as he sobbed uncontrollably.

Cecil and Elizabeth stared wide-eyed, unsure of what had happened, while the queen's guards stood by the doors, waiting for an order.

Elizabeth shook her head at them, then turned to Cecil, "Leave us," she commanded.

Cecil bowed his balding head and left, shooting one last bewildered look at Robert as he closed the doors behind him.

Robert continued to weep on the floor.

"Robert?" Elizabeth said carefully, taking a tentative step towards him.

"He is dead…" he mumbled into his hands, then cried out in anguish as he spoke the words aloud.

Elizabeth knelt beside him and raised her hand to comfort him. But she stopped mid-air, unsure of where they stood with one another.

He raised his head from his hands then and Elizabeth knew – simply from the pain in his eyes – of who he spoke.

"He is dead," he repeated quietly, staring blankly ahead as the tears continued to stream, "My boy…my little boy."

Elizabeth's throat closed in agony for her lifelong friend, the anger she had held for him over the years suddenly seeming futile compared to the heartache he was facing at the loss of his child.

She knelt down beside him and placed her hand on his head, stroking his greying hair, completely lost on how to comfort away such grief.

Robert turned towards her and embraced her then as he continued to sob, his shoulders shaking so intensely Elizabeth thought he may yet fall to pieces in her arms.

She tightened her grip around him, hoping it would be enough to hold him together.

"Shhh," she cooed, the only thing she could think of to do, "Shhh."

She held him for what felt like hours, though only minutes had passed when he pulled away and wiped his bloodshot eyes with his hands.

"Forgive me, your highness," he muttered, "I did not know who else to go to. My feet led me here."

"You don't need to explain, Robert," Elizabeth replied softly, "I know."

And she did.

Though they had been parted in anger for many years, their connection went beyond that.

Robert exhaled deeply then and shook his head, "My line has ended," he said, his voice serrated like the jagged side of a saw.

Elizabeth shuddered, thinking how both his and her death would signify the end of both their lines.

If only she had married him.

The thought came too forcefully, making her flinch.

So much could have been different if she had married Robert. If Amy had not died so mysteriously. If she had done as she had pleased and married him despite the scandal.

If Thomas Seymour hadn't raped me.

Her life could have been so different. She may have married Robert and had his children. And their bloodline would have continued.

The thought sent a shiver down Elizabeth's back, and Robert looked up from his lap and into her pale blue eyes.

"Are you cold?" he muttered, almost lifelessly, the sorrow of his loss having sucked the energy out of him.

Elizabeth shook her head lightly, and then she breathed a little laugh. How could he be thinking of her wellbeing in that moment? When his whole life had been ripped out from underneath him.

Because he still loves me.

"Robert –" she began, but then he leaned forward and pressed his lips to hers.

His kiss was urgent, as though Elizabeth were his anchor, keeping him from giving into his agony and letting go of this world.

His beard scratched at her chin as he kissed her forcefully, but Elizabeth didn't mind. In fact, she welcomed the pain. Anything to take away some of his.

After some moments, his urgency fell away and they settled into each other's embrace, and Elizabeth poured her strength into him with each gentle kiss. Her hands were in his thick hair, stroking it tenderly when she sensed his distress overcoming him again.

But she kept on kissing him – hoping to feed life back into him – even as his tears streamed down his face and their kisses turned bitter with grief.

January 1585

"Sugar?" Elizabeth gasped.

"Vast quantities, y' majesty," Walter Raleigh replied, flashing a wide, mischievous grin.

Elizabeth raised her eyebrows, "Is this how Spain is using their enslaved? Sugar plantations."

"Aye," Sir Francis Drake said, "So it would seem."

Walter Raleigh and Sir Francis Drake had returned to England after yet another successful raiding expedition in the Americas and Pacific Ocean, bringing back large quantities of sugar as well as tobacco from their plundering of Spanish ships.

And Elizabeth rewarded them grandly.

The handsome Walter Raleigh was promptly knighted, and both he and Drake were given official slave trade privileges and the right to continue to colonize the Americas, provoking the Spanish king further with England's obvious affront.

Sugar, though not a novel discovery to England, had previously been used only in the rarest of occasions, its scarcity deeming it a luxury even to the Queen of England.

But with its new import through regular plundering of Spanish ships, Elizabeth's court kitchen was quick to include it in most any feast when the queen expressed her love of it.

And it wasn't long before Elizabeth began carrying a little tin of the sweet ingredient with her everywhere she went, to avoid ever having to eat or drink another thing without a sprinkle of sugar on top.

"Wine, Bess," Elizabeth ordered over her shoulder during a council meeting some days later. Her young lady poured her a cup of wine, to which Elizabeth promptly added a pinch of sugar before draining the cup in one.

"The future of the Netherlands as a Protestant nation is significant to England," the Earl of Pembroke said passionately as he pushed his thinning white hair from his eyes.

"I don't dispute that, my lord," Robert replied, "But our direct involvement is not necessary. The queen has already sent a small army to aid their revolt. To continue to send arms would cause an even greater disagreement between us and Spain," he looked at Elizabeth as though for confirmation of agreement, but she only returned a neutral gaze, "Surely it is enough to send monetary support and offer sanctuary to Dutch rebels."

Elizabeth shook her head then, "Spain has gone too far within the Netherlands," she stated, "The assassination of their Prince Willem van Oranje by the Catholic supporter of Filipe II has caused much uproar. England must continue assisting in this rebellion with more than just financial support."

Cecil and Walsingham nodded in agreement.

"I put forth that more English troops be sent to aid the Dutch," she concluded.

Robert shook his head and scoffed, "Your majesty," he said disparagingly, "Spain will retaliate."

Elizabeth stared at him, her mouth pressed into a tight line, "Then I suggest you kill as many of them as you can when you, Lord Robert, lead our army to fight with the Dutch."

It was with those words that Elizabeth realised she had begun thinking like a man: proclaiming war as though it were a knee-jerk reaction. When just some years ago she had believed her advisors fools for threatening war on Spain.

At least with this war, Elizabeth thought in her defence, *England has a chance of winning.*

March 1585

Since Robert's young son's death four months prior, he and his wife had maintained very little communication, her banishment from court and Robert's continued devotion to Elizabeth causing a rift between the married couple.

His and Elizabeth's reconciliation since that day had helped to patch up his broken heart; and knowing that he was once again in the queen's favour was enough to warrant getting out of bed in the mornings.

And so, when the time came for Robert to depart to battle in the Netherlands, it was not of Lettice that he dreamt of on those long nights at sea; though he had tried his best to stay true to their marriage.

Lord Robert may have disagreed with his queen on England's need for involvement in a foreign war against Spain, but he understood her decision to ignore his warnings. The Spanish king was a tyrant. And a powerful one at that.

If Spain overpowered the Netherlands once more and increased their Catholic hold over it, it could be used as a direct base for an easy invasion of England in the future.

And though Robert did not like to vex Spain further – after nearly twenty years of England openly attacking Spanish ships for their treasures – he understood the other side of the coin too. And the fact of the matter remained the same: that while Elizabeth, as a Protestant ruler, continued to sit on the throne, Spain would prove a threat to England.

And Robert knew, that if the need ever arose, he would gladly give his life, knowing that he had fought and died to defend his Elizabeth.

June 1585
Amberley Castle, West Sussex

"Bess, bring me the new wig."

Queen Elizabeth and her court had moved to Amberley Castle, some sixty miles south of London, to avoid the city during the plague-riddled summer months.

Word had come from the Netherlands – after three months of silence due to bad weather at sea – that Robert had landed successfully, and that their troops had aided the Dutch Revolt enormously, leading Spain to retreat in fear.

But Elizabeth knew the truth.

Though the English army that she had sent, as well as the monetary aid, had no doubt helped to bulk out the Dutch army, Elizabeth had learned through Walsingham's spies that the true cause of the Spaniard's retreat to have been due to their own financial difficulties, rather than their fear of Elizabeth's army. Spain's inability to support their troops' needs in their ongoing war in the Netherlands was ultimately what had caused them to have to withdraw. And therefore, England's victory had been by default.

Elizabeth exhaled angrily as she thought of it, subconsciously stroking her thumb over her coronation ring with the miniature portrait of her mother hidden inside.

Bess brought the queen her newest wig in silence.

Elizabeth should be happy about the victorious news against Spain. And for a moment she had been. But it irked her to know that it had not been a deserving victory.

"In the years to come," Cecil had told her wisely, "No one will remember the specifics, your grace. They will remember only that England defeated Spain in the Dutch Revolt. History is never remembered in detail."

Elizabeth hoped he would be right. Though realising she would not know for many years to come gave her no peace.

But an unnerved disposition was becoming a common ailment for the queen of England; age and stress having caught up with her in recent years.

When Elizabeth thought of it now, she realised that her sudden need for wigs due to her thinning hair had begun soon after she had begun wearing her extravagant white paint. And she wondered now if perhaps something within it was causing her harm.

But she dismissed the notion almost as soon as it began to take form, for surely the only thing causing her harm was the incessant stressors of her life as England's monarch.

How I wish this fate had never fallen to me.

She sighed heavily then as Bess carefully placed the beautiful new wig over Elizabeth's balding head while Blanche stood beside her, ready to apply red rouge to her lips and cheeks.
Later, as Elizabeth and her ladies entered Amberley Castle's great hall to attend the Privy Council meeting, Elizabeth was surprised to see a new face sitting at the council table.

"Your majesty," the man said in greeting as he stood.

"Ambassador Mendoza, your grace," Cecil said in introduction, "He has been chosen to replace Feria who could not continue in his position due to his failing health."

"Mendoza," Elizabeth said coldly, caring little as to who would speak for Spain, knowing it did not matter when the communication was sour.

The members of the Privy Council took their seats with their old queen, and she was left shocked to see Mendoza resume his seat as though he were welcome.

"My lord," Walsingham said through gritted teeth, "You may leave."

"Leave?" Mendoza replied, dumbfounded, "As ambassador to *Espana* I have an obligation to my country to attend the meeting."

"Given our countries'...*disagreements* of late," Walsingham replied, "I should say you are not welcome."

Mendoza looked wide-eyed at England's queen as if he assumed she would jump to his defence, but she only stared him down icily.

He breathed a flabbergasted scoff but stood from his seat and made his way towards the exit.

"Now," Elizabeth said, turning her attention to her council, "Let us discuss our declaration to keep the Netherlands under England's protection."

She had said it purposefully loud enough for Mendoza to hear, unable to resist rubbing salt in Spain's fresh wounds.

Mendoza stopped in his tracks – where the former ambassador, Feria, would have feigned deafness – and Elizabeth was surprised to see the new imperial ambassador turning back around to face her.

"You speak of alliances against us," he called, "as though Spain will remain weak for long! But trust me, your grace, you will regret all this one day."

Walsingham, though old and frail, was up in a flash, his anger spurring him on, "You dare to threaten the queen of England in my presence!"

At the outburst, the queen's guards sprang into action, their swords drawn as though an army had come through the doors.

Mendoza smiled faintly, "It is no threat, sir," he replied calmly, though his eyes shone with arrogance, "King Filipe has been much disturbed by England for many years. Your pirates have done an excellent job at fuelling my master's rage. And your inability to punish them or return our stolen treasurers, well…it has been ignored for far too long. This business with the Dutch may have a positive outcome for you now, but *Espana* will regroup."

"I suggest you remove yourself from my presence, sir," Elizabeth called back casually, her lids heavy with boredom, "Your empty threats do not scare me."

Mendoza's face grew red, "Your majesty will regret the day you involved yourself in Spanish business! We know where the order comes from to sack our ships and steal our slaves –"

"Get him out of here!" Pembroke called loudly then, commanding the guards to remove the new and much feistier ambassador.

Two guards grabbed the man by the arms and began escorting him out, Mendoza raging angrily in Spanish.

Once he had quit the great hall and her council had resumed their seats, Elizabeth glanced over at her spymaster.

"Keep an eye on him, Walsingham," she mumbled emotionlessly, her mind heavy with the never-ending issues she had yet to address.

January 1586
Hampton Court Palace, London

"How goes the matter of religion?" Elizabeth asked as she lay a card down on the table.
Cecil, who sat opposite her, took his turn before replying, "The seminary priests continue to come, and we continue to execute them."
"And the people?"
Cecil sighed, the burden of the ongoing religious disputes throughout the country weighing him down in his old age.
"The Elizabethan Religious Settlement passed by your majesty has clearly failed to end religious disputes," he said.
Elizabeth nodded, "I had hoped that by now Catholicism would be a thing of the past within England."
Cecil raised his eyebrows and laid his cards down facing upwards, showing his winning hand, "Perhaps it would have been settled by now if we had followed in your sister's footsteps and simply removed those who opposed us… instead of allowing them to continue doing as they please as you have."
Elizabeth pursed her lips and shuffled the deck, "Mary failed during her reign," she replied sharply.
"No," Cecil replied, "Mary died before she had had time to succeed."
The statement hung between them heavily.
Elizabeth glanced up and him, her eyes narrowed threateningly, but Cecil continued.
"Your sister's rule may have been long and glorious as yours has been if only she had been well enough to continue on her

path," Cecil said, "and England may very well have been a fully Catholic nation yet again."

Elizabeth blinked and leaned forward, "What is your point?"

"My point, madam," he said with a knowing smile, "Is that we have been lucky that you have continued to thrive despite your resistance to marry and produce an heir. But the country remains within a religious crisis. Your sister Mary had a clear goal in mind – to regain Catholicism within England – and she might have very well succeeded had she lived. But what is your goal, your grace? When we are dead and gone, what will you leave behind but the same thing your sister left behind: a country fighting over how to pray."

Elizabeth raised her chin defiantly and stared her old advisor down, the truth in his words irking her more than even his continued winning streak, Cecil being the only person to have ever beaten her at cards.

"The people look to their monarch for direction," Cecil concluded with a bored sigh, "It is high time you give them it."

Chapter 23

March 1586

Cecil had, of course, been right. Elizabeth had known it for a long time.
Walking the cautious midway between Protestantism and Catholicism had been a beautiful idea, but the reality was that the common folk needed direction.
It was not their fault, Elizabeth thought. After all, they were not as educated or as intellectual as she; but it displeased her that even when they had been presented with the perfect consensus, they could not put their differences aside.
Her subjects' stupidity vexed Elizabeth. England could have been living harmoniously for so many years if they had only accepted her divine law of uniformity.
But Cecil had been right.
It seemed Catholicism would not simply die out and be forgotten as she had hoped it would, and Spanish and Italian martyrs would continue to plot against her as long as Catholics were allowed to live in her country.
Cecil had been right…her sister Mary had known how to deal with opposition: kill it before it could spread and infect the hearts of others.
Perhaps it was time to take a leaf out of her late sister's book.
Only…Elizabeth would have to take it that much further.

"What about heavy fines, your highness?" Pembroke suggested at the daily council meeting.

"Fines will not stop them," Walsingham replied, his wrinkled face creased in anger.

"Fines, threats of imprisonment, none of it will do," Elizabeth added, "It is time to be blunt. To *be* a Catholic must be, quite simply, high treason."

Pembroke – a Catholic – widened his eyes in shock, "My queen…"

Elizabeth waved her hand, as if to wipe the frightened look off his face, "You will be the exception, my lord," she said casually, and Pembroke's face drained of colour. Relief and dread running his blood cold.

Parliament, with a high majority of Protestants, passed the new law within the week.

And before long, a hundred and eighty Catholic priests, as well as civilians, were burned at the stake for denying the Protestant faith, joining the Spanish and Italian Catholic martyrs who died just the same way throughout the years.

April 1586

"I ask you to allow me leave from court, your majesty," Robert Dudley said a month later, unable to stomach the actions that were taking place right under his nose within London.

"Leave?" Elizabeth replied, her listless eyes flashing momentarily.

Robert only nodded his head once, maintaining eye contact with the queen.

He knew that she would know his reasons for wanting to distance himself. He had been quite vocal with his opinions on these new developments at council meetings, as well as in private.

He understood Elizabeth's fears and frustrations, perhaps more so than anyone else, but he believed there were other ways that she could protect herself without passing the death sentence to so many others.

Are their lives lesser than yours?

He had called the question out in a heated argument the night before, his stomach lurching with anxiety as the words left his mouth, for fear of confirmation for how he already knew she would answer.

Yes, she had hissed back.

It had been the moment he had dreaded for many years. The moment in which he realised that his Elizabeth was never to return, replaced by a hateful shadow of her former self.

And though there was nothing but a childless and loveless marriage awaiting him in the countryside, Robert knew there was far less left for him at court.

He only hoped now that she would grant him this one wish.

Elizabeth narrowed her eyes at him. Eyes he would have once happily stared into forever, but now they only made him shudder with unease.

He held his breath, praying she would offer him this one final act of kindness.

"No," she finally said.

And Robert considered if perhaps it would be less painful if he gave into death now, and to simply never breathed in again.

May 1586

Elizabeth had been suffering from a terrible toothache all week, and the side of her face had swollen up horribly.

She had retired to her chambers that midmorning, ordering all the shutters to be closed and not to be woken unless the Palace itself were on fire.

It came as a huge shock to the aging queen then when, not one hour into her rest, she was startled awake to the sound of thunderous banging on her door.

"Your majesty!" the male voice called, "Your majesty!"

Bess, who had been quietly sewing in the other room, hurried to the door while Blanche made Elizabeth presentable.

Once dressed, Elizabeth emerged from her chambers, "What is it?" she asked the messenger curtly, her tooth and gum throbbing uncontrollably.

"Walsingham," the messenger replied, "He has important news regarding Mary Queen of Scots."

Immediately, Elizabeth picked up her skirts, her pain no longer of significance, "Take me to him."

The queen was led through the Palace swiftly, the messenger leading her straight to Walsingham's chambers where he and two other men were leaning over a wooden table at its centre.

"My queen," Walsingham said in greeting and all three men bowed their heads as the messenger left, closing the door behind him.

"Speak," Elizabeth ordered with a slight lisp brought on by her swollen cheek and gums.

Walsingham extended his arm to the men beside him, "This is Gifford and Phelippes. They work for me," he said, and Elizabeth knew them then to be part of his network of spies, "Gifford here, he was placed in the Scottish Queen's household a year ago, working as a double agent to infiltrate the Scottish Queen's trust. He has been appointed within her household as her messenger."

Elizabeth nodded and Gifford bowed his head.

"He has copied many of Mary's letters and brought them to our attention whenever possible," Walsingham continued, "Phelippes here has been deciphering those letters."

"Deciphering?" Elizabeth parroted, furrowing her eyebrows.

"Some have been written in code, your highness," Phelippes replied with a grin, "A rather simple code."

Elizabeth ignored the remark and approached the table, "Show me," she said.

"So far there is not much to show, your grace," Walsingham replied as he handed her two letters with cyphers scribbled on them.

"What does it say?" she asked, looking at the three men before her.

Phelippes inhaled, "So far there is little of anything," he admitted, "But the cyphers alone are evidence enough that the queen of Scots aims to convey information in secret."

"Who were the letters intended for?" the queen asked, and all looked at Gifford.

"This one," Gifford said as he pointed one long finger at a letter, "was to Anthony Babington."

"Babington?" Elizabeth echoed, knowing him for a staunch Catholic. She looked at Walsingham for confirmation.

He nodded his head in response to her unspoken question, "I hear he continues loyal to the Catholic Church. He was recruited by a French Jesuit Priest some months ago according to my spies."

France.

"And the other?" the queen asked, looking down at the other letter.

Gifford cleared his throat, "This one was intended for imperial ambassador Mendoza."

"Mendoza..." Elizabeth breathed.

Spain.

"There is not much to go on yet," Walsingham said quickly as he noticed Elizabeth's mind working away, "There has been no mention of anything treasonous or of a plot."

"But the communication is open between her, a Catholic heir to my throne, and two Catholic nations who wish to depose me," Elizabeth replied.

Walsingham nodded, "We will continue to intercept their letters. Their code was easy to break according to Phelippes. We will know if they are planning anything."

Elizabeth flung the letters back down onto the table before gingerly placing her hand over her swollen cheek, her pain returned, "Yes," she said, "See to it that you do."

July 1586

Despite his mother being imprisoned for nineteen years and being investigated for high treason against queen Elizabeth, King James VI of Scotland had recently entered into correspondence with the queen of England.

Since he and his royal mother had had little to no relationship throughout the years due to her fleeing Scotland after his birth and being kept imprisoned in England, the young king felt no need to interfere with English matters in order to rescue her.

And though he would be eternally grateful to her for having brought him into this world, King James felt no familiarity to his natural mother. In fact, since his accession to the throne of Scotland at just one year old, he had received nothing but damning evidence to support his mother's misguided behaviour. And in truth, he was glad for her to remain where she was, so that he would not have to be the one to deal with the never-ending chaos that surrounded her.

And so, when queen Elizabeth herself made contact with him, proposing a peace agreement between their two countries, King James was eager to agree, if only to cease the long-standing dispute over Scotland and England's cross-border raiders.

An English diplomat, Thomas Randolph, was sent to Scotland to commence negotiations, and after a week of meetings, England and Scotland agreed on a final draft of their treaty.

The Treaty of Berwick, as it would be called, declared a mutual defensive alliance pact that would guarantee aid be sent to either country should they face foreign invasion. As largely Protestant countries, England and Scotland were therefore united should either be threatened by Catholic powers, such as Spain or France.

King James VI believed this treaty to be nothing but positive for him, his country gaining a powerful ally in England as well as opening communication with the heirless queen of England and the possibility of, one day, being named as her heir.

All he had to do, was maintain the peace between their two countries, and as a direct descendant of Henry VII, he may very well rule over Scotland *and* England one day...

Little did he know, that while he was blinded by the potential of ruling England in the future, with this new peace treaty, Elizabeth had strategically arranged for there to be no real repercussions from Scotland should the need arise for her to execute a certain Scottish Queen.

August 1586

While Elizabeth's inflamed gums and cheek subsided over the following month, her troubles regarding her cousin continued to intensify.

Walsingham's spies had uncovered many more letters between Mary Queen of Scots and her Spanish and French supporters in the past few weeks.

And through Phelippes' decoding, the depth of their plotting had emerged.

"The plan is to assassinate you," Walsingham stated late one night as he met the queen in her chambers.

Elizabeth's eyes glazed over, "Am I supposed to be shocked, Walsingham?" she asked, "It is not the first time there has been such a plan."

Walsingham shook his head, "No, but...this goes further. Spain and France support it. The Duke of Guise himself is readying sixty thousand men to invade England and put Mary on the throne. We *also* have the Scottish Queen's signed letter where she expressly agrees that you must be killed. At last, she openly orders her would-be rescuers to assassinate you."

Elizabeth inhaled deeply, then exhaled to calm her mind.

"Do we know of the traitors' whereabouts?" she asked coolly.

Walsingham grinned, flashing his crooked teeth, "We do."

September 1586

Thanks to the decoded letters, Elizabeth's order to arrest the traitors was met with much ease, Anthony Babington and his conspirators being completely unaware of their botched plans.

Babington and thirteen of his Catholic conspirators were arrested and tried at Westminster, and were found guilty of treason rather swiftly, the proof against them being undeniable.

They were all – wealthy courtiers as well as the Jesuit Priest who had recruited Babington – executed for their crimes before a crowd of thousands, so that everyone could witness the price paid for plotting against Elizabeth.

To follow were the arrests of Mary Queen of Scots' two secretaries and a clerk, who were all interrogated and sentenced to death for conspiracy against the crown.

They were hung, drawn, and quartered without mercy.

October 1586

"How goes my cousin's trial?" Elizabeth asked as she bent over and gently rolled her bowling ball along the lawn. The ball glided lazily towards a smaller ball upon the bowling greens, stopping just shy of its target.

The courtiers around her clapped at her roll, then the ladies beside her took their turns.

"The Scottish Queen continues to deny any involvement in the Babington Plot," Cecil said quietly, "Portions of the translated letters between herself and the conspirators were then read out in court. They were all signed by her. There is no room for denial."

"Good," Elizabeth replied, "I trust she will be convicted of treason soon."

"Walsingham has also produced Babington's written confession of the secret plot, as well as her secretaries'," Cecil continued as the courtiers surrounding them clapped at one of the bowlers beside Elizabeth.

The queen nodded, "Make sure she is dealt with," then she smiled, her brown teeth visible for all to see, "Soon, I shall rest easy at night knowing her conniving head has been stricken from her body."

January 1587

For several months since the signing of the Treaty of Berwick, forming a mutual alliance between England and Scotland, King James VI and Elizabeth had been participating in a friendly correspondence of letters.

Since his mother's official arrest and trial, however, king James had sent only the one letter, where he relinquished all words of friendship and addressed Elizabeth as a fellow monarch.

"He requests his mother be pardoned," Elizabeth mumbled as she handed Cecil the letter.

He scanned its contents, then looked up to meet his queen's tired gaze, "Will you oblige?"

Elizabeth raised her eyebrows, surprised at his need to ask the question.

"What do you think?"

February 1587

Elizabeth had not obliged, and just one month later, Mary Queen of Scots was condemned to die by the axe.

"Bess," the queen called, "Fetch me my fastest rider to convey a message."

Bess curtsied and left the queen's bedchamber as Elizabeth sat down at her writing desk.

"What is so important it cannot wait, your grace?" Blanche asked from her seat at the fireplace.

It was almost midnight, sleep having escaped Elizabeth of late since her cousin's execution had been scheduled.

By midday tomorrow, Mary Queen of Scots would be executed for treason against England's rightful queen, and though it gave Elizabeth a sense of calm, this night it had suddenly dawned on her that it would be a safer course of action to be rid of her cousin in a much less public manner. Scotland was unlikely to retaliate to the execution of their former sovereign, their love for her having evaporated many years ago. But Mary's Catholic allies in Spain and France would not take this act lightly, despite the fact that she had committed a mortal offence.

"This cannot wait," Elizabeth replied as she put quill to parchment.

Her messenger rode all night to deliver the letter to the Scottish Queen's custodian at Skipton Castle, where she was being held until her execution the following morning.

The custodian, Ralph Sadler, received the queen's messenger before the break of dawn, three hours before the scheduled execution.

He opened the letter in haste, wondering if perhaps the imprisoned queen would be pardoned at the last minute.

What he found instead was quite the opposite, and his eyes grew wide as he read the covert instruction for him to secretly assassinate his prisoner before her beheading.

Ralph Sadler looked up from the note and met the messenger's blank gaze, and it seemed not even he knew what heavy burden he had just delivered.

Sadler swallowed the acid rising in his throat and folded the note in half before nodding to the messenger, allowing him to leave.

He watched as the young man flung himself upon his steed and rode off, leaving behind nothing but a cloud of dust and an impossible decision.

8th February 1587
Fotheringhay Castle, Northamptonshire

Mary Queen of Scots was transported from Skipton Castle to Fotheringhay Castle, where her execution was to take place.

Ralph Sadler had decided to burn his queen's letter ordering him to murder her cousin before her public beheading.

As an old man of seventy-years of age, Sadler had believed it would be less dangerous in these, his final days, to refuse his queen in life, than to sully his soul for all eternity to do her bidding. Even if it meant imprisonment for his insubordination.

And so, the once queen of France and Scotland, mother to the noble king James VI of Scotland, entered the execution chamber.

She wore black robes as she approached the block, her head held high as she addressed her servants that they should not weep for her, for she would die a true woman to her religion.

Ralph Sadler realised then that queen Elizabeth had wanted to avoid this exact moment: where an executed Catholic queen became a Catholic martyr.

He was pulled out of his own thoughts when the lady was suddenly disrobed, her black garments falling to the ground to reveal a deep red dress underneath – the Catholic colour of martyrdom – confirming his suspicions.

Sadler's stomach lurched at the thought that perhaps he ought to have done as his queen had asked of him, after all.

But it was too late.

He would have to live with his choice and be damned for anything that may come from it.

Mary knelt on the cushion before the block then and laid her head down before stretching out her arms, signalling the axeman to do his duty.

"Into thy hands, O Lord, I commend my spirit!" the Queen of Scots called passionately then, and the axe came down heavily, landing – to the horror of the public – on the back of her head.

The crowd exclaimed in alarm before the axeman took another swing, this time to the neck. But the head remained attached.

With a third blow, the head became severed from the body and the executioner bent down to pick it up by its hair, only for it to fall to the ground with a wet *thump*.

The crowd gasped and cried out to see the axeman holding the dead queen's bright orange wig in his hand, then all eyes fell to the grey, short-haired head on the ground.

The room fell deathly still for a moment, and then a tiny mewling was heard.

The executioner looked around himself and followed the high-pitched sound to the headless body by the block. He lifted the red skirts then, and to the crowd's shock, revealed the Scottish Queen's little Skye terrier, trembling with fright and soaked in its owner's blood.

Chapter 24

February 1587
Hampton Court Palace, London

"We should keep her body hidden so it cannot be used as a relic," Cecil whispered to Elizabeth as soon as word arrived at Hampton Court Palace of Mary's successful beheading.
Elizabeth nodded as she stared, glassy-eyed, into the distance.
"See to it that her clothes are burned," the queen added as she rubbed her jawline gently, her toothache having returned once again, "I want nothing of hers to remain. Keep her body hidden at Fotheringhay for six months. Then bury it in a secret ceremony at Peterborough Cathedral."
Cecil bowed deeply and exited the queen's chambers.
Her cousin, Queen Mary of Scots, was finally dead. And with her death came an overwhelming sense of peace to know that there was no longer another claimant to her throne.
Elizabeth inhaled deeply and closed her eyes, a faint smile playing on her wrinkled lips despite the intense pain she felt.
Her abrupt wish for a secret assassination of her cousin had failed, for reasons Elizabeth was not yet entirely certain of. Perhaps the messenger had arrived too late, or Sadler had not had a chance with so little forewarning. It irritated Elizabeth slightly to know she could have avoided such a public execution, one where Mary Stuart had been created a martyr.
But her cousin was dead. The outcome had been the same. It was enough for Elizabeth.
Though, she would have to make sure no one would ever find out of her last-minute attempt to murder Mary. After all, her image of the innocent, virgin queen was at stake.

"Walsingham!" she called then, to which her young lady Bess hurried out the room and returned within minutes with the queen's spymaster.

"My queen?" he said.

"Leave us," she ordered her ladies, and watched patiently as they quit the room.

Then Elizabeth turned to her spymaster and smiled sweetly, though her rotting teeth did little to support the angelic look.

"I have two people I need taking care of, Walsingham."

The old man nodded once, awaiting his instructions.

"Ralph Sadler," she stated, "and the messenger boy who rode out to Skipton Castle on the eve of Mary's execution."

Walsingham swallowed, his Adam's apple bobbing up and down, "Any particular fashion, your grace?" he asked.

Elizabeth licked her red lips and smirked, "Discreetly."

March 1587

Just as she had hoped, Scotland did not retaliate after the execution of their former queen, their mutual defence against foreign invasion being too important to throw away over the death of someone they themselves did not deem important enough to rescue in the nineteen years she had been imprisoned.

The correspondence from king James VI, however, stopped entirely, dispelling his and Elizabeth's earlier friendship into the wind.

And before long, king James began to reconcile with other monarchs of Europe, in the hope of ridding himself of the need for an English alliance, in favour of alliances with monarchs who did not so easily commit regicide.

April 1587

The toothache had become unbearable, and Elizabeth would spend days groaning in pain, the side of her face swollen and tender.

"We must pull the offending tooth, your majesty," her physician told her.

Elizabeth shook her head wildly, her eyes wide with fear.

The queen's rotten, black teeth had become a popular talking point of late. And ladies of the court – and common folk alike – having even been reported to be purposefully blackening their teeth with soot to achieve the queen's famous look.

"It will hurt only for a moment," the queen's physician told her. But she continued to shake her head, tears welling in her eyes.

She was frightened, there was no denying it. Pain was something Elizabeth did not seek out willingly, her threshold for it being extremely low.

And the sharp pain she had been experiencing of late throughout the entire side of her face hurt more than any pain she had ever endured. Sometimes it even travelled down her neck or up into her ear. Piercing shooting pains, stabbing her from within.

Her doctors told her they had to pull it to alleviate the pain. And yet, the thought of it being pulled sent her into a panic.

How she wished Robert would be here to soothe her... but he was fighting his own ailment of late, claiming fatigue and retiring early in the evenings. In fact, she hardly ever saw him anymore.

And though it had previously upset her to think he was avoiding her, it only angered her now to think that he was not by her side when she needed his comfort.

The physician was still awaiting her consent to remove the tooth, his old watery eyes looking down at her sympathetically.

Elizabeth shook her head again, turning away from him like a petulant child.

"Might I be so bold as to offer up one of my own teeth for demonstration, your grace?" a voice spoke up from behind the physician.

It was the Bishop of London, John Aylmer, a man well into his seventies who had very few teeth left to spare.

"Demonstration?" Elizabeth slurred.

"To show your grace that, while it will hurt, it is not as bad as you may imagine," the bishop explained with a small smile.

Elizabeth looked from the bishop to the physician before her, unsure of how to respond.

But after a moment she realised it could not hurt – *her*, at least – if she were to observe the demonstration. After all, it didn't mean she would have to go through with her own extraction.

She nodded her head and sat upright in her bed for a better view of the procedure.

The old bishop sat down on a chair beside the queen's bed then and bravely opened his mouth.

"Which one?" the physician asked the bishop, unsure which of the four teeth to choose.

The bishop shrugged, it did not matter to him, having so few already.

Then he squeezed his eyes shut and prepared himself. The doctor reached inside the old man's gaping mouth with the pliers and, with a loud *crunch*, ripped out one of John Aylmer's perfectly healthy teeth.

The bishop cried out only for a moment before closing his mouth and swallowing hard – swallowing blood, Elizabeth assumed, and she grimaced at the thought.

"See?" the bishop said easily, as though it were nothing.

Elizabeth looked from the bishop's face to the tooth in the doctor's hand. It was longer than Elizabeth had imagined.

A sharp pain shot up Elizabeth's face then like a lightning bolt to the brain as her rotten tooth continued to attack her senses.

There was nothing left to do, she could not live with this pain for the rest of her life. The tooth had to come out.

She sighed and leaned her head back, "Just do it," she ordered before opening her mouth as wide as she could.

The physician tried not to recoil from the stench that wafted out from her majesty's mouth, and before she could change her mind, he reached inside and yanked the offending tooth out, causing Elizabeth to scream as though she had just been ripped apart limb by limb.

May 1587

Since Sir Walter Raleigh's return from his latest journey from the Americas, Elizabeth had grown rather fond of the handsome sailor.

His appeal had first come to the queen's attention when he and Sir Francis Drake had brought back their stolen shipment of Spanish sugar. At the time she had thought her excitement to derive principally from the product he had returned – sugar being by far her favourite thing to eat – but in recent months, queen Elizabeth had noticed that he too seemed to enjoy her company.

Though they had never spoken privately, Elizabeth had noticed a cheeky glint in his eyes whenever he addressed her in public. His lopsided smile from across the table at banquets too, felt to the queen as though he were openly flirting with her.

The idea was preposterous of course, and she told herself this on occasion, since she was a woman of fifty-four and he a striking young man of thirty.

But Elizabeth enjoyed the flirtation all the same and had even commanded that he no longer accompany Francis Drake on his travels and stay at her court instead. Her need to feel desired suddenly taking precedence even over her need to increase England's riches.

Robert had been fighting illness for many months now, and Elizabeth could not help but think his symptoms to be faked, or at least exaggerated, so that he would have an excuse to remain absent from her.

His obvious disappointment in her actions in most recent years exasperated her beyond measure, and so she did not always demand his presence when he locked himself away. However, she could also not bring herself to allow him to leave London to be with his wife, the hatred she felt for her former lady-in-waiting continuing to eat away at her.

In Robert's absence, Elizabeth would enjoy what little excitement was offered to her, especially if it came directly from a rugged adventurer.

"A puddle, your majesty," Raleigh pointed out then as he, Elizabeth and her ladies walked leisurely through the palace gardens.

Elizabeth looked down at the small puddle before her and raised her foot to step over it when Raleigh flung off his coat and laid it carefully on the ground, covering it.

"Your majesty," he said as he bowed and grinned, as though he had done a great deed.

Elizabeth furrowed her brows but laughed, before continuing her walk over his coat.

It was silly little things such as that which gave Elizabeth so much joy. When she was around Raleigh she felt as though all her queenly troubles did not matter. She felt young again, despite her ailing body.

"I'd like to create Sir Walter Raleigh, Captain of the Guard," Elizabeth proclaimed later that day to her Privy Council.

Cecil nodded and scribbled a note.

"Whatever for?" Robert asked then, his dark eyes narrowed in suspicion.

Elizabeth looked at him, "In your absence," she said, "He has proven to be a loyal servant. You would know that if you chose to grant me with your presence."

"I have not been well, El – your grace," Robert replied, his pained voice rattling in his chest.

Elizabeth raised her invisible eyebrows and waved his comment aside, indicating her disbelief.

"Nevertheless, see to it that it's done Sir William," Elizabeth continued, "Those who serve me well," she said as she glanced at Robert from the corner of her eyes, "Will be rewarded. And those who do not...well, they will be replaced."

December 1587

For a time, Elizabeth was at peace.

Though her body was achy and haggard – her black teeth causing her much pain – Elizabeth rested easily knowing that with her cousin's death, there would be no more cause for religious rebellion from her people. For without the Catholic's figurehead, Protestant England would continue victorious.

However, as time went on, the calm became increasingly perturbing, like a breeze whistling over motionless waters on a dark night at sea. And after some time, Elizabeth was restless once again, her many years as queen having taught her that peace never did last long.

Her increasingly uneasy feeling was confirmed when, on a repetitively quiet day, a messenger came thundering into the throne room.

"Your majesty!" he shouted at the top of his lungs as he pushed past the ignorant courtiers, "I bring urgent news! From Spain!"

At the mention of Spain, Elizabeth was up from her throne as quickly as her old body allowed, "Let him through!" she commanded, and the crowd parted like the red sea.

"Their plans are accelerating. There is talk of –"

"Invasion," Elizabeth mumbled, having known the news before it had been uttered.

Then a horrified cry echoed through the crowd before her.

"Our ships are longer 'n' faster, y' grace," Sir Francis Drake assured her as he, the queen, and her Privy Council walked hastily through the palace on their way to the council chambers, "They're more manoeuvrable than t' bulky Spanish ships," Drake continued, "The decks fore 'n' aft being longer also allow our ships t' carry more guns. They fire lethal broadsides!"

Elizabeth only continued to stare straight ahead, and Drake looked above her wigged head to Sir Walter Raleigh, who nodded in silent agreement.

Once they entered the council chambers and dispersed to their seats, Elizabeth took her seat at the head of the table and swallowed, "Suggestions?" she asked, her dread rendering her almost speechless.

She had known this day would come. She had been preparing England for it for decades.

And yet, the old queen could not deny that her blood was running cold ever since the messenger had brought the terrible news of war.

After twenty years of agonising the Spanish king with her support of the pirate raids of his ships, as well as her involvement in the war in the Netherlands, Elizabeth was actually surprised that this day had not come sooner.

One of Walsingham's spies entered the room then and whispered in the spymaster's ear, "The execution of the Scottish Queen is what seems to have influenced this attack," Walsingham said after the man had left once again, quick as a shadow, "She was their Catholic ally after all. They are avenging her."

And there it was: the repercussion Elizabeth knew would come from publicly executing her cousin, Mary Queen of Scots.

She exhaled sharply, "Regardless of their reasons," she said, as though it did not matter. But it did. For she only had herself to blame, "We need to ready our men," she ordered, "Walsingham, continue to gather intelligence about the timing and route of their attack. We must know the number of ships and troops they have sent."

Walsingham stood and bowed his head before quitting the room to spread the word to his network of spies.

"Sir William," Elizabeth continued.

"Your grace."

"I want imperial ambassador Mendoza removed from my court."

Cecil frowned, "Removed?"

"Thrown out," Elizabeth replied, "Expelled. He is a snake in the grass and an informant to Spain."

Cecil looked around at the council table as if to ask them for aid in this conversation, "That is his job," he said confusedly.

Elizabeth slammed her hands down upon the table and stood tall above them then, "*Cecil!*" she shrieked, "Get him out of my court or I swear to God, I will run him through myself if I come across him in my country!"

Elizabeth put Lord Howard of Effingham in charge of England's defence against the Spanish fleet. Though he was a much less experienced sailor than Sir Francis Drake,

Effingham was an able commander and had the support of the nobility.

Elizabeth also knew him for an open-minded man, with a willingness to listen to others who may be more experienced than he. His noble lineage also gave him the authority that would be needed to keep big egos, such as Drake's, in check.

Sir Francis Drake was appointed Vice-Admiral of the fleet instead, his expertise in navigating against the bulky Spanish ships being of vital importance.

Walsingham's spies continued to gather information from all corners of Europe, aiding Elizabeth to strategize before the inevitable attack took place.

And Lord Robert Earl of Leicester was put in charge of the land army at Tilbury, on the Thames, in case Spain successfully docked on English shores.

July 1588

Six months later, the Spanish Armada was sighted off the coast of Cornwall. England had had time to prepare, and a series of beacons were lit along the coast, the warning spreading – quite literally – like wildfire.

"Send in the fleet at Plymouth," Elizabeth ordered as soon as news reached London.

The English fleet was sent in and attempted to disrupt the Spanish ships' passage. Canons were shot and some damage was done to a handful of the heavy Spanish ships, but it was not enough to stop the Armada on their path.

That night, the queen and her council met in the empty throne room, lit only by a handful of torches along the stone walls, shadows flickering eerily in every corner.

"The Armada has anchored off of Calais," Walsingham informed Elizabeth, his voice echoing in the large hall, "They are no doubt awaiting another army to join their forces."

"We need to take advantage of this," Robert said passionately, his voice still sounding raw, his illness continuing to weaken him despite Elizabeth's initial disbelief of it.

He cleared his throat, hoping to sound stronger than he felt, "Send in the fireships," he said, "Burn them down in the night when they least expect it."

Elizabeth looked around at the four men before her, all of them nodding in agreement with Robert's suggestion. Then she raised her head, "Send in the fireships!" as though it had been her idea all along.

Although no Spanish ships caught fire, the swift attack in the night panicked the Spaniards, and all one-hundred-and-fifty ships scattered out to sea to avoid the English fireships.

A day of fighting ensued between the two fleets, one which saw English ships on the losing side of battle. As the sound of cannons and shouting continued into the evening, a strong wind had begun to pick up, blowing the Spanish ships dangerously close to shore. To avoid their heavy bottomed vessels wrecking on the rocks beneath the shallow waters, they had no other choice but to sail northward in disorder after several of their ships had already been lost due to the sudden change in weather.

"They are fleeing," Elizabeth mumbled when news came.

"Luck was on our side, your grace," Cecil remarked quietly as he leaned forward, "Our ships were taking heavy damage, and we were likely to be on the losing end of this attack. The winds were in our favour."

Elizabeth sighed and licked her lips while looking around her chambers, gauging her ladies' distance from the conversation far enough to allow a safe response.

"*God* was in our favour," she claimed, "It was not luck."

"Call it what you will, your grace," Cecil said wisely, "But it was not your strategy or manpower."

A muscle ticked in Elizabeth's jaw at the snub.

"And if they try to return," Cecil continued, too old to care about having to stroke the queen's ego, "you'd best pray to *God* that he sends another bought of wind to hold them off!"

Three days after the Spanish fleet had been blown to the North Sea by the heavy winds, Walsingham brought news that the Armada had tried to turn back around in direction of England to continue the onslaught.

"The winds at sea remain," he stated to his queen as she sat upon her throne in the great hall, "It will likely prevent them from successfully returning."

"Are you certain?" Elizabeth asked, her blue eyes narrowed pensively as she fumbled agitatedly with her coronation ring.

Perhaps God was on our side after all...

"Lord Howard of Effingham and his fleet pursued them for two days," Walsingham said, "He sent word that it appears they are retreating."

Elizabeth broke out in a wide, black-toothed smile. She would use this piece of information to her advantage.

"Spread the word of imminent invasion!" she bellowed, her voice reverberating off the high ceilings.

The members of the Privy Council looked at each other in confusion, "Your majesty?" Robert asked weakly.

"England must be ready for the worst," she continued as she walked down the three steps and past her puzzled advisors.

Pembroke looked at Cecil, silently asking if Elizabeth had perhaps not understood the good news.

Cecil shook his head and shrugged in response.

Not even he knew what the queen was planning.

❖

Within just a few hours, chaos had spread throughout London and its surrounding districts.

By now, word had circulated that England was moments away from impending doom at the hands of the terrifying Spaniards. And yet Elizabeth knew the truth: that England was safe, the winds having continued too strong for the bulky Spanish ships to navigate back to her shores.

With this knowledge, Elizabeth dressed slowly while Robert sent word for the queen's warhorse to be readied.

When the queen was comfortably sat in her saddle, she and her guards followed Robert's lead to Tilbury, where his army awaited, having been expecting a land attack for several days.

"What are you planning, Elizabeth?" Robert asked as they rode ahead in a slow trot.

"England is fear-stricken," she said, as though he were somehow unaware of the obvious, "I shall address my people and my soldiers and stand with them in this fight."

"But," Robert replied, "There will be no fight."

She waved his comment aside, "The people do not know that."

Robert frowned at her, "What are you doing, Elizabeth?" he asked, and the turmoil in his voice caused Elizabeth to slow her horse to a walk, and she looked at him, "I need this victory to be remembered," she admitted, sounding unexpectedly like a fearful child.

Robert blinked, "My queen," he said, "England has fought off the Spanish Armada. Of course, it shall be remembered."

The queen looked over her shoulder at the guards following some paces behind, then back at Robert, "I need this victory to be mine. My own," she admitted quietly, "Not the *wind's*. Not God's. Mine."

"And you need the country in chaos for that?" he asked, dumbfounded.

She spurred her horse ahead, resuming her trot. Robert followed suit.

"You don't understand," she said, "You never have."

Robert continued to look head, silent for a moment while he tried to suppress the sour taste in his mouth, "You're right," he admitted then, "I have never understood most of what you have done. You claimed the throne, though you seemed to not even have wanted it. You rejected my love time and time again though you appeared to need it. You feared Spain though you antagonized king Filipe with your antics. Tell me, your grace, how am I to understand when you continue to defy logic."

Elizabeth's expression was blank. She did not reply.

He looked down at her attire then, his anger having opened a floodgate, and he was finally unable to suppress his bitterness.

"Should you not have, at least, worn armour if you're to be believed that you're heading into battle?"

He glanced at the queen's white velvet dress, with only a small steel cuirass strapped to her chest, and then shook his head at her.

Elizabeth raised an eyebrow, "Perhaps," she admitted, feeling suddenly more worried that her ruse of imminent war would not be believed, above even the worry she felt at having lost Robert's love.

And though it pained her soul, she realised then that she had made the right decision in choosing her duty over her own happiness, for it appeared she was more like her late father than she had ever wanted to believe.

August 1588
Tilbury, Essex

"My loving people!" the queen called out when she and her riding party arrived before Robert's army at Tilbury, "I am come amongst you, as you see, at this time, not for my amusement or display, but being determined, in the midst and heat of the battle, to live and die amongst you all! To lay down for my God, and for my kingdom, and my people!"

A murmur of admiration began to bubble from among the crowd at the queen's noble presence and her words, many craning their necks to admire her bravery for themselves.

Elizabeth continued passionately, her voice booming above the crashing of the waves behind her, "I know I have the body of a weak and feeble woman... but I have the heart and stomach of a king! If Spain or any prince of Europe should dare to invade the borders of my realm, I myself will take up arms, and be your general, judge, and rewarder of every one of your virtues in the field," she paused and cast her eyes over the men, "We shall shortly have a famous victory over these enemies of my God, of my kingdom, and of my people!"

She had given her speech, the one she had prepared to pledge her life to support her soldiers if the need for battle arose. She had proclaimed herself one of them, showing strength and unity against the greatest threat England had faced in decades.

Her words and her grit would surely be remembered, even if an actual battle were never to occur.

The queen's party made camp near the shore of Tilbury, and the queen awaited the threat along with her loyal soldiers. Day and night they waited, warming themselves by the fires at night and watching the dark horizon for a glimpse of lit beacons.

But then the rays of the dawn began to pinken the night sky.

And as the sun rose, fabricated news came to inform them that Spain had fled in fear of their brave and glorious monarch and her army.

And so, Queen Elizabeth had proven victorious in her people's eyes, and soon word spread all over the country that in her might, their queen had defeated the Spanish Armada.

If only they had known the truth.

Chapter 25

September 1588

After Elizabeth's great success, she allowed Robert to return to his home in the country in the hope that he would finally recover from his ongoing ailment.
With the threat of Mary Queen of Scots, as well as the Spanish Armada, gone, Elizabeth had begun to believe that Robert's affection for her would surely return, now that her biggest enemies were defeated.
But she had noticed how he looked at her of late, his dark eyes emotionless and disinterested. It pained her to imagine that his love for her had ended, for it had been the one constant in her life that she had always known she could count on.
She hoped some time away would incite some of his former passion for her. At the very least, the clean air would do his health some good.
But, despite Elizabeth's hopes, Robert did not recover.
And soon after his departure to his home at Cornbury in Oxfordshire, the queen received word that her Master of Horse, her favourite, the love of her life, had died.

"It has been eight days!" Walsingham hissed as Cecil and he walked hastily through the Palace, on their way to a council meeting without its leader, their queen.
Upon receiving news of Robert Dudley's passing, Elizabeth had fallen to her knees and shrieked in agony, clutching the note to her chest as if it were a bandage that could stop the bleeding in her heart.
Her ladies had hurried her to her chambers, where she remained day and night, receiving no one except for Blanche and Bess.

"It cannot go on!" the queen's old spy master said now, shaking his head angrily.

Cecil stopped before opening the doors to the council chamber, "What would you have me do?" he asked, "Break down her majesty's doors and force her to rejoin the living?"

Walsingham raised his bushy, white eyebrows and nodded curtly, "She is the Virgin Queen!" he replied, "The death of her *married* courtier should not affect her so."

Cecil exhaled sharply through his nose, then nodded his balding head, his hand hovering over the door handle as he thought, "Perhaps it is time I coax her out of this melancholy."

"How?" Walsingham asked.

Cecil smiled, "You forget," he said, "I have access to all court documents. Many of which the late Robert Dudley wrote and signed himself."

Walsingham narrowed his eyes in confusion.

"If her majesty cannot rouse herself from her grief," Cecil explained as he turned the doorknob, "then perhaps a letter from beyond the grave from her beloved will give her the strength she needs to carry on."

The following day, a sheepish Cecil knocked on the queen's door only to be addressed by her lady Blanche, who spoke to him through the closed wooden door.

"Yes?" she called.

"I bring a letter for her majesty," he said.

"Slide it underneath, my lord," Blanche suggested.

Cecil smiled, knowing that would have been the answer. He did as he was bid.

"I beg you to tell her majesty," he called through the door, "That I pray for her forgiveness in the lateness of this letter."

He heard rustling as Blanche picked it up and turned the letter around in her hand before gasping at the wax seal.

"It is from Lord Robert," Blanche whispered to herself in shock.

It had been easy to procure Lord Robert's seal, since the queen had been too grief-stricken to order the removal of his possessions from his chambers.

He heard the lady scurry away to give the queen the letter. Then Cecil hung his head at the closed door before him and smiled sadly, silently praying that God would forgive him this small treachery to his queen.

He thought of a different betrayal then, one he had orchestrated many years ago to keep the queen from marrying that poor fool, Dudley. And Cecil wondered if God would forgive him for that, too.

He turned away from the queen's chambers then and shook his head at himself as he walked off through the dark corridors.

Surely God had already forgiven him for his actions – after all, they had been done for the good of the kingdom and the people. To sacrifice one woman's happiness surely did not measure up to the long-lasting wellbeing of an entire nation.

And yet, the old man thought, *Robert had been the only one she had been willing to marry. And if I had not interfered, England might have had at least one Protestant heir to succeed Elizabeth…*

He sighed deeply as he walked slowly towards his empty chambers, his old knees aching from the walk. He had acted on his best intentions at the time. How could he have known that she would never marry during her lifetime… no royal woman in her position had ever chosen that lonely path before.

God would forgive him. Cecil believed that He would.

But whether he would forgive himself…of that, he was not so sure.

"It is a letter, your majesty," Blanche said quietly as she handed it to Elizabeth, "Baron Burghley asks that you forgive its lateness."

The queen lay motionlessly in her great royal bed, its thick curtains drawn to enclose Elizabeth in her grief.

She lay there without her white ceruse and without her wig, looking twice as old as she was due to the pain of her loss.

The queen waved her hand in the air, signalling to Blanche that she was not interested.

"It is..." Blanche said, before pausing and clearing her throat, readying herself for her mistress' reaction, "It's from Lord Robert."

Elizabeth turned to look at her with bewildered eyes before forcing herself upright into a sitting position.

Blanche passed her the folded note and watched as Elizabeth's trembling hands tore open the seal.

Then Blanche took young Bess by the hand and exited the bedchamber to give their queen some privacy.

Elizabeth was alone, and while she had pealed the wax seal open, she continued only to stare at the letter, her chest heaving as she struggled with each intake of breath.

This would be Robert's last words to her. He had no doubt intended to send this before he had died...its late arrival proving that he had been unable to dispatch it in time.

She wanted to read it...more than anything...and yet she dreaded its contents.

Had he known he was dying as he had written this? Had he filled it with words of everlasting love and of meeting in the afterlife? Or had he remained true to his more recent feelings? Where he had quite clearly detested the person she had become.

Elizabeth could wonder no longer. She had to know.

And so, as she steeled herself for the worst, Elizabeth unfolded the letter, praying that she would find words of wisdom that would enlighten her on how to live in this world without him.

The following day, Elizabeth emerged from her chambers looking much recovered despite her thinner frame.
The dark circles under her eyes had been easily concealed with four layers of her white paint, her almost bald head hidden underneath a bright red, coiffed wig.
To the world she appeared the same as ever, and only her ladies and her council would know that she had been quite ready to give up on life not twenty-four hours prior.

"Whatever you have done has worked," Walsingham pointed out to Cecil quietly as the queen glided past them on her way to her throne in the great hall.
Cecil nodded, his guilt evaporating as he witnessed the positive outcome of his meddling.

"I would ask *what* you did," Walsingham whispered, "But I would prefer to be free of implication, should your interference come to light."
Cecil breathed a laugh as he watched Elizabeth sit down upon her throne and greet the noble lords and ladies with a great, black-toothed smile on her face.

"I am not worried," Cecil said smugly.
He had been right to be conceited, for their queen's lust for life had returned swiftly upon receiving that letter, as if the words had spurred her into believing that, though Robert was dead, their love would live on, eternal.
Yet, Cecil had known the truth; he had known it for many years:
That Robert Dudley had ceased to love the queen rather a long time ago.
But Cecil's letter had fooled her into believing differently. And in doing so, it had achieved its goal – to remind the queen of her duties to the realm. And that was all that mattered.

And so, Elizabeth had been fooled – just as she had been fooled over four decades prior – by a letter written in Robert's name, to achieve another man's earthly desires.

This time however, instead of ruining her, it had restored her.

1590

Life at court went on, though many of Elizabeth's courtiers and friends had started dying in quick succession. Their faces would be replaced by younger ones each month, their sons and daughters attending court in their stead, claiming their parent's titles with their passing.

It made Elizabeth feel old. And she did not like it, for it made her realise that her time, too, was fast approaching.

England's development had been on the rise once again since the retreat of the Spanish Armada, the influx of slaves and gold continuing through the queen's support of Drake's expeditions to the Americas.

And with that continuous influx of riches, Elizabeth chose to focus it entirely on the preservation of her memory.

Elizabeth understood the power her image could convey, having been a successful *female* powerhouse for over four decades; surviving assassination attempts, outsmarting other male monarchs, and even *defeating* the great Spanish Armada. Elizabeth knew she was seen as a power to be reckoned with. She had set many fashion trends, ladies blackening their teeth with soot being but one of the many examples she had set as a beauty standard over the years.

And yet, it was not enough for Elizabeth to be remembered in life. To make sure her glory – and therefore her mother's great sacrifice – would be remembered, Elizabeth would have to make sure to also be remembered in death.

She began by commissioning for great statues to be erected of her holding her coronation orb and sceptre – a reminder of how far she had come. She also contracted several painters to paint her portrait; grand images of her in all her glory, covered in jewels, diamonds and beautiful garments. Paintings that would live on throughout the centuries.

As well as imprinting her image upon the world, Elizabeth, through her great love of theatre since its permanent establishment in England some fifteen years prior, commissioned for many more playhouses to be built in London.

The queen's support of the arts throughout her reign had led to an impressive growth in the entertainment industry, and many playwrights and poets – such as William Shakespear and Edmund Spenser – showed their thanks for her support by contributing numerous references to their queen in their plays and poems.

Just as she had hoped they would.

One day, Edmund Spenser, a poet who had been employed as a secretary by nobles within the queen's court, went one step further from mere mentions, and published a poem he named 'The Faerie Queene'. This poem was set in a mythical 'Faerie Land' where the virginal Faerie Queene overcomes many symbolic struggles. And Spenser openly admitted that this 'Queene' was inspired directly by his own monarch, Queen Elizabeth.

"Tell me," Elizabeth said as she looked down at her subject with a smile upon his invitation to stand before her, "what gave you cause to write this work?"

Edmund Spenser bowed, "Your most gracious majesty," he drawled, starstruck at the sight of Elizabeth sitting grandly on her throne in the great hall, "I was particularly offended by the *disgusting* propaganda that circulated of late in the Catholic circles since your cousin's execution."

A muscle ticked in Elizabeth's jaw, but her frozen smile remained.

"Catholicism is the anti-religion, as we can all agree," he continued, and the court behind him murmured in agreement, "I used this sentiment as a backdrop for the battles in the poem, representing your majesty as the light – the Faerie Queene – and Rome as those who would oppose her."

The queen continued to smile at Spenser, blinking slowly as she took in his words, before grabbing the opportunity he had presented.

"I would like to see it continued," she declared.

"Your majesty?" Spenser asked, his brows furrowed.

"See to it that you publish more poems to follow the…Faerie Queene's… journey."

Spenser's eyes widened and he bowed, speechless at her grand request, his career as a poet being cemented for all eternity right before his very eyes.

"I shall also commission for a play to be created of it," Elizabeth continued as Spenser looked up at her, hanging onto her every word, "And it shall be shown in every theatre in London."

And that it did.

Edmund Spenser's work of the noble and virginal Faerie Queene was enjoyed throughout most of England, nobles and common folk alike hearing of the Faerie Queene which had been inspired by their very own. And within mere months, Elizabeth's favourite playwright, William Shakespeare, created a play with Edmund's Spenser's poem as inspiration.

A play where the strong and fierce Faerie Queene, Titania, rules over her country facing constant attacks from evil, and she fights them off nobly, light defeating dark.

This play would be shown for many years to come; Elizabeth even dubbing it her favourite play of all time, in the hope that it would be remembered throughout the ages.

This play was named: A Midsummer Night's Dream.

January 1591

Ever since Robert's passing two years prior, Elizabeth had begun waking up every morning before the dawn, under the guise of needing more time to apply the many layers of white paint to her face and body. But in truth, Elizabeth could not find peace in her sleep.

Her ladies buzzed around her for hours to ensure their queen looked her best, applying red rogue to her cheeks and bright red lipstick to her lips once the ceruse had had time to set.

Then they dressed her and applied one of her many extravagant wigs, several of which had beautiful feathers or jewels sewn into them.

Once the queen was ready for the day ahead, it was customary for her of late to stand before her mirror and assess their handiwork, Blanche and Bess having learned long ago that silence was their only form of thanks, for if she were displeased, there would be a barrage of insults.

On this day, Elizabeth remained silent as she observed herself in the looking glass, and her ladies behind her visibly relaxed knowing they had succeeded in avoiding reprimanding.

And yet, the queen continued to look for longer than was usual, up to a point where Bess stole a nervous glance at Blanche beside her. But then Elizabeth broke the silence.

"Have I done enough?" she asked quietly, her eyes glazed over as she stared back at herself hauntingly.

Bess opened her mouth to speak but Blanche nudged her gently with her elbow before shaking her head. Their queen was not addressing them.

The ladies watched as Elizabeth took a step closer to the full-length mirror and held out a hand, as though she would reach inside and pull out an answer to her own question.

Then she dropped her hand and clenched it closed before her, "Has it been enough to rewrite it?" she whispered eerily.

Blanche noticed Elizabeth stroking her coronation ring with her thumb as she continued to stare unseeingly into the mirror. She wore it on her wedding ring finger, symbolising her 'marriage to the country' as she had so passionately declared all those years ago.

Bess pulled at Blanche's sleeve then, "What do we do?" she whispered.

Blanche shook her head, *nothing.*

Then she looked back at Elizabeth, who continued to fumble with the ring, and Blanche noticed how it did not move about as it should. Perhaps she ought to suggest to her majesty to have it cleaned…since she had not once taken it off her finger in nearly fifteen years.

Elizabeth sighed deeply then, her eyes blinking quickly as though she were waking from a trance.

Then she turned to her ladies and smiled, before heading towards the door.

"Are you well, your grace?" Bess asked, unable to help herself.

Elizabeth frowned but ignored her entirely, and Bess looked over at Blanche who raised her eyebrows as if to say *told you.*

The queen's usher announced her, and the sea of courtiers parted to allow Elizabeth through.

As she sat down on her throne, two of her advisors, Cecil and Pembroke, approached her as the rest of the courtiers dispersed into various groups, gossiping or taking seats at game tables to try their luck at cards and backgammon.

"Where is Walsingham?" the queen asked, a deep frown etched between her invisible brows.

Cecil looked at Pembroke beside him before clearing his throat.

"Walsingham is dead, your grace."

Elizabeth froze, "Dead?" she echoed.

Cecil nodded.

The queen looked from Cecil to Pembroke as if in confirmation and Pembroke nodded. Then Elizabeth breathed a bitter laugh.

"Who gave him permission to die?" she said, to which Pembroke forced a smile, thinking his queen had meant it as a joke. But seeing her expression of confusion, Pembroke dropped his gaze.

"Madam," Cecil said calmly, "Walsingham was old. Nobody lives forever."

"Not even you."

She heard the whisper clearly, though no one had uttered it.

Elizabeth looked around at the courtiers within the great hall, her eyes narrowing in suspicion.

Then she shook the whisper from her mind, "Who shall replace him?"

Cecil raised one eyebrow at her lack of emotion at the loss of the man who had protected her fiercely for her entire reign, who had personally invested to the growth of her impeccable intelligence network – so much so that he had left behind nothing but debts.

"Your majesty," Cecil said then, unable to allow her to forget Sir Francis Walsingham so easily, "I beg you to take a moment to remember your most loyal spymaster. You will not find another such as he, ever again, and you will simply never 'replace him'."

Elizabeth was stunned into silence.

"He was a most subtle searcher of hidden secrets," Cecil went on, "He knew excellently well how to win men's minds unto him…He saw every man. And *none* saw him!"

Cecil stared up at his queen, his pale face glowing red with passion at the defence of his old friend's memory.

Elizabeth stared down at her old advisor, a man who had been more a father to her than her own had ever been, and though she was a woman of near sixty years old, she found herself feeling as small as a reprimanded child at his speech.

But his words had been truthful, and she had been wrong to think Walsingham could be replaceable.

"We shall hold a service for him," the queen announced quietly then, shame weighing down her words.

At that, Cecil nodded once, glad to have brought some sense back to his queen, and after a brief moment of silence, he presented her with a document, moving onto the next matter of business.

"The new French Protestant king Henry IV calls for our aid," he summarised as she skimmed the document before her, "He is planning to siege and capture the capital city of Normandy, Rouen, and believes he will need our support against his own Catholic subjects who do not recognize him as king."

"Why would he need England's involvement?" the queen asked, looking up from the document to see Sir Walter Raleigh entering the great hall and approaching them.

"His informants warn against a Catholic League against him," Cecil said, "which will attempt to resist the siege. There are rumours of Spain sending aid to defeat him. As a fellow Protestant ruler, your majesty should show your support as you did in the Netherlands."

Raleigh had reached earshot by now. He flashed Elizabeth a lopsided grin, which caused her cheeks to burn red – not that anyone would have noticed underneath all her paint.

"I'd be honoured to fight for this cause," Raleigh interjected. Cecil looked at him sideways, as though his presence were beneath him, and he ignored the pirate.

"You?" Elizabeth asked with a small laugh.

"Aye," Raleigh replied, focusing his dark eyes on her intently.

An image of Robert flashed before her then. So real it had felt like a slap to the face. She blinked her eyes, trying to free herself of the vision.

"Your majesty?" Raleigh asked as he took a cautious step towards her.

She raised a hand and looked away from him, hoping to avoid looking into his dark eyes, so much like Robert's.

"No," she mumbled, then waved him away.

She closed her eyes and inhaled deeply to steady her nerves. Then she addressed her two remaining council members directly.

"Send three thousand men under the command of John Norreys to aid the French king," she ordered coolly, avoiding Raleigh's pleading look.

Cecil and Pembroke bowed, "Majesty," they mumbled, and then swiftly walked away.

Raleigh remained for a moment longer, looking up at his queen, his mouth open slightly as though he wished to speak, but he did not dare to ask again. He exhaled through his nose then and shook his head as he took a step backwards. Then, just before he turned to leave, his gaze slid from the statue-like queen to her ladies beside her. He might have been mistaken, for their eyes had locked for but a moment, but it had looked as though one of them – the pretty, young one – had offered him a small smile.

November 1591

The siege of Rouen was failing miserably.

The three thousand soldiers Elizabeth had sent to aid Henry IV in battle, had not even made it long enough to be of use to fight, for shortly after their arrival, John Norreys had had to return to London to plead with his queen for food and supplies for her troops. And in his absence, while the queen deliberated his request for the most basic of human needs for her soldiers, word arrived that a Catholic force had slaughtered the leaderless and disorganised army.

"What was her gain from this?" Pembroke asked Cecil quietly as they walked side by side down the dark hallways of the Palace.

Cecil did not reply.

"England has the means to supply an army with the goods it needs," Pembroke continued, "Why was she reluctant?"

Cecil only shrugged.

"For God's sake, man!" Pembroke boomed then, grabbing the shorter, older man by the shoulder, "Did she deliberately send those men to their doom?"

Cecil stared angrily at his fellow advisor, "The queen does as she pleases," he said curtly, "We would do well not to question her reasons."

"But then, all their deaths were meaningless," Pembroke replied as Cecil shrugged his shoulders free of his grasp, "Surely she will have wanted to aid her fellow Protestant monarch."

Cecil turned his head to watch as two giggling young ladies walked past them then, he and Pembroke remaining silent until the ladies had walked out of earshot.

Then Cecil continued walking slowly, carefully looking over his shoulder as he spoke quietly.

"Her majesty received word prior to Norreys' return that the French king was, in fact, no longer a Protestant."

Pembroke choked on his own reply before he had had the chance to utter it, staring questioningly into Cecil's face instead.

Cecil raised his white eyebrows meaningfully.

Pembroke cleared his throat then, "You mean to say, she left her men to die, defenceless in battle, because she no longer wished to aid Henry IV?"

Cecil sighed, "Because she would not have been aiding a *fellow* Protestant. She would have been aiding a *Catholic* one."

Pembroke nodded, understanding her twisted reasoning. Though, at the same time, he realised that surely her own English soldiers need not have perished due to this turn of events.

After all, what wrong had they done but followed their most glorious queen's orders?

Pembroke sighed heavily and frowned, *Followed them right to their bloody end.*

Chapter 26

January 1592

The court was merry following the Christmastide and New Year festivities, and the masques and balls continued throughout the following weeks.
Elizabeth, though fifty-nine years old and practically toothless, enjoyed partaking in the dances as much as any lady.
On occasion she would enjoy a dance with the handsome Walter Raleigh, making eyes at him as his strong hands guided her into each step.
But on this day, she danced with her ladies, young Bess' smile lighting up the room as she and Blanche stepped in time to the music with their queen.
After what felt like hours, Elizabeth quit the dancefloor, signalling to her ladies that they may continue to dance if they wished.
Blanche followed her queen to the high table, while Bess stayed behind much to the male courtiers' delight.
Elizabeth sat down heavily on her cushioned gold seat and sipped her wine, flinching suddenly at its taste.
"Urgh," she mumbled before clicking her fingers at Blanche. Blanche leant forward and retrieved a small tin from her sleeve, opened it and sprinkled sugar into Elizabeth's wine cup.
Elizabeth sipped it again and nodded, approving of its sweetened taste, then grabbed a slice of her favourite almond paste candy, marchpane, as she watched Bess being twirled around by one male courtier after another.

The queen took a bite of her sugary treat, ignoring the pain it caused her rotten teeth, when she noticed Bess and Walter Raleigh sharing a lingering look from across the dancefloor.
Elizabeth, having herself tried to keep a romance secret, quickly noticed other tell-tale signs of two people trying desperately to not look besotted with one another.

"Blanche," Elizabeth called.

"My queen?"

"What is this?" she asked, pointing her pinkie finger at the dancers before her as she clung onto the slice of marchpane.

Blanche looked at the courtiers and frowned, "What, your grace?"

"This! Bess and Raleigh," the queen exclaimed.

Blanche blinked, "I – I don't know…"

The queen exhaled sharply and threw her favourite treat down onto the gold plate before her, "Useless," she muttered as she licked her fingers clean.

Then she stood from her seat and walked briskly out of the great hall, her heeled shoes clinking purposefully loud against the stone floor, signalling that the entertainment was over, their queen having deemed it concluded.

"Bess!" Elizabeth screeched once she had marched into her chambers, her ladies' footsteps growing louder as they attempted to catch up with her.

"BESS!" she hollered, her eyes ablaze with anger.

Blanche and Bess hurried inside, and Blanche closed the door behind her.

"Your majesty?" Bess muttered, curtsying quickly as her queen's fury vibrated through the air.

"Speak!" Elizabeth demanded.

Bess looked over her shoulder at Blanche, hoping for a lifeline. The older lady only raised her eyebrows as she took a step back against the wall, glad Elizabeth's anger was not aimed at her.

"I – I do not know w—what…"

"You and Raleigh," Elizabeth countered, "is there something you wish to tell me?"

Bess' face grew red as she stared wide-eyed at the queen before her, her mouth hanging open like a fish out of water.

"Well?" Elizabeth demanded, taking a step towards her threateningly.

"Your majesty," Bess whimpered as she took a step back and subconsciously snaked a hand over her belly protectively.

Elizabeth's eyes slid down the length of the young lady before resting suspiciously on her hand as it trembled over her belly in fear.

Bess immediately snapped her hand away, but it was too late, and she steeled herself as she met her queen's gaze.

"You're with child…" Elizabeth mumbled, and she was reminded of Robert's betrayal with Lettice, when her world had begun crumbling around her.

Bess raised her chin and swallowed, "We…are married, your grace."

All was still for a moment as Blanche watched from the shadows as the two ladies stare at each other, knowing from experience just how the queen would react to such insubordination.

Suddenly Elizabeth sprang towards Bess, her fingers sprawled out like claws as she tore at the lady's face and body.

Bess exclaimed in fear and cowered, raising her arms in self-defence as the queen continued to deliver blow after blow.

Then Elizabeth, her face contorted with anger, grabbed one of Bess' fingers and forced it backwards, a horrible *crack* erupting as the bone was snapped out of place.

Blanche flinched, one hand covering her mouth as she observed the altercation. And as Elizabeth stepped away from the lady on the floor, gasping for breath, Blanche saw the misshapen finger dangling gruesomely from Bess' hand.

Then Bess let out an agonising scream, one which echoed through chambers, and which led to the doors being flung open by the queen's guards, and Walter Raleigh storming inside. Half the court was hot on his heels, stopping in the hallway and craning their necks in the hope of catching a glimpse of what had occurred. But all they could see was their queen, huffing and puffing in her chambers, her wig crooked upon her balding head and her red lipstick smeared across her white cheek.

Raleigh rushed to Bess' side and helped her up, shooting a disgruntled look at his queen, who he had previously so admired.

"Guards!" Elizabeth ordered as she raised her arms to straighten her wig, "Seize them!"

The guards stormed towards Bess and Raleigh as the crowd of courtiers outside the queen's chambers gasped and muttered in horror.

"Your majesty!" Raleigh called over the kerfuffle, "Have mercy, she is with child!"

Another gasp from the crowd.

Elizabeth's fists were balled at her sides, "Get them out of my sight and into the Tower!" she screamed, practically stomping her foot with anger at their disrespect.

October 1592
Windsor Castle, outskirts of London

"The Black Death continues to claim lives throughout London and its surrounding parishes," Cecil informed the queen as they sat opposite each other in her private chambers. Elizabeth took a bite of the roasted pig before her and chewed as she thought.

"What can be done?" she asked eventually.

Cecil shrugged his slightly curved shoulders, his old age becoming more and more apparent with each passing day.

"It is quite unheard of," he said, "for plague to persist so long following the hot, summer months."

"I know."

"The people are becoming extremely restless. They see it as ominous that it should persist into the winter."

Elizabeth exhaled, bored of the topic, "What are the numbers?"

Cecil blinked his tired, watery eyes at her, "Total death count so far is nearing twenty thousand."

Elizabeth nodded and spooned more food into her mouth, flinching slightly as her teeth caused her pain to chew.

"What of the prisoners in the Tower, your grace?" Cecil asked then, hoping to reawaken compassion in his queen before his days on this earth came to an end.

"What of them?" she replied, barely looking up from her plate of food.

"We have received reports of many dying in the Fleet Prison due to its unhygienic circumstances. The Tower of London is not much better."

Elizabeth did not reply, remembering the moss that had grown in the corners of her own cell over four decades ago, when her sister had held her captive.

Queenship had hardened Elizabeth since then, power and fear of overthrowal having etched themselves into her very core.

And yet, she had never wished for any of it.

Not only has she never wished for the crown itself, but when she accepted her fate, she had never imagined herself to have become this kind of monarch, so much like her father.

It was almost as though, whenever news came, that Elizabeth was watching from a great height, and the queen that gave orders of death and destruction was someone else entirely.

"Perhaps you would like to show mercy to those who you once held dear?" Cecil pushed, knowing that she was aware of what he was insinuating to.

Elizabeth sighed and swallowed her mouthful, "No," she said, "Leave them where they are. I've had one too many ladies betray my trust in this lifetime. Lettice Knollys and now Bess Throckmorton…they can both be glad I didn't immediately condemn them to the block."

Cecil didn't even flinch, he was used to his queen's ruling by now. Instead, he stood and bowed before slowly shuffling out of the room, leaving Elizabeth to finish her meal in silence, and utterly alone.

The following week, one of the queen's servants was reported to have died in the night of the plague, fluid-filled boils having sprouted all over her body before bursting painfully in her sleep. And the alarm was raised in Windsor Castle.

"We should evacuate!" Pembroke said as he and Cecil entered the queen's chambers.

"No," Elizabeth mumbled but they did not hear her.

"We should make haste. God knows who else is infected…"

"No!" the queen said again, louder this time.

"My queen, it isn't safe," Cecil argued.

"We remain!" Elizabeth ordered, "This one death will not get in the way of my annual Accession Day festivities."

Cecil and Pembroke stared at their queen wide-eyed.

"Surely it would be safer to cancel – or at least, postpone – the annual celebration…" Pembroke pointed out logically.

"Theatres are shut down due to the plague, your grace," Cecil added, "Playwrights and actors will not want to risk their lives for entertainment purposes in a Castle where someone has been infected. We should leave –"

"Sir William," Elizabeth whispered menacingly, "I demand my Accession Day be celebrated as it has done every year since my coronation. Plague or no plague, see to it that it happens."

It was not a grand affair, and none of the festivity took place inside the Castle walls, the celebrations being held entirely outdoors and within the safety of fresh air.

The queen greatly enjoyed watching the theatrical performances held upon a makeshift stage on the lawns outside Windsor Castle.

Elizabeth cared little that no one but herself was pleased to be there and she knew they resented her for her decision to host the celebrations on this dangerous occasion.

But the idea of cancelling the very celebration of her accession, frightened her far more than the plague.

Her years were coming to an end, Elizabeth knew that with every fibre of her being.

Her youth was gone. And her lust for life had died along with her beloved Robert, though his final letter to her ignited a low burning flame in her soul on occasion.

The thought of him alone punched a hole in her heart, no matter how much she liked to pretend that Raleigh had somehow replaced him. He was a handsome man, full of wit and adventurous stories to tell. He clearly admired her – up until she locked him and his expectant wife in the Tower.

But he was not her Robert.

His final letter brought her much peace, at least, and she unfolded it every night before she retired to bed.

But with each year that passed, Elizabeth knew that it would not be long before she too would one day lay her head down and never again wake up.

And that thought troubled her more than anything.

It was for that reason that she could not fathom the idea of *not* celebrating this special day. The day that had marked the beginning of her glorious reign.

For when the time would come when God would call her to Him to be with Robert and her mother in Heaven, then she would want to be able to say that she lived her life as she had wanted.

Even if, in truth, her life had been nothing but what others had wanted for her instead.

1593
Hampton Court Palace, London

The plague had finally begun to subside the following year, and the queen and her court were able to safely return to London.

By some miracle, Bess and Raleigh had survived the onslaught of Plague that had ripped through the city, being part of the lucky few who had been spared while in unhygienic captivity.

But Bess' babe – who had been born in imprisonment – had not survived, the Tower's poor conditions causing the child to die soon after its birth.

Elizabeth, though still filled with anger at their betrayal, ordered for the couple to be released under grounds of having concluded their sentence. But in truth, Elizabeth felt to blame for their young son's demise – though she would never admit this to anyone but herself.

Instead, she added it to the list of things that were eating her up inside.

Raleigh was given a place at court as Captain of the Queen's Guard once again, the queen claiming to need his expertise as a former soldier. But Bess was not given such privileges.

And just like Lettice – who too had embarked on a secret relationship with Elizabeth's favourite without her queen's permission – Bess was banished from court, condemned to live out her days as a wife parted from her husband, and a mother without a living child.

Cecil cleared his throat, "There is news from Ireland, your majesty."

Elizabeth looked up from the cards in her hands, "Bad news?" she asked, tired of the never-ending conflict.

"There is tension in Ulster," Cecil explained slowly, his breathing coming in ragged, "The Irish are forming an alliance against –"

"English rule in Ireland," Elizabeth finished impatiently. She laid out her cards, "*Piquet*," she said, casually announcing her victory to Blanche who sat before her.

Then she sat back in her seat and sighed, "Is it so hard to simply give in to the new order of things?" she asked Cecil rhetorically, "Well, not new. I have been their queen for decades. Did the defeat of the Desmond Rebellions not teach them *not* to provoke me?"

Cecil did not reply but stole a glance at Blanche who sat rigidly in her seat, her age having become quite visible of late as the queen's only remaining lady-in-waiting, Elizabeth no longer trusting herself to appoint ladies who would remain loyal.

The queen sat forward then and grabbed the deck of cards before shuffling them absentmindedly, and Cecil continued to stand before her, waiting for her response to the news.

Elizabeth then dealt out the cards and looked up at Cecil as though she had forgotten he were there.

"Well," she said, her eyebrows raised in question, "What are you waiting for? Retaliate, of course."

May 1595

The queen's order to strike back against the rebellion in the north of Ireland sparked the beginning of a long-lasting conflict. Many battles ensued between the English and Irish soldiers, the Battle of Clontibret being one of the first of many losses for England during this war that would last for several years to come.

Elizabeth continued to supply more soldiers as others died, unwilling to give in to the Irish leaders' demands for independence from English lords and their Protestant laws.

"If they would just accept the Protestant faith, none of this would be happening," Elizabeth muttered as she rubbed her fingers distractedly over the smallpox scar over her eyebrow, which she felt she had gained another lifetime ago entirely.

She tried not to think about how this – as well as the conflict with Spain – may never have happened if her sister, Mary, had lived on to continue ruling as queen, her Catholic beliefs and Ireland's having been one and the same.

"The Irish are stubborn," Cecil mumbled, his energy failing him recently, "They will fall to their knees soon."

But they didn't.

And the war raged on, sweeping all over Ireland and forfeiting thousands of lives, of both soldiers and civilians.

Chapter 27

1596

"It is called 'Romeo and Juliet'," Elizabeth's newest lady-in-waiting said as she applied the queen's white ceruse to her face and neck.

Since Bess' banishment and Blanche's faltering ability to single-handedly attend to the queen in her old age of near seventy-years old, Elizabeth had chosen two new ladies to join her household.

Elizabeth Knollys was the daughter of Catherine Carey, who was the daughter of Mary Boleyn – her mother's sister.

"It is said to be very dramatic," Elizabeth Knollys said then as she applied the finishing touches, "A romance."

Elizabeth looked at herself in the mirror and nodded, pleased with the outcome, "Well done, Lady Knollys," she praised, to which the young lady smiled prettily and bobbed a curtsy.

Queen Elizabeth watched as she walked away to join the other new lady by the window, before picking up the bible she had previously discarded.

The other new lady was Frances Walsingham, the daughter of the queen's late spymaster, Sir Francis Walsingham. The queen had chosen her as a lady partly to make up for her lack of emotion at his passing, having since become quite disgusted at her own selfish reaction at the tragic news.

"Romeo and Juliet?" Blanche said as she approached Elizabeth then.

"Shakespeare's newest play," Elizabeth replied as she continued watching the young ladies giggling by the window, mesmerised by them – their youth, their carefree nature…

Blanche followed her gaze, "Do you wish to see it?"

Elizabeth swallowed, then nodded, "I think I shall," she said, "I could use the distraction."

It had been a mistake to watch Shakespeare's play of 'Romeo and Juliet', for not a day had gone by since where Elizabeth had not been haunted by the ghosts of her past.

As if the vivid memory of her mother – which had flashed before her eyes over the years at the slightest veering off track – wasn't enough, Elizabeth now saw glimpses of her Robert everywhere she looked. Whether in Sir Walter Raleigh's dark gaze, or as a silhouette lurking in the shadows, he was always there.

Watching her.

She walked the halls of the Palace on edge, fearful that she would somehow bump into him, and it be abruptly confirmed that she was, in fact, going mad.

She gained no reprieve in her sleep either, for the ghosts would follow her into her subconscious, tormenting her with visions of the life she could have led, had her sister lived on and produced an heir to replace her…

Elizabeth would wake several times in the night, covered in sweat and breathing frantically. Her new ladies would wake due to her flailing and rush to her side, wondering what had happened.

But Elizabeth would remain silent, shaking her head and blinking away the tears.

And after many nights of this, her ladies no longer came to her aid, knowing that they nor anyone could do anything to save Elizabeth from her own guilty conscience.

1597

"My queen," Cecil wheezed, as though he had just climbed a flight of stairs instead of merely entering the council chamber, "Parliament is restless."

Elizabeth watched as her oldest and most loyal advisor sank down into his chair.

"Restless?" she repeated.

Cecil nodded and exhaled dramatically, "The matter of your succession is being broached once more."

Elizabeth raised an eyebrow, "Do they expect me to die sometime soon, Sir William?"

"They expect you to name an heir, Elizabeth."

The queen looked at Pembroke, who too had aged drastically of late, his frail body looking almost skeletal.

"Do you wish me to name a successor, Pembroke?"

The old man sat back in his chair, eager to put distance between himself and his fiery queen during this subject.

He shrugged his brittle shoulders, "It would settle the people's minds," he replied tactfully.

Elizabeth breathed a laugh, "Coward," she stated half in jest, then turned her attention to Cecil, "What are my options?"

Cecil cleared his throat, "Your father's will stated a clear line of succession. As you know, after his son and first daughter he left the throne to you. Beyond that – as your grace chose never to marry or produce your own heir – the next in line would have been your cousins: Jane Grey, Katherine Grey, Mary Grey, and Margaret Clifford. You have outlived them all."

Elizabeth stiffened at the mention of her Grey cousins, one of which her sister, Mary, had executed for treason, and the other two whom Elizabeth herself had imprisoned for all of their adult lives, due to the risk they had posed as potential usurpers to her throne.

"You are the only remaining Tudor. Like your father," Cecil continued, "You must name your heir – or heirs – in your will."

Elizabeth nodded but did not reply. Pembroke and Cecil shared a look, hoping to have finally shown their queen the error of her ways in postponing the inevitable.

Perhaps now she would *finally* name her heir?

Elizabeth, now a woman of sixty-four, was tempting fate with every month that passed, and Parliament was right in pressing her for an answer to their long-standing question of her successor.

For without a clear plan for the future, England would be left in crisis, and other leaders of the world would attempt to cease power of the land through any means necessary.

Finally, she raised her chin.

"I will think on it," Elizabeth declared.

But her lips were pursed and her eyes remained lacklustre, and her advisors were left – yet again – without a real answer to their forty-year-old question.

1598

The war in Ireland continued.

It had raged on for four years already, Ireland never steering from their hope for independence from the exploitative English lords and their Protestant laws.

And Elizabeth persisted in England's retaliation.

"We cannot be seen to give in," she declared stubbornly as she walked the gardens with her advisors, hoping that the cold Spring breeze would help to keep her awake.

She had suffered another fitful night's sleep, tossing and turning as the nightmares taunted her every hour.

"They have made it quite clear it's a matter of religion," Cecil agreed, "If we give in, we allow other Catholic nations to do the same. It will appear that we are accepting of the Catholic faith."

Elizabeth nodded, "Has there been much development?" she asked then, wondering if she should send more reinforcements.

Cecil looked to Pembroke, who replied, "Our latest army of reinforcements of four-thousand men march to Blackwater Fort as we speak, led by Henry Bagenal. There they will re-supply the fort to reestablish it as one of our strongholds."

"Good," the queen replied, having only half listened, words of war meaning little to her, as long as the outcome meant victorious to England, "And Spain?"

Cecil sighed, "Spain continues to supply the Irish with more of their own men to raise their numbers against us."

The queen shook her head, "Filipe," she muttered angrily, "Will that man never cease to be a thorn in my side?!"

Henry Bagenal and his army of four-thousand men never did reach Blackwater Fort to reestablish it as an English stronghold, for he and his soldiers were ambushed by an Irish army under the command of the leader of the rebellion, Hugh O'Neill.

"It is our greatest loss so far since the beginning of this war, your grace," Cecil stated.

"How many casualties?"

"Near a thousand-five-hundred dead and three hundred deserted."

"And the Irish army?" the queen asked, her eyes blazing.

"It is reported that our army took out maybe two hundred," Cecil said, "But it is likely far less, the number we are being told is possibly an attempt to soften the blow of their failure."

Elizabeth shook her head, "We cannot continue with this war..."

"But Ireland will fall back into the darkness of Catholicism!" Cecil interjected.

"Might I be so bold as to say," Pembroke said then, "Ireland could continue to believe in their own way, and still be loyal to their queen."

He was, of course, referring to himself: A Catholic loyal to his Protestant monarch.

"You are an excellent example of loyalty, Pembroke," Elizabeth stated, "But Ireland is clearly not as loyal, to resort to such measures to begin with."

Pembroke hung his head, unwilling to push the matter further.

"England is running out of resources. Our monies are low, certainly too low to continue financing this war for much longer. And soon there will be no additional troops to send…"

The queen and her Privy Council fell silent for a while then, all trying desperately to come up with an outcome that would see to an English victory.

"Gentlemen," Elizabeth suddenly said, breaking the silence, "There's nothing left to do but to resort to old measures. Measures which have worked in our favour in the past."

Cecil was nodding, he knew what his queen was alluding to.

"Send the Earl of Essex with an army of 17-thousand men. Let them disperse all over the country and lay waste to the lands. The Scorched Earth Policy worked to quash the Desmond Rebellion, and it will work to quash this one. Let them burn their crops to the ground. Let them target civilians and their livestock. I will stamp out this rebellion if it's the last thing I do."

Elizabeth's plan to scorch the lands led to thousands of deaths. Innocent men, women and children starving to death from the aftermath of the destroyed lands.

But it did nothing to stop the war, and not long after the Earl of Essex and his army arrived in Ireland, many of the English soldiers were struck down with disease, thousands dying from typhoid and dysentery due to the unsanitary conditions of their garrisons.

"Essex has challenged O'Neill to single combat to settle the war," Cecil mumbled.

He was tired.

He was so tired.

Of this war. Of this life. And even, sometimes, of his stubborn queen.

The queen scoffed, "Single combat? O'Neill will not fall for that when Ireland is winning!"

And of course he did not, causing the Earl of Essex to sign a truce with O'Neill instead, agreeing to leave Ireland with his remaining English troops, against his Queen's instructions.

Upon the Earl of Essex' return to England in disgrace, the Queen was asked what was to become of him.

She was sitting upon her throne in the great hall, Cecil, Pembroke and Raleigh all looking up at her as she debated the Earl's fate.

There was a low hubbub from the crowd of courtiers within the great hall, some playing cards by the windows, while others stood bunched in groups, appearing to be deep in conversation instead of eavesdropping for their queen's decision.

Elizabeth breathed in deeply, anger boiling inside of her as she considered the man's failings. She cast her eyes over her advisors, avoiding Raleigh's dark-eyed stare entirely, for fear that it would cause an onslaught of painful memories of her Robert.

Her dead Robert.

Elizabeth squeezed her eyes shut and gritted her teeth.

"Elizabeth..."

She heard it. A whisper in the far corner of the hall. As clear as if it had been whispered right into her ear.

But he was not there.

Elizabeth shook her head and cleared her throat before looking down at the advisors before her.

"Arrest the Earl of Essex," she declared finally, "He is to be executed for treason."

A murmur vibrated through the crowd and Cecil and Pembroke nodded their heads before turning to walk away.

Then a shadow scurried past the open doorway of the great hall.

Elizabeth gasped and half stood from her throne.

"Your majesty?" Raleigh asked, his eyebrows furrowed together.

She raised her hand and shook her head slightly, "I thought I saw..."

What? A dead man's ghost?

"Nothing. I saw nothing," she concluded, but she continued to stare wide-eyed at the open doorway, "I shall retire, my lords."

The crowd bowed and curtsied as their old queen made her way through the throng of people, her hands clasped graciously before her.

On the surface, queen Elizabeth appeared regal and composed. But deep-down she was agitated, and she held her hands together tightly not to portray grace or strength, but to keep her people from noticing that they were trembling.

August 1598

Though Elizabeth had noticed the decline of Cecil's health, it nevertheless alarmed her when he asked to retire to his London house in Covent Garden.

The queen was reluctant to let him go, knowing that at seventy-seven years old, he would likely not recover from this latest bout of weakness he had been battling.

She gave her approval nonetheless, and in his absence, she prayed each day that her most loyal and trusted advisor, the father she never had, would return to her.

But God had not been listening, for just four days after his departure from court, word came that Sir William Cecil, Baron Burghley, had collapsed and been taken to bed.

Elizabeth wasted no time, and by that same afternoon, the queen arrived at Cecil's residence.

She sat by his bedside that evening, carefully feeding him broth. But when it was clear that his time had come, Elizabeth leaned over him and gently pecked a kiss on his clammy forehead.

"Thank you," Elizabeth whispered, a small smile on her lips, "You were like a father to me."

Cecil's lips twitched a tired smile as he blinked back at her slowly.

"You have been a loyal servant to your queen," Elizabeth went on, "But now it is time to rest, Sir William."

Cecil nodded his old head.

Tears sprang to Elizabeth's eyes then at the idea of his loss. Cecil had been by her side for almost forty years, and though she was an old woman herself, she felt suddenly like a small, frightened child.

"I do not wish to live much longer without you with me," she whispered shakily then, a lump stuck in her throat.

Cecil's brow furrowed, and his eyes shone with tears at his queen's emotional confession.

But then he closed his eyes and took in one last inhale.

And with his final breath, Elizabeth suddenly felt the cold air tightening around her.

She was alone.

Orphaned and childless, Queen Elizabeth glided through the halls of her Palace as if without direction, ever fearful of catching a glimpse of the ghosts that haunted her, day and night.

To replace those of her Privy Council that she had lost over the years, Elizabeth appointed William Cecil's son, Robert, to take his place as Secretary of State, knowing that he would follow in his father's footsteps well enough.

She also appointed Thomas Sackville as Lord High Treasurer. He was the son of Richard Sackville, who had been a cousin to her mother, Anne Boleyn.

She was with this new council when a messenger burst through the doors of her chambers one day, announcing the death of her life-long enemy, King Filipe II of Spain.

"Good news at last!" Pembroke called out, "Walsingham would have celebrated this day gloriously."

Elizabeth smiled at the mention of her former spymaster, a now familiar knot of guilt tightening her stomach at the same time.

"Good news indeed," she agreed calmly.

But it did little to lift her spirits, for death seemed to be on every corner these days, whether within her own council or far away in Spain, many of those she had known throughout her reign were perishing at an alarming rate.

And it made her wonder just how much longer she would have to wait until she would meet her mother and her Robert in the afterlife.

Chapter 28

January 1600

It was a new century, and England celebrated grandly.
But the festivities did not last long, for just a few weeks into the new year, Hugh O'Neill took up arms once more, raising a new army from the ashes of Ireland, and plunging it into war with England yet again.

Elizabeth pressed her fingers into her forehead at the news, shaking her head violently, "This cannot go on," she mumbled, her councilmen straining to hear her.

"O'Neill and his allies' objectives are much the same as ever," Robert Cecil informed her, "To keep their own personal power and that of their clans intact. They cannot foresee a place for themselves in the new order under your majesty's rule. It seems to go beyond a matter of religion or culture at this point. But not all of Ireland stands with them."

Elizabeth liked Sir William's son, his replacement. But his rambling irked her at times, and she began to miss Sir William's short and to-the-point replies.

"England does not have a large standing army," the queen said, "Our soldiers are depleted, and the country is not strong enough to extract enough taxation to pay for this long war. The war in the Netherlands as well as this ongoing one with Ireland has bled us dry."

"O'Neill is marching to Munster with his ever-growing army," Pembroke stated calmly, the last of Elizabeth's original advisors, "We must do something to quell this rebellion. If not by military force or by scorching their lands, then by reconciliation."

Elizabeth stared at him as she considered his advice. Then she slowly shook her head.

"No," she concluded, "we will not negotiate with traitors. We need someone to replace the disgraced and executed Earl of Essex, someone savvier and less of a coward."

Charles Blount, Lord Mountjoy, was an English soldier and lord deputy of Ireland, who had caught the queen's attention when he had accompanied Sir Walter Raleigh on a successful expedition to the Azores some years prior. They had returned to England with much Spanish treasure, proving his worth to his queen. Not long later, he had been sent to Ireland with the late Earl of Essex's army.

"Send word that Mountjoy is to assume command of our remaining army in Ireland," the queen ordered later that day.

"He already has, your grace," Robert Cecil replied, "He and our army are awaiting your orders. And there are rumours of Spanish reinforcements being sent to aid the Irish."

"Of course there is," Elizabeth mumbled, raising one invisible eyebrow.

The young Cecil maintained eye contact with the old queen, "What are your orders?"

Elizabeth inhaled as she considered her options, "We are outnumbered," she deduced, "But this is our final hope to quash the war, as we have no more troops to spare."

He swallowed, a bead of sweat trickling between his brow as he awaited his queen's verdict.

Elizabeth raised her chin then, "We must get O'Neill to submit," she announced, "The Spanish army will land at Kinsale. O'Neill and his men will likely march south to join them."

Robert Cecil nodded.

"Send word to Mountjoy to await their arrival outside Kinsale. Our final battle will be one of surprise. All we can do from here is pray that our army is successful."

June 1600

"Your majesty, you must rest," Elizabeth's lady, Frances, said as she stifled a yawn, "It is past midnight."
Elizabeth shook her head, "I cannot sleep."
She had been made ready for bed two hours prior, her bright orange wig with the white feather had been removed, her black and gold velvet dress was hung up in the other room. The white ceruse, red rogue and lipstick had been gently wiped off with rose and orange scented water, and she had been left to retire into her four-posted bed while her ladies brushed down her dress and carefully put away her wig.
But when they returned to extinguish the candles and close the queen's bed curtains, they had found her still sitting before her mirror, intently staring at her own reflection.
Lady Knollys and Frances had shared a confused look.
 "Are you well, your grace?" Lady Knollys had asked, but their queen had not replied.
In fact, it had seemed as though she was completely unaware that they were even there.
 "Should we fetch Blanche?" Frances had asked lady Knollys quietly.
Knollys had shaken her head, "Leave Blanche to rest. She needs it more than we do in her old age."
Frances had nodded, then Knollys had taken a step towards Elizabeth as she sat before the looking glass.
 "Your majesty?" she had called softly.
Elizabeth's chin had jutted slightly upwards, "Hm?" she had asked, suggesting she was not entirely oblivious of her surroundings.
But now, two hours later, the queen continued to simply stare at her aged reflection, unable – or unwilling – to give in to sleep.

Elizabeth was practically bald, with only four long strands on thin, white hair scraped back over her head. Her once fine lines around her eyes and mouth were now deep crevices which not even her white ceruse could hide of late.

Her pale blue eyes, while watery from old age, had lost their shine and vibrancy, leaving behind only two dull orbs staring back at her.

And yet, Elizabeth would rather face herself, timeworn and haggard, than face the images which would plague her if she succumbed to sleep.

The nightmares that plagued her at night had become more vivid in the last few months. Some nights she would dream of her mother, and of telling her what she had achieved. Her beautiful mother would smile sadly and ask her if she was happy, and Elizabeth would falter, unable to reply, before waking up in a cold sweat.

But most nights she would dream of him.

Snapshots of herself – younger, full of life – racing towards a shadowy figure in the distance. The joy that she felt as the figure solidified into a young Robert overwhelmed her and she could run faster, breathe easier.

And yet, every time, no matter the scenery, when her younger self was just about to reach out and touch him, he would disappear into a puff of black smoke.

Terror would engulf her as the sunlight melted from the sky above and she was left in darkness, turning this way and that to search her surroundings. But every time, she could see nothing.

She would call out for him, for her mother, for Kat, for anyone who had once loved her. Only to find that her voice was gone, and that her cries for help were in vain – silent gusts of air.

She would wake soaked in sweat with his name on her lips, trembling at the realisation of his loss, despite the fact he had been dead for many years.

Sometimes she would clutch the cushion beside her and hug it tightly as she wept in silence. But more often she would retrieve his letter from her nightstand and re-read it for what felt like the thousandth time.

How grateful she was for this note from her beloved, whom she had sacrificed to rule England as the Virgin Queen.

This final memento gave her peace beyond any other trinket she possessed – even more than her coronation ring with the hidden image of her mother inside.

How lucky she was that he had loved her until his dying breath, since it was this letter alone that kept her from losing touch with reality, and what kept her from thinking that it had all been in vain.

November 1601

Regret.

It was something that weighed heavily on Elizabeth's chest lately as she considered the choices she had made during her long reign.

True, many choices were made with leniency on those who had stood against her, who had prayed for her downfall.

But many were made in fear. And even more had been made in anger, with vengeance as their fuelling.

Robert had tried to warn her. He had stood by and watched her become more consumed with rage, hoping she would realise it herself. And when she did not, he had tried to hold up the mirror and show her a glimpse of herself in his eyes.

The way he had stopped looking at her. It had spoken volumes.

And still Elizabeth could not have been stopped on her path to achieve her ultimate goal.

Even when he left her for a lesser version of herself, Elizabeth had not wanted to believe that she had gone too far.

For how far was 'too far' when everlasting glory was at stake? But in his persistence to haunt her, she had finally begun to see the error of her ways.

Perhaps she could have reigned more with her heart instead of her head? Perhaps she could have sustained from aggravating Spain into a war? Perhaps she could have avoided executing her cousin, and imprisoned her more harshly instead?

In hindsight, so many different paths may have avoided much conflict, and she would be leaving behind a much less bloody legacy. And perhaps even an heir to continue the Tudor line – something her father had moved mountains for to achieve.

But who is to say the outcome would not have been the same? Would she have outlived all her enemies if she had been more loving instead of strong?

Elizabeth would never know.

But the regret weighed her down, nonetheless.

If the constant internal battle of her body and her mind told her anything, it was that the end of her life was nearing.

Her throat had been feeling scratchy in more recent weeks, her voice coming out ragged and hoarse, and she knew that if she were to address her country one last time, and alleviate some of her guilt, it would have to be before her deteriorating body failed her.

She called a meeting of Parliament – where she would address all one-hundred and forty-one members of the House of Commons, and her council – under the guise of discussing the matter of the country's economic issues.

"Gentlemen!" the queen called out, silencing the gentle hubbub that reverberated from the crowd of the House of Commons, "I have come to address you all, and my kingdom, today, to give thanks to all who have supported my claim, and what you bestowed onto me."

The men before her looked around at one another, confusion painted over their faces as they realised their queen was not tackling the economic issues after all but addressing them personally – a gift to the people from their almighty queen.

"My heart was never set on any worldly goods," Elizabeth continued, casting her voice as far as she could, "Therefore I shall not hoard it up, but instead bestow them onto you again in form of thanks, such thanks as you imagine my heart yields, but my tongue cannot express. Had I not received knowledge from all of you," and she glanced into the faces of her councilmen, and imagined those who had died along the way, standing beside them, "I might have fallen into the lapse of error."

A lump formed in her throat as the regret crept up and tightened a hand around her neck.

"Soon, the day will come where I will be called to answer before a higher judge – God – and if I abused my kingly bounties and somehow turned them to the hurt of my people, I hope God will not lay blame at my feet. I know the title of King is a glorious title, but I assure you that the shining glory of princely authority does not deny that I will also yield an account of my actions before the great judge."

Tears pricked her eyes as she continued, finally admitting to a truth she had been carrying with her all her life, "To be a king and wear a crown is a thing more glorious to you than it is to its bearer… for myself I was never much enticed by it… but I pray I did my duty well enough to defend this kingdom from peril, dishonour and oppression."

She felt a weight lifting off her shoulders at the confession, and there was a murmur from the crowd before her.

But she continued, "There will never be a king or queen to sit in my seat with more passion for my country and care to my subjects. And I willingly venture on in this life and reign for no longer than it shall be for your good, above even my own."

With that, the queen fell silent along with the members of the House of Commons, her speech having rendered them stunned into silence.

She had thrown away the Tudor legacy, for the sake of being remembered eternally – the daughter of Queen Anne Boleyn.

And she hoped her mother would have been proud of what she had accomplished in her name.

But, even with her own acknowledgement of some of her failings, the nightmares continued to haunt her.

And a taunting voice, which she quickly realized was her own, became a constant fixture in her mind.

Was it all really worth it?

December 1601

Despite the queen's personal turmoil, her strategy to attack the Irish unexpectedly at Kinsdale by night proved victorious.

The Irish troops were defeated, and the small army of Spaniards surrendered.

"They have been forced into submission," Pembroke summarised with a tight-lipped smile, "But O'Neill has fled to Ulster."

"He is of no more threat to us," Elizabeth said, waving a frail hand in the air, "We have him in our sight. He cannot rally another army without us knowing."

Pembroke nodded.

"This victory will surely put an end to Spanish help in Ireland," Robert Cecil added.

The queen sighed heavily, her eyelids feeling heavy due to lack of sleep.

"Let us pray you are right," she mumbled, "But until they formally surrender, we must remain vigilant. They may yet take advantage of England in its current state."

She did not need to say it, but her council knew what she was referring to: that England's queen was old and frail – and would likely not survive much longer – while continuing to be as stubborn as ever and heading towards her grave without naming an heir.

May 1602

Though France and England had traditionally been rivals for many decades, king Henry IV of France had recently been openly gushing over queen Elizabeth, announcing his great admiration and respect for her as a female sovereign in a man's world.

"He is no doubt feeling guilty over his betrayal of when he converted to Catholicism after I sent him Protestant troops to fight his cause," Elizabeth said, remembering the unsuccessful siege of Rouen.

"Our English ambassador in France informs me," the queen's new Secretary of State, Robert Cecil said, sidestepping Elizabeth's remark, "that he speaks highly of your highness, and continues to do so even while in talks with the Scottish ambassadors."

"The Scottish ambassadors?" Pembroke asked.

"It seems France and Scotland have begun negotiations for an alliance once more," Cecil said, "They have their sights set on bringing down Spain."

Elizabeth's interest was piqued.

"We should send our ambassador to Scotland to join their league," Elizabeth declared then, an opportunity for reconciliation with Scotland springing to mind, "This may be an opportunity to finally bring Spain to their knees."

Pembroke nodded, "Excellent idea, your grace," he said approvingly.

"I shall write to King James myself," Elizabeth declared as she stood from the council table and glided towards the exit, eager to join forces with Scotland and France against her greatest foe.

My good Brother,
I offer you my assistance, should you need it, in your union against our common enemy, Spain.
I know your alliance with France offers much in aid for your cause, but since I know King Henry IV has so good reflection of me, I ask you to consider allowing England to join.
While I will not forget that Spain and Scotland united in a League against me in the past, I believe this union between us old enemies would be a good step in the direction in regaining our mutual friendship, and in looking to the future.
I ask you to consider this for the good of both our countries.
   Your most loving and affectionate sister,
   Elizabeth the Queen

Elizabeth sent her messenger away with a great smile on her weathered face.
This potential union with Scotland could not have come at a better time, and she only hoped that the Scottish king would accept her offer of a renewed friendship.
She knew that king James had long hoped to rule England as her heir. She had known it to be the true reason for his agreement to the Treaty of Berwick all those years ago, as well as the reason why he had not declared war on England after the execution of his mother.
If she could broker an official alliance between England and Scotland that would draw a line under their previous discord, perhaps the issue of her successor could finally begin to be addressed.

Naming king James as her heir – a Scottish king with noble English blood running through his veins, with direct lineage to her own grandfather, Henry VII – would unify their two countries under one ruler.

As a Protestant king, it would cement the true religion into the next generation, and hopefully bury Catholicism for good.

Elizabeth inhaled deeply to quench the tightness of her chest as she watched the messenger hurry away.

The future of her country hung in the balance as to how king James would reply to her offer of aid.

So much was at stake for a positive response: Her country's future, her legacy, her people's peace.

But there was one thing she hoped to achieve above all else with this sudden stroke of genius, and that was to alleviate some of the ever-growing remorse that troubled her soul.

For in leaving her country to James VI, perhaps this way Elizabeth would be forgiven for the gruesome execution of her own cousin, his mother.

March 1603
Richmond Palace, Richmond

Elizabeth knew her time was near.

But though she longed to be reunited with her Robert and her mother, she dreaded the idea of death.

"Your majesty must rest!" Blanche fretted around her old queen, "You have not slept in three days."

The queen had become increasingly ill in the months that followed her rekindled friendship with king James of Scotland. Her throat had become inflamed and raw, rendering her completely mute, as well as causing her great pain even just to swallow.

Because of this, Elizabeth had also rejected any food that had been brought to her, living solely off watery broth, small ale and honey mead.

The queen shook her head at Blanche, jerking her hand away when her lady tried to plead with her.

Elizabeth, now an old, frail lady of sixty-nine years old, stood before her looking-glass – much as she had done for most of the past three days and nights – occasionally swaying from fatigue as she continued to simply stand, too frightened to lie down and close her eyes.

What if I never wake up...?

The thought tormented her with every breath.

Her ladies had begged and pleaded with her, but nothing they had said would change their mistress' mind. Instead, they laid out dozens of cushions and fur blankets on the ground all around her, in the hope of breaking her fall when their queen did eventually pass out from exhaustion.

A shadow flickered past Elizabeth then as she continued to force her eyes from drooping, and she turned her head to search the bedchamber, eager to catch a glimpse of Robert's ghost, who had been appearing more often in recent weeks.

"What is it, your grace?" Lady Knollys asked, her forehead creased with worry for her queen.

Elizabeth opened her mouth, but no sound would follow, her throat burning with the attempt at speech.

"It's alright," Knollys soothed, "I know," she said with a reassuring smile, though of course she had no idea.

Elizabeth frowned and returned to staring at herself in the mirror.

It would be on the rising of the sun on the fourth day without sleep, that Queen Elizabeth collapsed to the ground, the cushions her ladies had lain out being the only thing to break her heavy fall onto the hard floor.

"The physicians say she will not accept their remedies," Pembroke whispered to Robert Cecil as they hurried towards the queen's bedchamber upon hearing of her collapse.

"They say she could have recovered from this illness by now if she would only accept administration from her doctors."

Robert Cecil raised his eyebrows, "Perhaps she does not wish to."

Pembroke looked at his fellow advisor and frowned as they neared the queen's chamber, "Does not wish to what?"

Robert Cecil grabbed the heavy doorhandle and looked Pembroke in the eyes before pushing open the door, "Recover."

Elizabeth's Archbishop was called to her side that same afternoon, the queen clinging to his hand as he spoke to her of the joys of Heaven.

Her ladies and her advisors had gathered around her, Robert Cecil and Pembroke looking more concerned than she had ever seen them as they fidgeted with the documents in their hands.

They wished to speak, Elizabeth could tell by the way their eyes darted back and forth between her ashen face and each other.

No doubt it would be the matter of my successor, Elizabeth thought, since no other issue mattered more on this, her death day.

And yet she did not wish to name him.

King James knew he would succeed her. She had written to him personally not five days prior, that when her coronation ring would be sent to him, that he would know she was dead, and that he would henceforth be known as King James I of England.

But even if Elizabeth still had the use of her voice, she would likely not voice this piece of information to her advisors, their concerned faces bringing her one final moment of entertainment.

How odd men could be, she thought as she watched them shaking with worry. After decades under the leadership of a woman, they had not yet learned that she was just as capable – if not more so – than any man who had come before her.

The only issue they would have to face, would be to somehow remove her coronation ring from her finger...

They may have to cut it from my skin, Elizabeth thought as she looked down at her hand, where her skin had grown over parts of the ring.

It would be the only cutting she had allowed in the making of her will, having officially declared her body to be kept intact and untouched upon her death, waiving her rights to embalmment or any other acts concluded post-mortem.

She had spent the past four decades moulding herself into a strong and pure leader. One that had denied needing a man by her side to rule gloriously – The Virgin Queen.

She was not stupid enough to have that legacy destroyed after her death, where the mortician would learn that she was not, in fact, intact due to the acts of her stepfather, Thomas Seymour, so many years ago.

No.

Elizabeth had dedicated her whole life to be remembered purely. And she would die happy, with the hope that all her struggles had been worth it to clear her mother's name.

And though her father had changed the course of history and turned the country upside down for the sake of a son and the continuation of the Tudor line, Elizabeth had knowingly put an end to that same bloodline in the hope of achieving *her* goal. Surely, after everything Elizabeth had done to rewrite Anne Boleyn's memory in history, it had been enough.

It had to have been enough.

...It had to be.

End of Book 2

Acknowledgements:

I would like to give special thanks to my brother who, despite not being into historical fiction *or* Tudor history, has shown me his support by offering his services as the nitpicky, fault-finding, negative reviewer I believe is needed to cast an eye over a book before it can be shared with the world.

I am extremely grateful to him for powering through The Saddest Princess and The Haunted Queen for no pay and maximum pressure.

I would also like to thank my best friend who ARC read the first draft for me and picked me up when I was feeling down or worried over a certain chapter. The pictures she sent me of her crying hysterically at the end will live in my mind rent free forever…

Of course, I would also like to thank my husband, who has supported my dream without fail and has been there from the very start.

    I couldn't have done it without any of you.

Author's note:

I set out on this journey to shed light onto Mary I's traumatic life, and I quickly realised that I have a passion for exposing certain aspects of history and historical figures that modern media tries not to broach.
In the case of Elizabeth's story, I found it interesting to learn through my ARC readers that most of the events that occurred during Elizabeth I's reign, were completely unknown to them.
And so, with The Haunted Queen, I hope to have created a well-rounded story which showed that while her reign saw to many advantages and prosperity for England, that there were also negative aspects to her ruling, as well as her personality.
That doesn't mean that I am anti-Elizabeth, or pro-Mary.
Both made errors in judgement.
Both were human.

While this is a fiction book, almost all events mentioned pre and post Elizabeth's coronation are factual. In fact, I only altered very little to accommodate the fiction side of storytelling in The Haunted Queen, since Elizabeth's life was so rich and eventful, there was not much need for fictitious dramatization.

However, as in The Saddest Princess, I leave it up to you to decide who, or what, those made up aspects may be.

Printed in Great Britain
by Amazon